CLASSIC
SPANISH
RECIPES

Elisabeth Luard

Elisabeth Luard

CLASSIC SPANISH RECIPES

75 SIGNATURE DISHES

An Hachette UK Company
www.hachette.co.uk

First published in Great Britain in 2012 by Hamlyn
a division of Octopus Publishing Group Ltd

This edition published in 2014 by Bounty Books,
a division of Octopus Publishing Group Ltd,
Endeavour House, 189 Shaftesbury Avenue
London WC2H 8JY

www.octopusbooks.co.uk

ISBN 978-0-753726-11-2

A CIP catalogue record for this book is available from the British Library

Printed and bound in China

Both metric and imperial measurements are given for the recipes.
Use one set of measures only, not a mixture of both.

Ovens should be preheated to the specified temperature. If using a
fan-assisted oven, follow the manufacturer's instructions for adjusting
the time and temperature. Grills should also be preheated.

This book includes dishes made with nuts and nut derivatives. It is advisable
for those with known allergic reactions to nuts and nut derivatives and those
who may be potentially vulnerable to these allergies, such as pregnant and
nursing mothers, invalids, the elderly, babies and children, to avoid dishes
made with nuts and nut oils. It is also prudent to check the labels of
pre-prepared ingredients for the possible inclusion of nut derivatives.

The Department of Health advises that eggs should not be consumed raw.
This book contains some dishes made with raw or lightly cooked eggs. It is
prudent for more vulnerable people such as pregnant and nursing mothers,
invalids, the elderly, babies and young children to avoid uncooked or lightly
cooked dishes made with eggs.

Meat and poultry should be cooked thoroughly. To test if poultry is cooked,
pierce the flesh through the thickest part with a skewer or fork – the juices
should run clear, never pink or red.

Contents

Introduction

Behind the Spain of the tourist resorts and Mediterranean beaches, the elegant shopping streets of Madrid and Barcelona, the traveller will be aware of older traditions: hilltop villages shaded by olive trees first planted by the Romans; rice paddies watered by aqueducts set in place by the Moors; minarets as well as monasteries; and ports whose jetties were built by Phoenician sailors and that, in time, provided safe-harbour for treasure-ships laden with far more valuable cargo than gold – the botanical riches of the New World including potatoes, tomatoes, capsicums and all the storecupboard beans.

If history, geography and latitude dictate the daily dinner in Spain, the strength of traditional Spanish cooking lies in good raw materials simply and honestly prepared. Until recent times, safe behind the barrier of the Pyrenees and unaffected by what was happening in the rest of Europe, Spanish cooks preferred to concentrate on perfecting their own ingredients and culinary habits rather than take up anything fancy or foreign. Nevertheless, while recipes are fiercely regional – no Catalan would trust a Castilian to cook a *fideu*, and no Galician would trust a Valencian to prepare a *pote* – certain dishes are universal. Rich and poor eat alike, and the tortilla and the bean pot are the staples of the midday meal throughout the land.

The Spanish menu, as I learned when I was a schoolgirl in Madrid and later when I took my own young family to live and attend school in a remote valley in Andalusia, begins in the market place. By ten o'clock of a morning the inhabitants of Tarifa, my local market town, knew just what to expect of their daily rations. If the butcher had had a delivery of young beef from the Cádiz bull ranchers, that evening the town's earthenware *cazuelas* would fill the air with scented steam from a thousand tomato-rich stews. When the inshore fleet came in with a fine haul of silvery sardines or ivory-fleshed cuttlefish, or the migratory tuna shoals were running though the Straits on a spring tide, the breeze carried the fragrance of olive oil heating in a thousand frying pans. The Andaluz housewife has a reputation for skill with the raw-iron frying pan – she could, says the rest of Spain, fritter the sea spray if that was all there was.

Key ingredients

The quality of what's available in the market place allows the food to taste recognizably of itself. Meats are preferred sauced with their own juices, fish and shellfish are prized if they taste of the sea and vegetables are prepared as dishes in their own right and eaten in the proper season, as is fresh fruit for dessert. With this strong appreciation of quality comes a willingness to pay for excellence. Even the poorest will choose a little of the best if the occasion demands: a sliver of *pata negra* cut from the bone on the Whitsun pilgrimage to Our Lady of the Dew in the marshes of the river Guadalquivir, a few threads of real saffron to perfume the Sunday paella. Perhaps it's this, the certainty that comes from a long tradition of knowing how things should really taste, that allowed Ferran Adrià of the El Bulli restaurant, the most influential cook of our time, to change the way every chef now thinks and cooks.

7

Olive oil The defining ingredient of the Spanish kitchen is the pure raw juice of the olive. It's eaten with bread in much the same way as butter, used to dress vegetables and salads, in cakes and pastries and for frying, as well as stirred into the bean pot to thicken the juices. Home cooks rarely deep-fry, preferring to use a finger's depth of fresh oil to shallow-fry in a raw-iron pan. Spain's oil-production is traditionally geared to bulk, though this is changing as regional oils with a known and valued provenance have entered the market. The non-virgins are best for anything that involves the application of high heat, while cold-pressed extra-virgins are good for dressings, marinades and to enrich a cooking broth.

Jamón serrano Serrano ham, or mountain ham, is salt-cured and wind-dried without the application of heat or smoke, followed by a prolonged period of cellaring to develop the moulds that deliver the flavour. Most prized are the hams from the semi-wild ibérico, also known as *pata negra* (black foot) for its ebony trotters, which, when permitted to forage among the scrub oaks, earns the additional distinction *de bellota*, acorn fed. When judging excellence, flavour and texture matter more than tenderness. The best cuts are sliced off very finely from the bone (traditionally in short curls – *lonchas*) and eaten in the fingers with bread. The chewy little scraps are used to flavour soups, sauces and *croquetas*, or combined with eggs; the bone is sawn into short lengths and used in much the same way as a stock cube.

Chorizo The most obvious difference between the Spanish chorizo and Italy's salami, while both are all-meat sausages of similar preparation, is the inclusion of *pimentón*, or Spanish paprika, an ingredient that adds sweetness as well as colour. Salt is the main preservative along with (though not always) a light smoking. Additional flavourings include garlic, cumin, black pepper, oregano and red wine. If eaten fresh and soft, chorizos must be cooked; if allowed to mature – a natural process – the meat darkens and firms, and the casing grows a soft white bloom, when they can be sliced and eaten raw.

Garlic is the distinctive fragrance of the Mediterranean kitchen. Spanish garlic is mild and sweet, maturing on spring rain and early sunshine, and coming to Spanish markets fresh in the form of what looks like plump white onions. Nestling at the base of each layer are tiny pearl-like seeds, infant cloves that, when bunched and hung on a hook to mature, draw the juice from their coverings and swell. Once formed, the cloves are used raw as a rub for bread to eat with olive oil, or finely sliced as a dressing for marinated fish and salads (particularly tomato, beetroot and red peppers) or pounded to a mush with salt and olive oil to make an alioli; raw garlic is used in pickling marinades for everything from anchovies to olives. In cooking, their mildness and sweetness soften the flavour of anything cooked in olive oil; when high heat is applied, they caramelize deliciously. Spanish cooks pop whole heads of garlic into the bean pot and add handfuls of unpeeled cloves to anything roasted in the oven.

Spices and herbs Saffron, the stamens of an indigenous crocus, and pimentón, ground capsicums, are the home-grown spicings of the Spanish kitchen. Pimentón is available in mild, spicy or smoked varieties and is used in rice, stews and soups. Dried chillies, the poor man's pepper, and mild sweet peppers, *ñoras*, are used whole or ground to add flavour and colour to sauces, stews, rice dishes and preserved meats including pork dripping. Imported spices popular in cooking are peppercorns, cumin, nutmeg, cloves, coriander seeds, vanilla and cinnamon. Of the leaf herbs, flat leaf parsley is the universal favourite, with oregano, thyme and bay used both fresh and dried. Mint is partnered with broad beans in the Granada region, tarragon appears in salads in Seville and fresh leaf coriander replaces parsley on the borders of Portugal. Camomile, or manzanilla, is the most popular of the digestive infusions.

9

Olives To the Spanish way of thinking, olives are inseparable from bread and wine and should always be provided free in any bar. This suits the bartender, since a salt-pickled olive promotes thirst while lining the stomach with its oily juices – which, in theory, keeps the customer sober enough to carry on drinking. Spain's eating olives are gathered while still green and firm (or, if left a little longer, lightly tinged with purple) before they have a chance to ripen to black, the stage at which they are pressed for oil. In Andalusia, olives have long been a major export industry: the commercial olive canners of Seville export pitted and stuffed green olives all over the world; their canned black olives, however, are the result of deliberate oxidization rather than natural sun-ripening, so best avoided.

Sherry vinegar This is made with sherry wine that has been aged and matured by the solera method, and is mostly produced in the Spanish province of Cádiz. The flavour is stronger and more acidic than Italian balsamic vinegar, with a distinctive spiciness and a rich, oaky flavour. It's delicious used on salads but best used sparingly – dilute with its own volume of water when using to make a dressing or sharpen a mayonnaise.

Cheese The main protein source of the rural poor, cheese is prized in its own right and rarely used in cooking. In spring it's eaten as *queso fresco*, or fresh cheese, as a dessert with honey. The raw material can be goats', cows' or sheep's milk that, once renneted, is drained, pressed and comes to market as mature or semi-mature. Of the many regional variations, Manchego, the cheese of La Mancha, the central plateau, is deservedly most famous. Dairy country – Asturias and the land of the Basques – produces a pair of distinguished blue-veins, Cabrales and Idiazabal.

Almonds The Moors, the colonial power in Andalusia for seven centuries, planted their borrowed hillside with stock from the Jordan Valley. As a result, almonds, both ground and whole, are used a great deal in the Spanish kitchen. They are used to thicken sauces and in nut milk preparations, such as Granada's *ajo blanco* (see page 36), and in the making of nougats, marzipans and two Christmas sweetmeats – *polverones* (see page 147), powdery cinnamon-flavoured cookies shortened with lard, and the halva-like *turron*.

Bread Country loaves, or *pan candela* – round or oval for portability, raised with leaven from the day before and baked in a wood-fired oven (although rarely these days) – are rough-textured, chewy and robust, with an elastic, creamy-white crumb and a thick golden-brown crust. They are sold by weight rather than volume. It dries to palatable crusts which are used for stale bread dishes – *migas* and other soaked-bread preparations including the original gazpacho, a thick bread porridge eaten hot in winter and cold in summer. The most popular town bread is the torpedo-shaped *bolillo*, a bread roll with a snowy, dense-textured crumb and a thick, soft brown crust. Breakfast breads include the Mallorcan *saimaza*, snail-shaped buns enriched with lard and sweetened with dried fruits, and *churros*, tubular doughnuts made with naturally leavened batter fried to order in street kiosks and eaten with steaming cups of coffee or hot chocolate.

Lard *Manteca*, pure pork lard, is used in baking and to enrich stews and sauces instead of butter. It comes in three forms: pure white and plain for pastry and cookies; *manteca colorada*, lightly salted lard coloured red with pimentón (Spanish paprika), flavoured with garlic and used as a spread on bread or for stirring into the bean pot; and *manteca colorada con carne*, flavoured lard in which small pieces of pork or chorizo are preserved.

Tapas

Mushrooms with Garlic and Parsley
Setas a la parilla

SERVES 4

500 g (1 lb) fresh large,
open-capped wild or
cultivated mushrooms

1 tablespoon olive oil

2 garlic cloves, finely
chopped

1 tablespoon dried
oregano

2 tablespoons finely
chopped parsley

salt and freshly milled
black pepper

toasted sourdough
bread, to serve

The Basques and Catalans are the mushroom fanciers of Spain. An astonishing variety of wild fungi are gathered, the most popular being the saffron milk cap – a meaty mushroom found in pine woods that produces a milky juice and has an alarming habit of bruising blue.

1 Shake the mushrooms to evacuate any unwelcome residents and wipe the caps – don't rinse or peel. Trim off the stalks close to the base.

2 Trickle the mushrooms with the oil and salt lightly. Place them on a preheated griddle or barbecue, cap-side to the heat, and grill fiercely until the juices pool in the gills. If you want to use an overhead grill, you will have to cook the undersides of the mushrooms first.

3 Sprinkle the gills with the garlic, oregano and parsley, season with plenty of pepper and cook for another couple of minutes. Serve on thick slabs of toasted sourdough bread to catch the juices.

Toasted Almonds
Almendras tostadas

SERVES 8 − 10

500 g (1 lb) whole unblanched almonds

1 tablespoon olive oil

1 teaspoon salt

1 free-range egg white, beaten with its own volume of water

1 tablespoon pimentón (Spanish paprika)

1 teaspoon ground coriander

1 teaspoon ground cumin

Although these are available commercially, almonds warm from the oven are irresistible. Prepare them fresh.

1 Scald the almonds with boiling water and pop them out of their skins as soon as the water is cool enough for your fingers – my children loved the task as much as they appreciated the result.

2 Brush a baking tray with the oil. Spread the skinned almonds out in the oiled baking tray, shake to coat the nuts with the oil and sprinkle with the salt. Place in a preheated oven, 180°C (350°F), Gas Mark 4, for 15–20 minutes, or until just golden – shake regularly to avoid sticking and don't let them brown. A perfectly toasted almond squeaks when you bite it. Alternatively, place in a cooler preheated oven, 150°C (300°F), Gas Mark 2, and double the roasting time – temperature is not as important as a watchful eye.

3 Allow to cool to finger-hot, then toss with the egg white mixture – a precaution that allows the spices to stick to the almonds. Sprinkle with the spices, shake to coat and return to the oven for a moment to set the coating. Leave to cool before storing in an airtight tin.

Green Olives with Herbs and Spices

Aceitunas aromatisadas

SERVES 8–10

about 1 litre (1¾ pints) water

500 g (1 lb) plain-brined green olives

3–4 garlic cloves, unpeeled and roughly chopped

1 teaspoon crumbled dried thyme

1 teaspoon aniseed or fennel seeds

1 Seville orange or lemon

3–4 tablespoons sherry or white wine vinegar

This is an easy method of giving commercially prepared green olives a home-pickled flavour, particularly if made with the big green olives of Seville. Choose Spanish olives for this dish such as manzanillas, gordal or reina, if you can.

1 Boil the water and then leave it to cool.

2 Drain the olives and mix them with the garlic, thyme and aniseed or fennel seeds.

3 Cut a thick slice from the middle of the orange or lemon and set it aside, then chop the rest of the fruit, skin and all. Add the chopped fruit to the olives and pack everything in a well-scrubbed and scalded jar. Pour in the sherry or vinegar and enough of the cooled water to cover, then top with the reserved slice of fruit, pushing it down to keep the olives submerged.

4 Seal tightly and leave in the refrigerator for at least a week to take the flavours. The olives keep well, refrigerated, for 3–4 weeks.

Chilli-roasted Chickpeas
Garbanzos tostados picantes

SERVES 8

500 g (1 lb) dried chickpeas, soaked overnight in cold water

olive oil, for oiling

1 teaspoon chilli flakes

sea salt

My children loved these crisp, nutty little nibbles, although I had to go easy on the chilli. Sold hot from the roasting pan at féria time (the annual summer festival) in the villages of Andalusia, they are the poor man's salted almond.

1 Drain the chickpeas thoroughly and dry them in a clean cloth or with kitchen paper.

2 Spread them in a single layer on a lightly oiled baking tray. Place in a preheated oven, 150°C (300°F), Gas Mark 2, for about an hour until dry, crisp and golden. Shake regularly to avoid sticking. Alternatively, dry-fry the drained chickpeas over the lowest possible heat – be careful, as they jump like popcorn.

3 Toss with the chilli flakes and a little sea salt. To store, leave to cool (don't salt or add chilli) and pack in a jar with a well-fitting lid.

Chilli Potatoes
Patatas bravas

SERVES 4
small bottle olive oil,
  about 200 ml (7 fl oz)
12 dried chillies
1 kg (2 lb) floury
  potatoes, peeled and
  cut into fat fingers
  or cubes
oil, for frying
salt

There are many versions of this recipe, but here's how they make them at the Bar Tomás in Barcelona, where everyone who's anyone goes for their midday treat. Allow at least a week for the chilli to impart its fire and colour to the oil.

1 Pour most of the olive oil from the bottle into a jug. Pack the chillies into the bottle and top up with as much of the olive oil as will fit. Seal tightly and leave for a week before using.

2 Salt the potatoes and leave them to drain in a sieve for about 10 minutes. Shake to remove excess moisture, but don't rinse.

3 Heat the oil for frying in a deep frying pan until a faint blue haze rises. Slip in the potatoes and fry gently, a batch at a time, until soft. Remove and drain. Reheat the oil and fry them again until crisp and golden. Repeat if necessary – which, depending on the choice of potato, it may well be.

4 Dress the potatoes with the chilli-infused olive oil – or hand round separately, for dipping. You can hand round a garlicky mayonnaise as well, just for good measure.

Meatballs in Tomato Sauce
Albondigas en salsa

SERVES 4

SAUCE

500 g (1 lb) ripe fresh or canned tomatoes

2 tablespoons olive oil

1 onion, finely chopped

1 garlic clove, finely chopped

1 red pepper, cored, deseeded and finely chopped

1 small glass dry sherry or red wine

1 small cinnamon stick

1 bay leaf

salt

MEATBALLS

350 g (11½ oz) minced meat (pork and beef)

1 free-range egg, beaten

100 g (3½ oz) fresh breadcrumbs

1 garlic clove, very finely chopped

1 onion, very finely chopped

1 tablespoon chopped parsley

1 teaspoon ground cumin

1 teaspoon ground coriander

salt and freshly milled black pepper

seasoned plain flour, for dusting

2–3 tablespoons olive oil, for frying

Tasty meatballs are the frugal Spanish housewife's standby. Cheap and easy to divide into small portions, they're the perfect tapa. The proportion of breadcrumbs to meat can be varied to suit your purse.

1 Attend to the sauce first. If using fresh tomatoes, scald, skin and chop the flesh. In a small saucepan, heat the oil and fry the onion and garlic until they soften and take a little colour. Add the tomatoes, red pepper, sherry or wine and the cinnamon stick. Add the bay leaf and season with salt. Bubble up for a moment, then turn down the heat and leave the sauce to simmer and reduce while you make the meatballs.

2 Work all the meatball ingredients together thoroughly – the more you work it, the better. With wet hands (keep a bowl of warm water handy for dipping your fingers), form the mixture into little bite-sized balls. Dust them through a plateful of seasoned flour.

3 Heat the oil for frying in a deep roomy frying pan, slip in the meatballs and fry, turning carefully, until firm and lightly browned on all sides. Add the tomato sauce, bubble up and simmer gently for about 20 minutes until the meatballs are tender. Serve with crisp lettuce leaves for scooping or, for a more substantial meal, chunks of crusty country bread or plain white rice.

Chicken Croquettes
Croquetas de pollo

SERVES 6

4 tablespoons olive oil

125 g (4 oz) plain flour

600 ml (1 pint) hot chicken stock (from the puchero pot, or freshly made)

1 teaspoon ground allspice

½ teaspoon freshly grated nutmeg

seasoned plain flour, for dusting

1–2 free-range eggs, lightly beaten with a little water

plateful of fresh breadcrumbs

oil, for frying

salt and freshly milled black pepper

Croquetas *require dexterity and patience, but a crisp coating and a melting, creamy interior reward the effort. The basis is a thick panada made with a well-flavoured broth, which may or may not be combined with additional flavourings: diced serrano ham, crabmeat, chopped prawns or grated cheese.*

1 Heat the olive oil in a small saucepan and stir in the flour. Lower the heat and stir for a moment or two until it looks sandy (don't let it brown). Whisk in the hot stock in a steady stream until you have a smooth, thick sauce. Season with salt and pepper, the allspice and nutmeg. Beat the sauce over a gentle heat for 10 minutes to cook the flour. Spread in a dish, then leave to cool, cover with clingfilm and set in the refrigerator to firm – overnight is best.

2 With wet hands (keep a bowl of warm water handy for dipping your fingers), form the mixture into little bite-sized bolsters. Dust them through the flour, coat with the egg mixture and then press into the breadcrumbs to make a perfect jacket. Refrigerate for at least another hour – overnight, if possible – to set the coating. You can, if you wish, freeze a batch ready for later.

3 When you're ready to serve, heat enough oil to submerge the *croquetas* completely until a faint blue haze rises. Slip in the *croquetas* straight from the refrigerator, a few at a time to avoid lowering the temperature of the oil. If the coating splits open, the oil is too hot; if it doesn't crisp and seal within a minute, it's too cool. Remove the *croquetas* with a slotted spoon as soon as they're crisp and brown, and transfer to kitchen paper. Serve without delay, while they're still piping hot.

Moorish Kebabs

Pinchitos moruños

SERVES 6−8

500 g (1 lb) lamb or
  pork, trimmed and
  diced into small
  pieces

2 tablespoons olive oil

1 teaspoon ground
  cumin

1 teaspoon ground
  coriander

1 teaspoon pimentón
  (Spanish paprika)

1 teaspoon turmeric

½ teaspoon salt

½ teaspoon freshly
  milled black pepper

baguette or ciabatta
  bread, cubed, to serve

*Long skewers threaded with scraps of spiced meat rarely appear on
restaurant menus unless aimed at tourists, but they are a speciality
of* féria *time (summer fiesta), cooked to order on a little charcoal
brazier by an itinerant peddler resplendent in a scarlet fez.*

1 Check over the meat – all the pieces should be neatly
trimmed and no bigger than a baby's mouthful.

2 Combine the oil with the flavourings and turn the
mixture thoroughly with the meat. Cover and leave in
a cool place overnight to take the flavours.

3 Thread the meat on to 8 bamboo or fine metal skewers –
about 6–7 little pieces each. If using bamboo skewers, soak
them in water for 30 minutes first.

4 Cook the meat under a preheated grill or on a preheated
barbecue over a high heat, turning the skewers frequently,
until well browned but still juicy. Serve on the skewers,
with a cube of bread speared on the end of each so that
people can pull the meat off without burning their fingers.

Grilled Sardines
Sardinas a la parilla

SERVES 4-6

1 kg (2 lb) whole fresh
   sardines

sea salt

This is the most popular way of preparing the fat sardines trawled by the inshore fleets. Fresh-caught sardines flash a brilliant rainbow of colour, their eyes bright and shiny. Don't scale them – the scales and the natural oil in the skin stop them sticking to the grate.

1 Gut the sardines, leaving their heads and tails in place – easily done with your forefinger through the soft bellies – and rinse to remove the loose scales. Salt generously.

2 Place the fish under a preheated grill or on a preheated griddle (Spanish cooks use a steel plate heated from beneath) and grill fiercely, turning once, until the skin blisters black and bubbly. The thicker the fish, the longer they will need, but 3–4 minutes on each side should be ample.

3 Serve one fish per tapa, with a lemon quarter. To eat, pick up the fish by the tail, holding the head with the fingers and thumb of the other hand, and eat straight down the bone, removing the fillets with your teeth. No one with any sense eats a grilled sardine with a knife and fork. You'll need chunks of bread for wiping fishy fingers.

Roast Red Peppers with Anchovies

Pimientos asados con anchoas

SERVES 4

4 red peppers

2 tablespoons extra-virgin olive oil

50 g (2 oz) can salt-pickled anchovies in oil, drained

black pepper

The sweet flesh of the peppers perfectly complements the salty fillets of anchovy – the best are packed straight from the cold waters of the Bay of Biscay in the canneries of Asturias and Galicia. Choose ripe red bell peppers or the scarlet triangular peppers from sunny Rioja.

1 Roast the peppers whole by holding them over a gas or candle flame, speared on the end of a knife, until the skin blisters and blackens. Alternatively, place them in a preheated oven, 240°C (475°F), Gas Mark 9, for 15–20 minutes, turning them halfway through.

2 Seal the peppers in a plastic food bag, wait for 10 minutes for the skin to loosen, then peel with your fingers. Deseed and cut the flesh into triangles or ribbons, depending on the original shape of the pepper.

3 Place the peppers in a single layer on a plate and trickle with the olive oil. Arrange the anchovies decoratively over the top and finish with a grinding of black pepper. Serve accompanied with plenty of crusty bread to mop up all the delicious juices.

Prawns with Garlic and Chilli
Gambas pilpil

SERVES 4

350 g (11½ oz) raw
  peeled prawns
4 tablespoons olive oil
1 garlic clove, sliced
1 teaspoon small dried
  chillies, deseeded
sea salt

Tapa bars that specialize in these mouth-scalding preparations provide customers with little wooden forks so that they don't burn their lips. Angulas, or baby eels, are prepared in the same way, as are hake throats, kokochas, a speciality of the Basque Country.

1 Pick over the prawns and remove any stray whiskers.

2 The important thing about this simple dish is that the prawns must be sizzling hot when they are served, ideally in the dish in which they are cooked. With this in mind, choose small individual earthenware casseroles (*cazuelas*) that have been tempered to withstand direct heat (see page 41). Alternatively, use a frying pan to cook the prawns, and heat individual ramekin dishes in the oven for serving.

3 Heat the oil until a faint blue haze rises and add the garlic and chillies. Reheat until sizzling, then add the prawns and let them cook. They'll turn opaque almost immediately. Serve as soon as the oil spits and bubbles in their individual casseroles or heated ramekins, with chunky bread for mopping up the fiery oil. Hand the sea salt round separately.

Clams in Sherry
Almejas en vino de Jerez

SERVES 4 6

2 tablespoons olive oil

2 garlic cloves, finely chopped

1 kg (2 lb) live bivalves, such as clams, cockles, mussels or razor shells, cleaned (see page 99)

1 large glass dry sherry or white wine

2 tablespoons chopped parsley

a little sugar

salt and freshly milled black pepper

Bivalves have a relatively long shell life, surviving for as long as they can keep water in their shells – hence the need to reject those with cracked shells or that remain closed when cooked. Spanish housewives expect to buy them live in the shell, the only guarantee of freshness.

1 Heat the oil in a saucepan, add the garlic and let it soften for a moment. Tip in the shellfish, then add the sherry or wine and the parsley. Season with salt and pepper and the sugar, and turn up the heat. As soon as steam rises, cover with a lid and leave to cook, shaking the pan to redistribute the shells. Allow 3–4 minutes for all the shells to open – check and turn them over if necessary. Discard any shells that remain closed.

2 Remove the pan from the heat as soon as the shells are open and serve straight from the pot – never mind if they cool down to room temperature, which happens very swiftly. Don't reheat or they'll be rubbery. Leftovers can be served with a little dressing of chopped tomato, parsley and onion.

3 Serve in deep plates and eat with your fingers, providing plenty of country bread for mopping up the juices.

Frittered Squid

Calamares a la romana

SERVES 4 – 6

500 g (1 lb) cleaned squid or cuttlefish, sliced into rings, tentacles left whole (see page 94)

about 4 tablespoons strong bread flour

1 tablespoon semolina

oil, for deep-frying (a mixture of olive and sunflower is good)

sea salt

quartered lemons, to serve

Squid (calamares) and cuttlefish (chocos) are both suitable for the treatment – simply flipping the prepared fish through flour to give it a light coating that crisps in the fryer. Small specimens (no bigger than a teaspoon) can be fried whole, just as they come from the sea.

1 Rinse, drain and shake the fish to remove excess moisture (don't dry it completely).

2 Spread the flour mixed with the semolina on a plate (no salt). Working quickly, dust the fish through the flour a few pieces at a time – the surface should be damp enough for the flour to form a coating – then drop into a sieve and shake to remove the excess flour.

3 Meanwhile, heat the oil in a deep-fryer or heavy frying pan. Test the temperature of the oil with a bread cube: it's ready for frying when bubbles form around the edge immediately and the crumb turns golden within a few seconds. Drop the coated fish into the hot oil quickly in batches and fry until golden and crisp, turning once. Transfer to kitchen paper to drain.

4 Serve piping hot and without reheating (reheating makes cephalopods rubbery), lightly salted and accompanied by lemon quarters.

Chilled Tomato and Garlic Soup

Gazpacho

SERVES 4

2 slices of day-old bread (about 50 g/2 oz)

ice-cold spring water, for soaking and thinning

2 tablespoons wine vinegar

2 garlic cloves, crushed

2 tablespoons olive oil

1 small or ½ large cucumber, peeled and roughly chopped

1 kg (2 lb) ripe tomatoes, skinned, deseeded and chopped

1 green pepper, cored, deseeded and roughly chopped

a little sugar

salt

In its modern form, this is a refreshing chilled tomato soup. In Spain, it's a way of making last week's bread palatable by soaking it with fresh water and flavouring it with a sprinkle of vinegar, garlic and oil. Here's the modern version; embellish it as you please.

1 Put the bread to soak in a few tablespoons of ice-cold spring water with the vinegar and garlic. Drop into a liquidizer or food processor and process to a purée, or pound in a mortar with a pestle. Add the oil and remaining vegetables. Add ice-cold spring water until you have the consistency you like – thick or thin, depending on whether you mean to serve it as a refreshment or a soup.

2 Adjust the seasoning with salt and the sugar. Transfer to a jug and cover securely. Set in a cool place or the refrigerator for 2–3 hours, or until well chilled. No ice – it just dilutes the delicate flavour and replaces it with the taste of the refrigerator instead.

3 As a refreshment, serve in a chilled glass, with a little olive oil drizzled on top. As a first-course soup, ladle into bowls and hand round any extras separately. Choose from diced bread croutons fried in a little olive oil (only worth it if you make your own), chopped hard-boiled egg, diced serrano ham, cucumber, peppers, tomato or mild Spanish onion.

White Gazpacho
Ajo blanco

SERVES 6–8

- 1 slice of yesterday's bread, crusts removed
- 100 g (3½ oz) whole blanched almonds
- 2 garlic cloves, peeled
- 1 tablespoon olive oil
- 1 tablespoon white wine vinegar
- 1 litre (1¾ pints) cold water
- sugar, to taste
- salt
- a few small white grapes, peeled and deseeded, to serve

A sophisticated summer refresher from Granada, white gazpacho is made with an infusion of almond milk heavily perfumed with garlic. You don't need much of it – it has a kick like a mule. I like to serve it in a little tumbler with another of red gazpacho and a glass of chilled dry sherry.

1 Put the bread, almonds, garlic, oil, vinegar and 500 ml (17 fl oz) of the water into a liquidizer or food processor and process thoroughly. Add enough water – another 500 ml (17 fl oz) or so – to give the consistency of thin milk. Season with sugar and salt to taste. Transfer to a jug, cover, and chill thoroughly.

2 To serve, pour into small bowls or glasses and try to float a couple of grapes on top of each serving. Mine always drop to the bottom. No matter – it'll make a nice surprise at the end. Warn participants that this is a high-garlic area.

Garlic Soup

Sopa de ajo

SERVES 4

6 tablespoons olive oil

6 thick slices of robust country bread, cut into cubes

12 fine fat garlic cloves, crushed

1 tablespoon pimentón (Spanish paprika)

about 1 litre (1¾ pints) chicken stock or water

4 free-range eggs

salt and freshly milled black pepper

More than a flavouring, garlic is a philosophy, a declaration of otherness, a way of life. Here, in a simple soup that is given to invalids and babies as well as their elderly relatives, it's cooked to a gentle sweetness that soothes the spirit and calms the stomach.

1 Warm the oil in a heavy pan, and as soon as it's hot enough to fry, drop in the bread cubes and the garlic. Fry gently and patiently until the garlic softens and the bread is golden – don't let it brown. Stir in the pimentón and add the stock or water. Season lightly with salt and pepper, then bring to the boil, cover and cook for 5 minutes, or until the bread is spongy and has soaked up most of the juice.

2 Meanwhile, heat 4 small individual earthenware casseroles (*cazuelas*) either on the hob (see page 41 for instructions on tempering *cazuelas* to withstand direct heat) or in a preheated oven, 180°C (350°F), Gas Mark 4. Ladle in the soupy bread with its broth and crack in the eggs – one for each casserole. You can return them to the oven for the eggs to set, or serve immediately, for people to stir the egg into the boiling soup.

Shellfish Soup with Sherry
Sopa de mariscos con vino de Jerez

SERVES 4

500 g (1 lb) soup fish (or ask your fishmonger for bones and heads)

about 1 litre (1¾ pints) water

about 200 ml (7 fl oz) dry sherry

1 onion, quartered but unpeeled

1 carrot, roughly chopped

3–4 parsley sprigs

1–2 bay leaves

½ teaspoon crushed peppercorns

12 saffron threads soaked in 1 tablespoon boiling water

1 kg (2 lb) live shellfish, cleaned (see page 99)

1 tablespoon diced serrano ham

1 tablespoon pimentón (Spanish paprika)

salt and freshly milled black pepper

1 teaspoon grated lemon rind

1 teaspoon finely chopped garlic

1 tablespoon chopped parsley

You need fresh live shellfish on the shell for this dish – ready-cooked won't do. If this proves impossible, a combination of firm-fleshed white fish – monkfish, swordfish – and oysters gives good results. Shuck the oysters first, naturally, and slip them in right at the end to heat through.

1 Rinse the soup fish (or the bones and heads – if using the latter, be careful to remove the gills or the stock will become bitter) and transfer to a roomy saucepan with the water and sherry. Bring to the boil and skim off the foam. Add the onion, carrot, aromatics and 1 teaspoon salt. Return everything to the boil, turn the heat down immediately and simmer for 20 minutes – no longer or the broth will be bitter.

2 Strain the broth and return it to the pan. Stir in the saffron and its soaking water – first crushed either with the back of the spoon or given a quick whizz in a liquidizer.

3 Reheat to just boiling and add the shellfish, ham and pimentón. Return everything to the boil, cover and cook for about 3–4 minutes until the shellfish open. Discard any that remain closed. Remove from the heat and taste and adjust the seasoning. Finish by sprinkling over the lemon rind, garlic and parsley. Serve without reheating.

Scrambled Eggs with Mushrooms
Revuelto de setas

SERVES 3-4

4 tablespoons olive oil

1-2 garlic cloves, finely chopped

about 350 g (11½ oz) fresh woodland mushrooms, such as saffron milk caps, porcini, chanterelles or oysters, sliced

2 tablespoons diced serrano ham

6 free-range eggs

1 tablespoon finely chopped parsley

salt and freshly milled black pepper

Scrambling eggs with olive oil is the perfect way to stretch the gatherings of any firm-fleshed wild fungi. In spring, a fresh-flavoured revuelto *is made with asparagus sprue – chewy little green shoots gathered from beneath the prickly bushes of the native wild asparagus.*

1 Heat the oil in a flameproof earthenware casserole (*cazuela*) or a heavy iron frying pan and add the garlic. Allow to sizzle for a minute or two until the garlic softens, then add the mushrooms and ham. Sprinkle with a little salt and turn up the heat until the mushrooms absorb the oil. Turn down the heat and cook gently until the fungi yield up their juices, then begin to fry again.

2 Meanwhile, lightly beat the eggs with the parsley, and season with a little salt and plenty of pepper. Stir the eggs into the mushrooms and continue to stir over a gentle heat until the eggs form soft curds – no more than 1-2 minutes. Remove the cooking implement from the heat just before the egg sets. Stir again and serve in the cooking dish, with plenty of crusty bread for mopping.

Ham and Eggs with Red Peppers
Huevos al plato con pimientos

SERVES 4

2 garlic cloves, halved
2 red peppers
4 tablespoons olive oil
4 slices of serrano ham
8 free-range eggs
freshly milled black
  pepper

This makes an easy evening meal for townies who have been out on a tapa bar round with friends after work. Spaniards prefer to lunch prodigiously and take a relatively light supper.

1 For the proper presentation of this simple recipe, you will need 4 individual earthenware casseroles (*cazuelas*) that have been tempered to withstand direct heat. To temper, rub the surface inside and out with the garlic (the inside is glazed, the outside unglazed), fill the *cazuela* with water and place it over direct heat – gas or electric, or any open flame. Bring to the boil and boil steadily until the water has completely evaporated.

2 Roast the peppers whole by holding them over a gas or candle flame, speared on the end of a knife, or cook under a preheated hot grill, until the skin blisters and blackens.

3 Seal the peppers in a plastic food bag, wait 10 minutes for the skin to loosen, then peel with your fingers. Deseed and cut the flesh into strips.

4 Pour a tablespoon of oil into each individual *cazuela* and place them carefully on direct heat. When the oil is smoking hot, lay in the peppers and a slice of ham and crack in the eggs – 2 for each *cazuela*. Cook for 3–4 minutes to set the white. Give each dish a turn of the pepper mill and then serve. The eggs will continue to cook in their dish.

Potato Tortilla
Tortilla española

SERVES 4
about 750 g (1½ lb)
potatoes (allow
1 medium potato
per egg)

olive oil, for frying

1 tablespoon finely
chopped onion

4 large free-range eggs

½ teaspoon salt

Call it egg and chips, Spanish-style: same ingredients, different method of attack. Opinions vary about the inclusion of parsley and onion; I leave the first one out and put the second one in. Some like the potatoes cut into thin rounds, others like them chip-shaped or cubed.

1 Peel and dice or slice the potatoes. Heat enough oil to submerge the potatoes completely – choose a frying pan in which you would usually cook a one-person omelette. Add the potatoes and fry gently until absolutely soft – don't let them colour. Add the onion for the last few minutes, just long enough to soften it.

2 Transfer the potato and onion to a sieve placed over a bowl to catch the drippings. Allow to cool to finger temperature. Lightly beat the eggs with the salt, then stir in the potatoes. At this point, the volume of the cooked potato should equal the volume of egg.

3 Pour all but a tablespoon of the oil out of the pan and add the drippings from the bowl (the rest of the oil can be used again). Reheat the pan and tip in the egg and potato mixture. Prod down the potato so that it's all submerged. Use a fork to pull the egg into the middle as soon as the edges begin to set. Fry gently, loosely lidded, until the surface no longer looks absolutely runny. The heat should be low or the base will burn before the egg is cooked. Don't overcook it – the centre should remain juicy. If the heat is too high, the egg will be leathery.

4 Place a clean plate over the pan and invert the whole thing with one quick movement so that the tortilla lands juicy-side up. Be brave: it's no harder than flipping a pancake. Reheat the pan with a little more oil and slip the

tortilla, soft-side down, back into the pan and set the other side. When the underside is done, reverse the tortilla back on to the plate and pat off the excess oil with kitchen paper. Serve at room temperature, cut into neat wedges or cubes.

Chickpea and Chorizo Tortilla

Tortilla catalana

SERVES 4

2 tablespoons olive oil

2 tablespoons diced butifarra or chorizo

6 tablespoons cooked chickpeas, well drained

4 large free-range eggs

salt and freshly milled black pepper

This spicy winter tortilla is made with leftovers from the bean pot and a handful of diced butifarra negro – black pudding spiced with cinnamon, cloves and nutmeg. If you can't find butifarra, use chorizo. Haricot or butter beans can replace the chickpeas, depending on what's available.

1 Warm a tablespoon of the oil in a one-person omelette pan. Fry the sausage for a few minutes until the edges brown and the fat runs. Add the chickpeas and warm them through.

2 Beat the eggs lightly with salt and pepper. Mix in the contents of the omelette pan. Wipe the pan and heat the rest of the oil. Tip in the egg mixture, stir to blend the ingredients as the egg sets a little and cook gently until it takes the form of a thick pancake, loosely covered, neatening the side as the curds firm up.

3 Turn it by reversing the whole panful on to a plate so that the contents end up soft-side down. Slip it back into the hot pan (add a little more oil if necessary) to allow the other side to set – a couple of minutes. The whole operation should be very gentle and take no more than 7–8 minutes in all.

Scrambled Eggs with Vegetables
Piperrada

SERVES 4

4 tablespoons olive oil

1 onion, finely sliced into half-moons

1 garlic clove, finely chopped

1 aubergine, diced

1 red pepper, cored, deseeded and diced

1 large tomato, skinned, deseeded and chopped

4 free-range eggs, lightly beaten to blend

a little chilli powder

salt

In this speciality of the Basque Country, eggs are scrambled into a juicy combination of aubergine, tomato and garlic cooked in oil. The vegetables can be prepared ahead and the eggs scrambled at the last minute.

1 Heat half the oil in a flameproof earthenware casserole (*cazuela*) or heavy iron frying pan. Add the onion and garlic, salt lightly and cook very gently for at least 20 minutes until the onion slices soften and brown a little – don't let them burn. Remove to a sieve placed over a bowl to catch the drippings.

2 Reheat the pan with the remaining oil and add the aubergine. Cook until soft and lightly caramelized at the edges (return the drippings to the pan as soon as they are available). Remove the aubergine and reserve.

3 Add the red pepper and turn it in the hot oil until it has softened and taken a little colour. Add the tomato and bubble up for a minute or two until the flesh begins to collapse. Return the reserved vegetables to the pan and reheat. Season with salt and the chilli powder.

4 Fold the eggs into the vegetables and stir over a gentle heat while the eggs form soft curds – about 1–2 minutes, no more. Remove from the heat immediately.

5 If you like, serve with toasted country bread and a garlic clove for rubbing over the crisp crumb – this is a *campesino* dish, nothing fancy. One countryman can manage the whole thing; townies have more delicate appetites.

Meat & Poultry

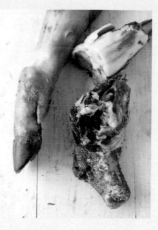

Chicken with Garlic
Pollo al ajillo

SERVES 4

1 small free-range chicken, jointed into bite-sized pieces

1–2 tablespoons seasoned plain flour

about 8 tablespoons olive oil

8–12 garlic cloves, unpeeled

about 150 ml (¼ pint) dry sherry or white wine

This is the Andalusian housewife's way with a tender young chicken. Pick a small bird with a high ratio of bone to flesh – more chewable and easier to eat with fingers. The olive oil must be mild and golden, not leafy, which will taste bitter once subjected to high heat.

1 Dust the chicken joints through the seasoned flour.

2 Heat the oil in a heavy frying pan until a faint blue haze rises. Add the chicken joints, turn down the heat and fry gently for about 10 minutes, turning to brown all sides. Add the garlic cloves and fry them for about 5 minutes until the papery coverings brown a little.

3 Add the sherry or wine and allow to bubble up until the steam no longer smells winey. Turn down the heat and simmer gently for another 15 minutes, or until the chicken is cooked right through, the sherry or wine has completely evaporated and the juices are reduced to a thick, oily little dressing. To test the chicken for doneness, push a sharp knife through the thickest part of one of the thigh joints: when the juices run clear rather than pink, it's ready.

4 Allow to cool a little, then serve with chunks of country bread and eat it with your fingers.

Breaded Escalopes
Filete a la milanesa

SERVES 4

500 g (1 lb) veal, beef or pork escalopes

2 tablespoons seasoned plain flour

2 free-range eggs

2 tablespoons milk

4 heaped tablespoons fresh breadcrumbs

olive oil, for frying

1 lemon, quartered, to serve

Thrifty Spanish cooks would be lost without this easy way to make a little go a long way. There was a time when fresh meat, a luxury until modern and more prosperous times, was eaten only on Sundays, and even then only by city folk.

1 Place each escalope between 2 large sheets of clingfilm and flatten with a rolling pin. The meat should be extremely thin.

2 Spread the seasoned flour on one plate, beat the eggs and milk together on another and spread the breadcrumbs on a third. Dust the escalopes through the flour (shake off the excess), then flip them through the egg and milk to coat both sides. Press well into the breadcrumbs, making sure that both surfaces are well jacketed.

3 Heat a finger's depth of oil in a frying pan – you'll need just enough depth to submerge the meat. The oil should be hot but not yet smoking – test with a bread cube, which should form bubbles around the edges and become golden within a moment. Slip in the escalopes, 1–2 at a time so that the temperature doesn't drop. Turn to fry the other side. Transfer to kitchen paper to drain. Serve with the lemon quarters. Mashed potato, beaten with oil rather than butter and flavoured with ground allspice, is the perfect accompaniment.

Mincemeat with Saffron and Raisins

Picadillo valenciana

SERVES 4

750 g (1½ lb) minced meat (best done by hand with a knife, but no matter)

1 tablespoon finely diced serrano ham

2 tablespoons olive oil

1 large onion, diced

1 large carrot, diced

1 garlic clove, peeled

6–8 saffron threads

2 large ripe tomatoes, skinned, deseeded and diced, or 2 tablespoons tomato purée

1 tablespoon raisins

500 g (1 lb) potatoes, peeled and cut into bite-sized cubes

½ teaspoon ground cinnamon

1 bay leaf

salt and freshly milled black pepper

TO GARNISH

1 tablespoon toasted pine nuts

2 hard-boiled free-range eggs, shelled and quartered

Moorish spicing and a touch of sweetness enlivens Monday's mince. I loved this dish when I was a teenager in Madrid. My mother's cook came from Valencia and included saffron, cinnamon and raisins whenever she could. This is perfect spoon food for toothless grannies and hungry children.

1 Mix the minced meat with the ham. Heat the oil in a flameproof casserole or heavy saucepan. When it is good and hot, stir in the meat, onion and carrot and let everything cook gently until it loses its water, begins to fry and takes a little colour.

2 Meanwhile, crush the garlic and saffron with a little salt, dilute with a splash of water and stir this paste into the meat as soon as it begins to fry.

3 Add the tomatoes and bubble up until the flesh softens and collapses or stir in the tomato purée. Add the raisins, potatoes, cinnamon and bay leaf, and turn to blend with the meat. Add enough water to just cover everything.

4 Bubble up again and turn down the heat. Cover loosely and leave to simmer gently for 25–30 minutes, or until the meat is tender and the potatoes are soft. Taste and adjust the seasoning, turn up the heat and let it bubble up to evaporate the extra moisture – it should be juicy but not soupy.

5 To finish, scatter over the toasted pine nuts and hard-boiled egg quarters.

Boned Stuffed Chicken
Galantina de gallina

SERVES 6–8

1 free-range chicken,
about 1.5 kg (3 lb)

450 g (14½ oz) minced
pork (choose a fatty
cut – shoulder or belly)

450 g (14½ oz) minced
veal or young beef

4 heaped tablespoons
fresh breadcrumbs

300 ml (½ pint) white
wine

2 free-range eggs, lightly
beaten

¼ teaspoon freshly
grated nutmeg

1 onion, quartered

1 large carrot, cut into
chunks

2–3 green celery sticks

1–2 bay leaves

½ teaspoon peppercorns

salt and freshly milled
black pepper

A poached stuffed chicken, eaten cold and served in much the same way as French pâté, is well worth the effort of boning out the bird. You'll find the commercially prepared version on the cold meats stall in Spanish markets, along with the serrano hams.

1 To bone out the chicken, lay the bird on its breast, back uppermost, and make a long slit with a sharp, slender-bladed knife right down the broad backbone. Ease the flesh from the skeleton as if opening a book, first one side and then the other, using the knife to separate the skin and flesh from the carcass. Pull the flesh up the legs, severing the skin where it joins the drumsticks. Trim off the wings at the second joint – no need to bone them out. Work your way up the carcass and over the breast, releasing the meat from the ribcage. Free the breastbone by slicing through the soft cartilage, keeping the skin intact.

2 Lay the boned-out chicken on the table with its flesh side uppermost. Remove most of the breast fillets and the thick leg meat. Chop this roughly and mix with the minced meats and breadcrumbs – enough to make a firm mixture. Moisten with 2–3 tablespoons of the wine, work in the eggs and then season with salt and pepper and the nutmeg.

3 Pat the mixture into a sausage shape and place on the boned-out chicken. How much you need depends on the meatiness of the bird (save any left over stuffing to fry as patties.) Re-form the casing over the stuffing and sew up the openings with a sturdy needle and strong thread. Wrap in a clean cloth and tie or sew to make a neat chicken-shaped bolster.

4 Place the bolster in a roomy flameproof pot just large enough to hold it comfortably. Add the remaining ingredients including the rest of the wine and some salt, and pour in enough water to submerge everything.

5 Bring to the boil, then turn down the heat, cover and leave to simmer very gently for 1½ hours or so until firm and cooked right through. Remove from the heat and leave to cool in its poaching water.

6 Once cooled, unwrap the gallatine and pack it into a loaf tin into which it will just fit. Weight down under a board and leave overnight in the refrigerator to firm and set. Cut into slices to serve, with a potato salad dressed with a homemade mayonnaise as a starter or light summer lunch.

Turkey with Red Peppers

Pavo chilindrón

SERVES 6

1 kg (2 lb) turkey meat, diced

2 garlic cloves, crushed

4 tablespoons olive oil

1 large mild onion, sliced into half-moons

6 red peppers, cored, deseeded and sliced into strips

1 tablespoon diced ham

500 g (1 lb) tomatoes, skinned and chopped

1 small cinnamon stick

about 200 ml (7 fl oz) red wine

a little sugar (optional)

salt and freshly milled black pepper

This is a classic dish from Saragossa in Aragón, where they grow particularly succulent red peppers. You can also make it with chicken or rabbit. If using turkey, the robust flavour of the leg meat is preferable to the softer flesh of the breast. A pretty dish for a party.

1 Fold the turkey meat with the garlic and season with salt and pepper.

2 Heat the oil in a roomy frying pan and fry the onion and peppers until they soften and take a little colour. Turn down the heat and cook very gently for 20 minutes or so until the water has evaporated and the vegetables are soft and thick.

3 Add the turkey meat and ham. Fry for 5–10 minutes until the meat seizes and takes a little colour. Add the tomatoes, cinnamon stick and wine and allow to bubble up until the steam no longer smells of alcohol.

4 Turn down the heat, cover tightly and simmer for 30–40 minutes – you may need to add a little more water if it looks like drying out – until the turkey meat is perfectly tender and the juices are well reduced. If it looks a little watery, remove the lid and let it bubble up fiercely for 1–2 minutes, or until the sauce is thick and shiny. Taste and adjust the seasoning – you might need a little sugar if the tomatoes were not particularly ripe. Bubble up for a few minutes more to marry the flavours.

5 Serve with white rice or plenty of bread. Good on the first day, better on the second.

Pasta Paella
Fideos a la catalana

SERVES 4

2 tablespoons olive oil

2 garlic cloves, chopped

2 tablespoons chopped parsley

1 tablespoon roughly chopped blanched almonds

about 150 ml (¼ pint) dry sherry or white wine

1 tablespoon pimentón (Spanish paprika)

1 teaspoon ground cinnamon

½ teaspoon ground cloves

12 saffron threads, soaked in 1 tablespoon boiling water

250 g (8 oz) dried pasta, such as small elbow macaroni, spaghettini broken into short lengths or thicker varieties of soup vermicelli

225 g (7½ oz) pork, diced

1 large onion, finely chopped

500 g (1 lb) tomatoes, skinned and chopped

300 ml (½ pint) water

salt

In this Catalan version of paella, rice is replaced by pasta of much the same volume and similar shape. Pork is the usual meat, but you can include prawns, shellfish, morcilla or chorizo. The almonds for the sauce, another strictly Catalan preparation, can be replaced by cubed bread.

1 Heat the oil in a frying pan and fry the garlic, parsley and almonds until the garlic and almonds are golden. Add the sherry or wine and allow to bubble up. Transfer all the solids to a food processor and process with the ground spices and saffron and its soaking water until you have a smooth paste, or pound in a mortar with a pestle. Reserve the oil.

2 In a paella pan or large frying pan, heat the reserved oil until a faint blue haze rises. Add the pasta and turn it in the hot oil until it takes a little colour.

3 Add the pork and onion, sprinkle with a little salt and continue to fry until the meat and the onion lose their water and begin to caramelize.

4 Add the tomatoes and the almond paste diluted with the water. Bubble up and cook gently until the meat is cooked through, the pasta is tender and the surface of the *fideu* is beginning to look dry rather than soupy. Add another splash of boiling water if it looks like drying out before the pasta is soft.

5 If you wish to eat in traditional style, serve as you would a paella, unplated but with forks for everyone to eat the portion in front of them.

Chicken with Almonds and Saffron

Pollo con almendras y azafràn

SERVES 4

1 free-range chicken
  1.5 k (3 lb), jointed
  into about 12 pieces

4 tablespoons pure pork
  lard or olive oil

2 garlic cloves, chopped

1 thick slice of day-old
  bread

1 tablespoon chopped
  parsley

2 tablespoons ground
  almonds

1 teaspoon ground
  cinnamon

½ teaspoon ground
  cloves

12 saffron threads,
  soaked in 1 tablespoon
  boiling water

juice and grated rind of
  1 lemon

about 150 ml (¼ pint)
  dry sherry or white
  wine

1 large onion, finely
  sliced

salt and freshly milled
  black pepper

1 tablespoon toasted
  flaked almonds, to
  garnish (optional)

This dish of tender chicken cooked in a saffron sauce spiced with cinnamon and thickened with pounded almonds is from the days of the Moors.

1 Trim the chicken joints, removing any whiskery feathers and flaps of skin, and season with salt and pepper.

2 Heat half the lard or oil in a frying pan and fry the garlic and bread until both are golden. Add the parsley and fry for a moment longer.

3 Transfer the contents of the pan to a food processor and process briefly, or pound in a mortar with a pestle. Add the ground almonds, cinnamon and cloves, the saffron and its soaking water, lemon juice and rind and the sherry or wine. Continue to process to a smooth purée.

4 Meanwhile, reheat the pan and add the remaining lard or oil. Gently fry the onion and chicken joints until the skin has browned a little and the onion is soft and golden. Stir in the nut purée and allow to bubble up. Cover, turn down the heat and simmer gently until the chicken joints are cooked right through and the sauce is concentrated to a couple of spoonfuls – add a little boiling water only if needed. To test the chicken for doneness, push a sharp knife through the thickest part of one of the thigh joints: when the juices run clear rather than pink, it's ready. Taste and adjust the seasoning, if necessary.

5 Heap on a warm serving dish and sprinkle with toasted flaked almonds, if you like.

Grilled Steaks with Hazelnut Salsa

Chuletas de ternera a la parilla con salsa de avellanas

SERVES 4

4 beef or veal T-bone steaks

1–2 tablespoons olive oil

1 garlic clove, finely chopped

salt and freshly milled black pepper

SALSA

100 g (3½ oz) toasted hazelnuts (skinned or not, as you please)

1 shallot or small onion, roughly chopped

2 tablespoons cider vinegar

4 tablespoons finely chopped parsley

1 tablespoon water

4 tablespoons olive oil

dry crust of bread (optional)

In the Basque Country, young thick beef steaks on the bone are the great luxury, a taste that can only be satisfied by a trip to one of the asadores that specialize in grilled meats and nothing else. T-bone steaks cut from young beef come closest to the real thing.

1 Wipe over the steaks and rub the surfaces with the oil. Sprinkle with the garlic and season with salt and pepper. Cover and leave for 1–2 hours at room temperature to take the flavours.

2 Put all the salsa ingredients except the oil into a liquidizer or food processor and process to a smooth purée. Add the oil gradually in a thin stream, as if making a mayonnaise, and process until you have a creamy sauce. If it's a hot day, add a dry crust of bread to maintain the emulsion.

3 Grill the meat on a preheated barbecue or under a preheated grill over fierce heat, turning it once, until done to your liking. To test for doneness, prod the meat with your finger – if it feels soft, the meat will be rare; if the surface still has a little elasticity, it will be medium done; if firm, it's well done. To check, place your forefinger on the tip of your thumb and feel the firmness of the thumb ball; replace the forefinger with the second finger and feel again, and so on until you reach the little finger. The forefinger produces the softest thumb ball, corresponding to meat cooked rare, and the little finger produces the hardest, corresponding to well done.

4 Serve each steak with a thick slab of country bread and hand round the salsa separately. Cider is the appropriate accompaniment: this is apple country.

Quail with Parsley and Garlic Sauce

Codornices a la parilla con salsa verde

SERVES 4

8 quails

MARINADE

2 tablespoons olive oil

juice of 1 lemon

2 garlic cloves, finely
slivered

1 tablespoon dried
oregano

salt and freshly milled
black pepper

SAUCE

2 slices of country
bread, crusts
removed, soaked
in water and
squeezed dry

2 garlic cloves, roughly
crushed with a little
salt

2 handfuls or 300 ml
(½ pint) loosely-
packed flat leaf
parsley leaves,
chopped

2 tablespoons white
wine or sherry vinegar

150 ml (¼ pint) olive oil

*Farmed quail, with their delicate, pale and tender meat inclined to
blandness, take well to a robust parsley and garlic sauce from the
Basque Country.*

1 First spatchcock the quail. Split each carcass in half
right down the back, open it out and press firmly on the
breastbone to flatten – it'll look like a squashed frog but
will cook in double-quick time.

2 Thread the quail on skewers to keep them spread out
flat. Sprinkle both sides with the marinade ingredients.
Cover and leave for 1–2 hours at room temperature or
overnight in the refrigerator to take the flavours.

3 Cook the birds under a grill preheated to maximum
heat, or roast in a preheated oven, 240°C (475°F), Gas
Mark 9, for 10 minutes on one side. Turn, baste and allow
another 5–8 minutes on the other side until the flesh is
firm and the skin beautifully browned. Test by pushing
a larding needle or fine skewer into the breast and thigh
of one of the birds – the juices should run clear.

4 Meanwhile, make the sauce. Put all the ingredients
except the oil in a liquidizer or food processor and process
to a smooth purée. Add the oil gradually in a thin stream,
as if making a mayonnaise, and process until you have a
creamy sauce. If it splits, a splash of boiling water will
bring it back.

5 Serve the birds with the sauce handed round separately.
For a more substantial dish, place each bird on a thick slab
of toasted country bread spread with the sauce.

Spiced Pork and Onion Pie
Empanada gallega

SERVES 4−6

FILLING

300 g (10 oz) lean pork, trimmed and diced

1 tablespoon pimentón (Spanish paprika)

½ tablespoon dried oregano

1 garlic clove, crushed

2 tablespoons olive oil

1 onion, diced

2 red peppers, cored, deseeded and diced

about 75 ml (3 fl oz) white wine

½ teaspoon saffron threads, soaked in 1 tablespoon boiling water

500 g (1 lb) tomatoes, skinned, deseeded and diced

1 tablespoon diced serrano ham or lean bacon

1 teaspoon dried thyme

2−3 anchovy fillets, chopped

½ teaspoon chilli flakes

salt (optional)

A juicy meat pie spiced with pimentón and baked between two layers of pastry makes excellent picnic food. This particular filling is typically Galician, other regions having their own versions. Although the pastry can be of your own choosing, a yeast pastry is more common in the region.

1 Make the pastry first. Sift the flour with the salt into a warm bowl and mix in the dried yeast. Make a well in the middle and pour in the warm water. Sprinkle the surface with a handful of flour and leave for 10 minutes in a warm place to allow the yeast to begin working. Add the oil (it should be as warm as your hand) and work the dry and wet ingredients together with the hook of your hand until you have soft, elastic dough. Drop the ball of dough back into the bowl, cover the bowl with clingfilm and set in a warm place for 1−2 hours until it has doubled in size.

2 Meanwhile, make the filling. Turn the pork in the pimentón, oregano and garlic. Heat half the oil in a frying pan and gently fry the meat until it stiffens and browns a little. Remove and reserve.

3 Reheat the pan with the remaining oil and fry the onion and peppers for at least 10 minutes until they soften. Add the wine, saffron and its soaking water, tomatoes, ham or bacon, thyme and anchovies. Bubble up for a moment.

4 Return the meat to the pan and let it bubble up again. Cover loosely and simmer for about 20 minutes, or until the liquid has evaporated and the meat is tender. Taste and add the chilli flakes and salt if necessary (the anchovies provide salt). Leave to cool while you finish the pastry.

5 Knock back the dough to distribute the air bubbles by punching it with your fist. Knead until elastic and springy – you'll feel the dough continue to rise as you work. Cut the dough into 2 pieces, one a little larger than the other. Brush a baking tray (about 34 x 22 cm/13½ x 8½ inches) with oil and dust with a little flour (nonstick needs no such attention). Work each piece of dough into a smooth ball.

6 On a floured surface, pat out or roll each ball to form 2 rectangles, one roughly the same size as the baking tray, the other a little smaller. Lay the larger piece in the baking tray, bringing it comfortably up the sides. Spread the filling over the pastry in an even layer. Dampen the edges of the pastry and top with the remaining dough. Work the 2 edges together in a rope pattern with a damp finger. Prick the top in a few places with a fork and paint with beaten egg to give the pie a pretty glaze.

7 Place in a preheated oven, 180°C (350°F), Gas Mark 4, for 40–50 minutes, or until the pastry is well risen and browned. Serve at room temperature.

PASTRY

300 g (10 oz) strong bread flour, plus extra for dusting

½ teaspoon salt

1 teaspoon easy-blend dried yeast

150 ml (¼ pint) warm water

4 tablespoons oil, plus extra for oiling

beaten egg, to glaze

Pot-roast Lamb with Almonds

Cordero estofado en salsa de almendras

SERVES 4

1.5 kg (3 lb) thick lamb steaks (shoulder or leg), chopped right across the bone

200 g (7 oz) whole unblanched almonds

4 tablespoons olive oil

1 whole head of garlic (about 12 cloves), cloves separated but not peeled

1–2 bay leaves

1 thyme sprig

200 ml (7 fl oz) white wine or dry sherry

200 ml (7 fl oz) water

1 tablespoon pimentón (Spanish paprika), preferably smoked

salt and freshly milled black pepper

1 tablespoon toasted flaked almonds (optional)

In this recipe from the shepherding regions of Spain (anywhere north of Andalusia), lamb on the bone is flavoured with garlic and finished with a thick paste of toasted almonds and pimentón. In the south, where the goat is the usual milk animal, it's made with kid.

1 Wipe over the lamb and season with salt and pepper.

2 Toast the almonds gently in a heavy, flameproof earthenware or enamel casserole with a teaspoon of the oil. As soon as the skins loosen and the nuts begin to brown, remove and set aside.

3 Reheat the casserole with the remaining oil and fry the meat, turning to brown all sides. Add the garlic cloves and fry for another few minutes. Add the herbs, wine or sherry and the water, and allow to bubble up.

4 Turn down the heat and leave to simmer gently, loosely covered, for 1 hour until the meat is tender enough to eat with a spoon. Alternatively, place in a preheated oven, 160°C (325°F), Gas Mark 3, for the same amount of time. Check occasionally and add another glassful of water if necessary. The cooking broth should be well reduced by the end, but the meat should never be allowed to dry out.

5 Remove a spoonful of the broth, put it with the reserved almonds and pimentón into a liquidizer and process to a paste, or pound in a mortar with a pestle. Stir the paste into the cooking juices and bubble up again to thicken.

6 Heap everything on to a warm serving dish and scatter with the toasted flaked almonds, if you like.

Braised Lamb Shanks
Caldereta de piernas de cordero

SERVES 4

4 lamb shanks

2 tablespoons olive oil

1 tablespoon diced serrano ham or lean bacon

250 g (8 oz) small shallots or baby onions

1 large carrot, cut into chunks

500 g (1 lb) ripe tomatoes, skinned, deseeded and diced

2–3 garlic cloves, crushed with a little salt

1–2 rosemary sprigs

1–2 thyme sprigs

½ teaspoon peppercorns, crushed

about 200 ml (7 fl oz) dry sherry or white wine

salt

The shank – the end piece of the shoulder – cooks to a gluey softness when subject to gentle braising. Although the cooking time is long, the preparation is short – slow food at its most succulent. You can even leave it, tightly covered, in a low oven overnight.

1 Wipe over the lamb shanks and season with salt.

2 Heat the oil in a roomy, flameproof earthenware or enamel casserole that will just accommodate the lamb shanks in a single layer. Brown the meat lightly, turning to sear on all sides. Settle the shanks bone-end upwards.

3 Add the remaining ingredients, packing them around the sides of the casserole. Bring all to the boil, cover tightly (seal with a layer of foil, shiny-side downwards, if you're uncertain about the fit) and place in a preheated oven, 150°C (300°F), Gas Mark 2, for at least 3 hours – longer if that's more convenient – without unsealing, unless your nose and ears tell you that the meat is beginning to fry, when you'll need to add a splash of water. The meat should be tender enough to eat with a spoon and the sauce reduced to a thick jammy slick – very delicious indeed.

Wild Duck with Olives and Oranges
Pato a la sevillana

SERVES 4

2 mallard, quartered, or 4 smaller wild duck, halved

2 tablespoons olive oil

2 garlic cloves, finely chopped

2 tablespoons diced serrano ham

1 teaspoon ground cinnamon

½ teaspoon ground cloves

1 tablespoon green olives, pitted or not as you please

2 Seville oranges or small, thin-skinned lemons, diced

about 150 ml (¼ pint) dry sherry or white wine

salt (optional) and freshly milled black pepper

The wetlands of the Guadalquivir and Valencia attract all manner of overwintering duck, an attraction for the hunters. If you prefer, make this with a domestic duck, quartered. Seville oranges, thin-skinned and sharp, are available only in January and February; other times of the year use lemons or limes.

1 Wipe the duck joints and season with pepper. Trickle with half the oil and sprinkle with the garlic. Cover and leave for about 30 minutes at room temperature to take the flavours.

2 Heat the remaining oil in a heavy flameproof casserole and gently fry the duck joints until the skin takes a little colour. Add the ham, spices, olives and citrus fruit and turn over the heat for 1–2 minutes.

3 Pour in the sherry or wine and just enough water to cover and allow to bubble up. Cover loosely, turn down the heat and leave to simmer gently for 30–40 minutes, or until the birds are perfectly tender and the sauce reduced to a thick, rich citrus sludge.

4 Taste and add salt if necessary (the ham and olives are already salty) before serving. The duck is good accompanied by crisp twice-fried chips cooked in olive oil and a salad of curly endive tossed, as they like it in Seville, with a little sherry vinegar, olive oil, coarse salt and a few sprigs of tarragon.

Spiced Oxtail Hotpot
Estofado de rabo de buey

SERVES 4–6

1–2 oxtails (depending on size), cut into sections

2 tablespoons olive oil

1 tablespoon diced serrano ham or lean bacon

1 large onion, diced

2 garlic cloves, crushed with a little salt

1 green celery stick, chopped

1 large carrot, scrubbed and diced

500 g (1 lb) ripe tomatoes, skinned, deseeded and diced

1 tablespoon hot pimentón (Spanish chilli powder)

1 small cinnamon stick

½ teaspoon crushed allspice berries

3–4 cloves

1 bay leaf

1 bottle red wine

handful of cooked chickpeas (optional)

salt and freshly milled black pepper

Oxtail dishes are found in Spain wherever there was once leather-working, since the skins came with the tail still attached. This delicious version, perfumed with the spices beloved by the Moors, is how they like it in the city of Cordova, famed for hand-tooled leather since the days when Andalusia was ruled from Baghdad.

1 Rinse the oxtail and trim off the excess fat.

2 Heat the oil in a flameproof casserole that is large enough to comfortably accommodate all the pieces. Turn the oxtail pieces in the hot oil until the edges brown a little. Remove from the casserole. Add the ham or bacon, onion, garlic, celery and carrot to the casserole and fry gently until the vegetables soften. Add the tomatoes, spices and bay leaf and allow to bubble up to soften the tomatoes. Add the red wine and bubble up again until the steam no longer smells winey.

3 Return the oxtail to the pot and add enough water to barely cover all the pieces. Season with salt and pepper. Bring back to the boil, then turn down the heat, cover tightly and place in a preheated oven, 150°C (300°F), Gas Mark 2, for 3–4 hours, or until the meat is falling off the bones (or leave to cook on the hob on a very low heat). Check from time to time and add more water if necessary.

4 To finish, transfer the oxtail to a warm serving dish and bubble up the juices in the pot to concentrate the flavour. Check the seasoning. You can, if you like, stir in a ladleful of cooked chickpeas to make the oxtail go further. Good today, even better tomorrow.

Liver and Onions
Higado encebollado

500 g (1 lb) veal liver,
finely sliced

1–2 tablespoons milk

4 tablespoons pure pork
lard or butter

500 g (1 lb) onions, finely
sliced

1 heaped tablespoon
seasoned plain flour

½ teaspoon fennel seeds

salt and freshly milled
black pepper

Here, a great deal of onion makes a sauce for the tender meat, which is cooked rare. This is a classic combination from the Basque Country, very simple and very good.

1 Cut the liver into fine strips and leave it to soak in the milk for 30 minutes.

2 Heat 3 tablespoons of the lard or butter in a heavy frying pan. Add the onions, salt lightly and let them cook very slowly for 25–30 minutes, turning them regularly, until soft and lightly caramelized. Remove to a sieve placed over a bowl to catch the drippings.

3 Drain the liver strips and flip them quickly through the seasoned flour. Reheat the pan with the remaining lard or butter and the drippings from the bowl. Drop in the liver and sear the strips briefly but fiercely, shaking the pan so that the heat reaches all sides, allowing no more than a couple of minutes.

4 Return the onions to the pan and sprinkle with the fennel seeds. Turn to blend the onion and the meat and cook gently for another 5 minutes to blend the flavours. Taste and adjust the seasoning. That's all.

Rabbit with Prunes
Conejo con ciruelas pasas

SERVES 4–6

1 large rabbit (2 if wild and small), jointed

2 tablespoons seasoned plain flour

2 tablespoons pure pork lard or butter

250 g (8 oz) small onions or shallots

3–4 garlic cloves, roughly chopped

300 ml (½ pint) red wine

1 thyme sprig

1–2 bay leaves

2–3 cloves

1 short cinnamon stick

250 g (8 oz) prunes, soaked to swell

salt and freshly milled black pepper

A recipe from the Basque Country, where rabbits fatten in the orchards and plums are dried for winter stores, this works almost as well with duck or chicken. If you should have any pacharán, Basque plum brandy, add a splash at the end and set it alight to burn off the alcohol.

1 If preparing the rabbit yourself, don't forget to lift off the bluish membrane that covers the back and legs, using a sharp knife, or the meat will never be tender. Dust the rabbit joints through the seasoned flour.

2 Heat the lard or butter in a roomy flameproof casserole and fry the onions or shallots and garlic gently until they take a little colour. Push to one side, then turn the rabbit joints in the hot fat and let them brown a little.

3 Add the wine, herbs and spices and a glass or two of water – just enough to cover everything. Allow to bubble up, turn down the heat and cover loosely. Leave to simmer gently for an hour until the meat is perfectly tender. Check every now and then in case you need to top up with a little more water.

4 After 30 minutes, add the prunes. Remove the lid at the end and bubble up to reduce the juices to a shiny little sauce. Taste and adjust the seasoning.

5 Serve in the cooking dish, or pile everything on a warm serving platter. Eat with a spoon and use your fingers – no one can eat a bony little rabbit with a knife and fork.

Chickpea and Chicken Stew
Puchero andaluz

SERVES 4–6

500 g (1 lb) dried
  chickpeas, soaked
  overnight

½ head of garlic (about
  6 cloves)

1 short length of ham
  bone or bacon knuckle

2 free-range chicken
  quarters (a boiling
  fowl is best, a chicken
  will do)

1 bay leaf

½ teaspoon coriander
  seeds

6–8 black peppercorns

1 onion, roughly
  chopped

1 bay leaf

1 marjoram sprig

1–2 large potatoes,
  peeled and cut into
  bite-sized pieces

generous handful of
  spinach or chard
  leaves, shredded

2 tablespoons olive oil

salt

Spain's pucheros *and* cocidos *– generic names for anything that combines pulses with a scrap of meat or bones and is cooked in a boiling pot – have their origin in Moorish Andalusia. The dish is now naturalized throughout the land, each region having its own particular recipe.*

1 Drain the chickpeas and put them into a saucepan of water. Bring to the boil and skim off the grey foam that rises to the surface.

2 Spear the garlic head on a knife and hold over a gas or candle flame until the paper skin singes and blackens a little and the flesh is lightly caramelized. Drop it into the chickpea pan with the ham bone or bacon knuckle, chicken quarters, bay leaf, coriander seeds and peppercorns. Add the onion and herbs, but no salt.

3 Bring to the boil, then turn down the heat. Cover and cook for 1½–3 hours, or until the chickpeas are quite soft.

4 Keep the soup at a gentle boil – don't let the temperature drop or add salt, otherwise the chickpeas never seem to soften. If you need to add water, make sure it is boiling.

5 Thirty minutes before the end of cooking, add the potatoes. Ten minutes before the end, stir in the spinach or chard. Just before you are ready to serve, add salt and stir in the oil.

6 Serve in deep plates, accompanied by plenty of bread and a cos lettuce and onion salad on the side, if you like.

Bean Pot with Chorizo, Chicken and Beef
Olla podrida

SERVES 6–8

750 g (1½ lb) dried
  haricot beans, soaked
  overnight in cold water

½ head of garlic (6 cloves)

1 short length of serrano
  ham bone or bacon
  knuckle

5 tablespoons olive oil

1–2 bay leaves

2 dried red peppers,
  deseeded and torn,
  or 1 fresh red pepper,
  deseeded and sliced

½ teaspoon peppercorns,
  crushed

1 small free-range
  chicken about 1.5 kg
  (3 lb) (an old hen has
  the best flavour, a
  young one will do)

750 g (1½ lb) stewing
  beef in a single piece
  (preferably shin)

500 g (1 lb) pork belly,
  salted or fresh

1–2 carrots, chopped

1 onion, stuck with
  2–3 cloves

250 g (8 oz) chorizo

250 g (8 oz) morcilla
  or black pudding

1 large sweet potato,
  peeled and cut into
  chunks

1 small green cabbage

2 green apples, peeled,
  cored and cut into
  chunks

salt and freshly milled
  black pepper

This is the stupendous bean pot as served in Madrid, which is as extravagant as can be expected from the nation's political capital, and is just as variable in its notions of what's acceptable. Chickpeas are traditional, but this version is based on white haricot beans.

1 Drain the beans, put them in a heavy saucepan and pour in enough cold water to submerge them to a depth of 2 fingers. Bring to the boil and skim off the grey foam that rises to the surface.

2 Spear the garlic head on a knife and hold over a gas or candle flame until the paper skin singes and blackens a little and the flesh is lightly caramelized. Drop it into the bean pot along with the ham bone or bacon knuckle, 4 tablespoons of the oil, bay leaves, red peppers and peppercorns. Bring all to the boil, and then turn down to a fast simmer. Cover loosely and leave to bubble gently, adding boiling water during the course of the cooking when needed. Beans are variable in the length of time they need to soften and can take anything from 1–3 hours to cook.

3 Meanwhile, put the chicken, beef and pork in another saucepan with the carrots and the onion stuck with the cloves and add enough water to submerge all completely. Season with salt and pepper. Bring to the boil, skim off the grey foam that rises to the surface and turn down the heat. Cover loosely and leave to simmer until all is tender.

4 In a small saucepan, make the tomato sauce: fry the onion gently in the oil until it softens and browns a little, then add the tomatoes. Allow to bubble up and then squash down with a fork until you have a thick, shiny deep red sauce. Season and reserve.

5 When the beans are soft but not yet mushy, add the
chorizo, morcilla or black pudding and sweet potato.
Bubble up again and turn down the heat to a simmer.
Test for doneness after 20 minutes.

6 Meanwhile, prepare the cabbage: with a sharp knife,
nick out the hard centre of the core, then slice thickly,
making sure that each slice is held together by a strip of
stalk. Pack the cabbage slices in a roomy saucepan and
add a couple of ladlefuls of broth from the meats. Bring
to the boil and drop in the apples. Cover tightly and cook
for about 5 minutes until tender but still bright green.

7 Taste and add salt (if you have used salt pork it will have
contributed to the saltiness), then stir in the remaining oil.
Remove the chorizo and morcilla from the bean pot
and heap them on a serving dish with the meats
from the other pot. Moisten with cooking
broth. Heap the meats, vegetables and
beans in separate piles on another
serving plate.

8 Serve the bean broth combined
with the meat broth first in deep
plates in which you may, if you
like, place a slice of toasted
bread rubbed with garlic, then
serve the real food – beans,
meats and vegetables
including the cabbage and
apples – as a second course.
Serve the tomato sauce
separately.

TOMATO SAUCE

1 onion, diced

2 tablespoons olive oil

1 kg (2 lb) ripe
tomatoes, skinned
and chopped

Venison Stewed with Chocolate

Venado estofado con chocolate

SERVES 4

1 kg (2 lb) shoulder venison, diced

2 tablespoons oil

1 thick slice of serrano ham fat or fatty bacon, cubed

500 g (1 lb) baby onions or shallots

1 large carrot, diced

plain flour, for dusting (optional)

50 g (2 oz) bitter dark chocolate, grated

1 tablespoon flaked almonds

salt and freshly milled black pepper

MARINADE

1 bottle red wine

2 tablespoons olive oil

1 tablespoon sherry or red wine vinegar

2 garlic cloves, crushed

1–2 bay leaves

1 teaspoon crushed allspice berries

½ teaspoon crushed peppercorns

½ teaspoon salt

Furry game is always improved by a night in a marinade: the meat is invariably lean and dry, and the flavours must be well developed to be convincing. The chocolate is used at the end to thicken and darken the sauce, much as blood does if making a civet.

1 Put the diced venison in a bowl and cover with the marinade ingredients, turning to blend. Cover and leave overnight in a cool place – 2 days is even better.

2 Next day, remove the venison from the marinade, drain and shake dry, reserving the marinade.

3 Heat a tablespoon of the oil in a deep saucepan and add the ham fat or bacon, half the onions or shallots and the carrot. Let everything fry for a few minutes, then push it all to one side and add the meat (you can dust the pieces with flour first if you want a thicker sauce). Let the meat seize and brown a little in the hot oil.

4 Add the marinade with all its bits, allow everything to bubble up and then turn down the heat. Leave to simmer gently, loosely covered, for an hour or so until the venison is quite tender. You may need to add a little water – not too much since you want a thick, rich sauce. Ten minutes before end of the cooking, stir in the grated chocolate and bubble up to blend and thicken. Taste and adjust the seasoning if necessary.

5 Meanwhile, cook the remaining onions or shallots gently in a closed pan with the remaining oil until they are golden and tender, then remove and reserve. Fry the almonds gently in the pan drippings until golden.

6 Heap the meat on a warm serving dish, spoon over the sauce and finish with the onions or shallots and almonds.

Braised Veal with Serrano Ham

Guiso de ternera mechada

SERVES 6−8

2 kg (4 lb) boned-out veal or young beef, rolled and tied as for a pot-roast

50 g (2 oz) thick-cut serrano ham with plenty of golden fat

500 g (1 lb) mature carrots

4 tablespoons olive oil

500 g (1 lb) shallots or baby onions

4 garlic cloves, crushed with a little salt

125 g (4 oz) fresh mushrooms (wild is best), sliced

a few thyme and oregano sprigs

1 bay leaf

½ teaspoon crushed black pepper

¼ teaspoon crushed allspice berries

1 bottle red wine

a little sugar

salt

In Spain, veal is usually young beef rather than milk-fed calf, and is naturally dry and mild flavoured. It benefits from larding – threading the meat with strips of fatty pork or some other meat – which adds richness and flavour.

1 Insert a sharp knife right through the heart of the joint to make a deep incision from end to end – starting at the blunt end, the knife point should appear at the tip. Cut the ham into matchsticks and cut one of the carrots into narrow batons. Push the ham and carrot batons into the incisions of the joint – be patient and use a skewer or larding needle to help you on your way.

2 Heat the oil in a roomy flameproof casserole and brown the meat on all sides. Pack in the shallots or onions, garlic and remaining carrots, cut into chunks the same size as the shallots or onions. Add the mushrooms.

3 Tuck in the herbs (in a little bunch, if that's convenient) and the spices. Add the wine and season with salt and the sugar to balance the acidity of the wine.

4 Bring to the boil, remove from the heat and cover tightly – use foil as well as a lid. Place the casserole in a preheated oven, 150°C (300°F), Gas Mark 2, and leave to cook gently in its own juices for 2–3 hours – overnight is not too long, although if this is your choice, you should drop the temperature to 140°C (275°F), Gas Mark 1.

5 When the meat is perfectly tender, remove and leave to rest before slicing. Serve at room temperature, with its sauce.

Butter Beans with Pork

Fabada asturiana

SERVES 6–8

750 g (1½ lb) smallish dried butter beans, soaked overnight in cold water

½ head of garlic

1 large carrot, diced

2 small turnips, peeled and diced

2 celery sticks, diced

500 g (1 lb) pork spare rib

250 g (8 oz) chorizo

250 g (8 oz) morcilla or black pudding (optional)

sea salt and freshly milled black pepper

TO GARNISH

chopped parsley

½ onion, finely chopped

The Asturians – dairy-herding upland farmers with a tradition of self-sufficiency – prefer the Peruvian native bean, the butter bean, to the other storable beans. Not only does it thrive in the cold climate of the highest mountain range in Spain but it also melts to a comforting creaminess in a stew.

1 Drain the beans and rinse them. Put them in a soup pot with the rest of the ingredients and enough water to cover them to a depth of 2 fingers. No salt yet.

2 Bring to the boil and then turn down to a simmer. Cover loosely and leave to bubble gently for 1–2 hours, or until the beans are perfectly soft and the meats tender enough to eat with a spoon. Season with salt and pepper.

3 Serve in deep soup plates. If you like, hand round a bowl of chopped parsley and raw onion for people to add their own.

Fish & Shellfish

Catalan Fish Soup

Zarzuela catalana

SERVES 4 AS A
MAIN DISH

- 500 g (1 lb) monkfish tail, filleted
- 500 g (1 lb) sea bream, filleted
- 350 g (11½ oz) squid, cleaned (see page 94)
- 500 g (1 lb) live mussels, cleaned (see page 99)
- 500 ml (17 fl oz) water
- 2–3 tablespoons seasoned plain flour
- 100 ml (3½ fl oz) olive oil
- 1 small onion, finely sliced
- 2 garlic cloves, finely slivered
- 500 g (1 lb) ripe tomatoes, skinned, deseeded and diced
- 1 short cinnamon stick
- about 12 saffron threads, lightly toasted in a dry pan
- about 150 ml (¼ pint) dry sherry or white wine
- 12 large raw unpeeled prawns or langoustines
- salt and freshly milled black pepper
- 2 tablespoons chopped parsley, to garnish

This is the Catalan version of Provence's bouillabaisse, a member of that venerable tribe of traditional Mediterranean fish soups that makes the most of whatever comes to hand. These delicious one-pot stews remain popular, their content becoming grander all the time.

1 Chop the fish fillets into bite-sized pieces and slice the squid into rings, leaving the tentacles in a bunch. Set aside. Put the mussels in a roomy saucepan with the water, lightly salted. Bring to the boil, cover and cook for 5 minutes or so until the shells open.

2 Remove the pan from the heat and transfer the mussels with a slotted spoon to a warm serving dish. Discard any that remain closed. Strain the broth through a cloth-lined sieve – mussels are hard to rid of all their sand – and reserve.

3 Place the seasoned flour on a plate and dust through the fish pieces. Heat the oil in a roomy frying pan and fry the floured fish for 2–3 minutes on each side until firm and golden. Transfer to the serving dish with the mussels.

4 Reheat the pan and gently fry the onion and garlic until they soften – don't let them brown. Add the tomatoes, cinnamon stick and saffron and bubble up for a few minutes until the tomato softens, mashing down to make a thick sauce. Add the sherry or wine and bubble up to evaporate the alcohol. Add the mussel broth and bubble up, stirring to blend. Taste and season with pepper – you probably won't need more salt.

5 Lay the prawns or langoustines in the hot broth. Allow to bubble up and cook briefly until they turn opaque. Transfer to the serving dish. Bubble up the sauce again until thick and rich. Ladle the sauce over the fish and finish with a generous shower of parsley.

Seafood Paella

Paella marinera

knife tip of saffron threads (12–18), lightly toasted in a dry pan

4 large ripe tomatoes

6–8 tablespoons olive oil

4 garlic cloves, unpeeled and roughly chopped

1 rabbit (or 1 small chicken), jointed into 16–20 bite-sized pieces

500 g (1 lb) paella or risotto rice (although pudding rice will do)

handful of thin green asparagus (sprue) or young green beans, chopped

1 kg (2 lb) live clams and mussels, cleaned (see page 99)

250 g (8 oz) unpeeled prawns (freshwater crayfish ideally)

salt and freshly milled black pepper

A paella is traditionally prepared over a campfire in the open air, though Spanish cooks have access to a specially-wide gas ring which does the job just as well. Failing this, light a barbecue and let the coals die down to an even heat.

1 You'll need a 7-person paella pan, 45 cm/17¾ inches in diameter, and a heat source to match. In order for the rice to cook evenly in a single layer, the pan requires an even bed of heat that allows the full expanse of metal to come into contact with the heat source. If this is not available, use a large frying pan and remember to stir the rice as it cooks.

2 Put the saffron to soak in a splash of boiling water for 15 minutes or so. Meanwhile, grate the flesh of the tomatoes: cut each tomato through its equator and empty out the seeds. Holding the skin side firmly in your palm, rub the cut side through the coarse holes of the grater on to a plate. You should be left with an emptied-out shell in your hand and a juicy heap of pulp on the plate.

3 Set the pan on the fire and wait until it is hot. Preheating the pan avoids food sticking later. Add the oil and wait until it smokes. Immediately add the garlic and the jointed rabbit (or chicken) and turn the pieces over the heat. Cook gently until tender and no longer pink, turning regularly – this will take at least 20 minutes.

4 Add the rice and stir until all the grains are coated and transparent. Stir the tomato pulp into the rice. Add the saffron and its soaking water and top up with as much water as will cover the layer of rice to a depth of one finger – the liquid should be level with the screws that fix the handles to the pan. Allow all to bubble up, season with salt and pepper and leave to cook for 15–18 minutes.

Move the pan over the heat and add more water when necessary, but don't stir again. After 10 minutes, add the asparagus or green beans and the shellfish – the clams and mussels will open in the steam. Discard any shells that remain closed.

5 When it's ready, most of the liquid will have evaporated and little craters, like worm holes, will begin to appear on the surface. Test the rice for doneness by biting into a grain – it should be soft but still retain a nutty little heart.

6 Remove the pan from the heat, cover with a clean cloth or a couple of sheets of newspaper and leave for 10 minutes to allow the rice to finish swelling. A paella should be moist and succulent, never dry.

7 Settle everyone in a circle around the pan. Traditionally you should eat the portion in front of you straight from the pan. You may use clean fingers, or a spoon or lettuce leaves for scooping. Provide plenty of robust country bread for the faint-hearted who would otherwise go hungry.

Cuttlefish with Broad Beans
Sepia con habas

SERVES 4–6

1 kg (2 lb) **whole squid or cuttlefish**

2 tablespoons olive oil

2 garlic cloves, finely sliced

250 g (8 oz) shelled, skinned broad beans

about 150 ml (¼ pint) dry sherry

about 150 ml (¼ pint) water

1 teaspoon marjoram or oregano leaves

salt and freshly milled black pepper

The creamy chewiness of the fish marries perfectly with the tender greenness of the beans. Squid can be substituted for the cuttlefish, and white beans – the large, floury pochas *or the smaller kidney-shaped* habichuelas *– can replace the broad beans.*

1 Rinse the squid or cuttlefish. Remove the bone (a long sheet of clear plastic in the squid; a chalky oval disc in the cuttlefish) and the soft innards with the tentacles and body attached. Discard the innards and the eye portion as well as the hard little beak-like mouthpiece. Slice the body and remaining head parts into rings. Rinse the tentacles in water and scrape off the little 'toenails'. If large, divide the tentacles into singles; if small, the tentacles look pretty left in their bunches.

2 Heat the oil gently in a flameproof casserole. Add the garlic and let it soften but not take on any colour. Add the fish and let it cook very gently for about 10 minutes until it yields up its juices.

3 Add the beans, sherry and the water and let it all bubble up. Sprinkle in the marjoram or oregano and season with pepper. Turn down the heat, cover loosely and leave to simmer for about 20–30 minutes, or until the beans and fish are tender.

4 Remove the lid, turn up the heat and bubble up to reduce the juices to an oily sauce. Taste and add salt. Serve with chunks of robust country bread for mopping.

Octopus with Onions and Potatoes

Pulpo encebollado con patatas

SERVES 4

1 smallish octopus, about 1 kg (2 lb), ready-cleaned

4 tablespoons olive oil

2 large onions, thinly sliced

1 tablespoon chopped parsley

about 12 saffron threads, soaked in 1 tablespoon boiling water

500 g (1 lb) yellow-fleshed potatoes, peeled and sliced

hot pimentón (Spanish chilli powder) or chilli flakes, to taste

salt

Octopus must be tenderized by bashing it thoroughly before you cook it – fishermen say to throw it 40 times against the rocks until the tentacles curl. Older specimens need lengthier tenderizing than young ones. Make it easy for yourself and pop it in the freezer for 48 hours.

1 Rinse the octopus and slice it into bite-sized pieces.

2 Heat the oil in a roomy frying pan and fry the onions very gently for 10 minutes until soft and golden – salt lightly to get the juices running.

3 Add the parsley and the saffron with its soaking water and allow to bubble up. Add the octopus and cook gently in its own juices (these are copious), loosely covered, for an hour. You may need to add a little water.

4 When the octopus is tender, add the potatoes, make sure that there's enough liquid to cover and continue to cook for another 15 minutes or so until the potatoes are perfectly tender. Taste and season with salt and hot pimentón or chilli flakes.

5 Serve the octopus in deep bowls, sauced with its own lovely juices.

Two-dish Rice
Arroz abanda

SERVES 6

1.5 litres (2½ pints) water

1 thyme sprig

1 bay leaf

about 150 ml (¼ pint) white wine

8 tablespoons olive oil

1 kg (2 lb) mixed fish fillets, divided into firm-fleshed and soft-fleshed

handful each of raw peeled prawns, live mussels and clams, cleaned (see page 99), (optional)

2 garlic cloves

2 tablespoons pimentón (Spanish paprika) or the pulp from 2 dried red peppers, soaked to soften

1 teaspoon salt

about 12 saffron threads, toasted in a dry pan

2 tablespoons chopped parsley

500 g (1 lb) paella or risotto rice

500 g (1 lb) tomatoes, skinned, deseeded and diced

ALIOLI

6 garlic cloves, crushed

1 teaspoon sea salt

about 300 ml (½ pint) extra-virgin olive oil

This is one of the two great rice dishes of the Levant – the other is paella – for which the rice and seafood are served separately. The firm-fleshed fish (monkfish, conger eel and weever fish are most favoured) and soft-fleshed fish (mackerel, bream and gallo, a Mediterranean plaice) are cooked in separate batches.

1 Bring the water to the boil in a roomy saucepan with the herbs, wine and half the oil. Add the firm-fleshed fish and bring back to the boil. Turn down the heat and leave to simmer for 5 minutes.

2 Add the soft-fleshed fish and prawns and shellfish, if using, and cook for a further 10 minutes. Carefully lift out the seafood and keep warm. Strain the fish stock and reserve.

3 Pound the garlic, pimentón or soaked peppers and salt in a mortar with a pestle. Heat the remainder of the oil in a paella pan – a large frying pan will do – add the garlic mixture, saffron and parsley and fry gently for a few minutes until the garlic softens.

4 Add the rice and turn it in the hot oil for a moment. Add the tomatoes and 1 litre (1¾ pints) of the fish stock – the volume of stock should be double that of the rice. Bring to the boil and let it bubble fiercely for 5 minutes, then turn down the heat and simmer for another 12 minutes. Add a little more fish stock as it dries out. Leave it to rest for 10–15 minutes after you take it off the heat. The rice should be juicy but with the grains visibly separate.

5 Meanwhile, to make the alioli, pound the garlic with the salt in a mortar with a pestle. Slowly trickle in the oil, working the paste so that the garlic acts like an emulsifier to make a rich, spoonable sauce for the fish.

6 Serve the sauce with the fish and shellfish. By the time the fish has all been eaten, the rice will be ready. The traditional way to eat the first course is by spearing the fish on a knife straight from the communal dish. The rice, too, can be eaten directly from the pan, scooping it up with a spoon and confining yourself to the portion directly in front of you – no poaching.

Clams in Tomato Sauce with Garlic

Almejas en salsa de tomate con ajo

SERVES 4

2 kg (4 lb) live bivalves, such as clams, mussels, cockles, razor shells or queen scallops

½ teaspoon saffron threads (about 12)

4 tablespoons olive oil

1 onion, finely chopped

3–4 garlic cloves, finely chopped

1 kg (2 lb) ripe tomatoes, skinned, deseeded and diced

1 tablespoon pimentón (Spanish paprika)

about 150 ml (¼ pint) red wine

salt and freshly milled black pepper

This recipe comprises a garlicky tomato sauce into which the shellfish are dropped raw. The cooking is very brief, since they only take a minute or two to open in the steam, releasing their fresh juices into the sauce.

1 Wash the shellfish in plenty of cold water, checking over and discarding any that are broken or weigh unusually heavy – they're probably dead and filled with sand. Also discard any that do not close when sharply tapped. If using mussels, scrape the shells and remove their sandy little beards. If using razor shells, remove their sandy little bag of intestine and rinse well. Leave the shellfish to spit out their sand in a bucket of cold water for a few hours – overnight is even better.

2 Toast the saffron in a dry pan for 1–2 minutes until it releases its scent – don't let it burn or it will be bitter – and drop into a cup with a little boiling water. Leave to infuse for 15 minutes or so.

3 Heat the oil in a roomy frying pan and fry the chopped onion and garlic until soft and golden – don't let them brown.

4 Add the tomatoes and allow to bubble up, mashing them until they soften. Add the pimentón, the saffron with its soaking water and the wine. Bubble up again, then turn down the heat and leave to simmer for 20 minutes or so until the sauce is thick and rich. Taste and season with salt and pepper.

5 Add the shellfish – check first to see that all are looking lively. Bubble up again, then turn down the heat, cover loosely and leave the shells to open in the steam, shaking the pan now and again to allow the top layer to drop to the bottom. Take the pan off the heat as soon as all the shells open – about 4–6 minutes, depending on size of pan and thickness of shells. Discard any shells that remain closed.

Squid Cooked in its Own Ink

Calamares en su tinta

SERVES 4

1 kg (2 lb) whole squid, including their ink

3–4 tablespoons olive oil

4–5 garlic cloves, chopped

1 teaspoon dried thyme (or a handsome fresh sprig)

1 teaspoon dried oregano (it dries naturally on the stalk; just shake it in)

2–3 bay leaves

1 small red chilli, deseeded and finely chopped

handful of celery leaves or green celery sticks, finely chopped

about 12 saffron threads

½ bottle red wine

a little sugar (optional)

salt and freshly milled black pepper

A remarkably good dish, delicate and elegant, the ink that colours and flavours the sauce has a faint taste of violets. Cuttlefish can be used instead, and some say they're even better. Fishmongers who sell the fish ready prepared will usually, if asked, provide a little bagful of ink.

1 Rinse the squid thoroughly (cephalopods are sandy creatures). If preparing your own, follow the instructions on page 94, but before discarding the innards, pick through them and rescue the silvery little ink sacks, then crush them through a sieve and reserve the liquid. If large, chop the tentacles after scraping off any 'toenails'; if small, leave them in their little bunches. Rinse your hands in cold water and they won't smell fishy.

2 Warm the oil in a roomy saucepan and add the garlic. When it begins to sizzle, add the prepared squid. Turn up the heat and stir until the flesh stiffens and turns opaque.

3 Add the herbs, chilli, celery leaves or sticks, saffron and a generous amount of pepper. Pour in the wine and bring to the boil, then turn down the heat, cover loosely and leave to simmer gently for about 40 minutes, or until the flesh is perfectly tender and the juices well reduced.

4 Stir in the reserved ink, taste and season with salt and pepper – perhaps adding a little sugar if the wine was a bit rough. Serve immediately.

Grilled Salt Cod with Red Pepper Salsa

Bacalao a la brasa con salsa romesco

250 g (8 oz) salt cod, soaked for 48 hours in several changes of water

bitter leaves, to serve

SALSA ROMESCO

2 dried red peppers (ñoras), deseeded and soaked to swell (if you can't find these, replace with 2 tablespoons pimentón, or Spanish paprika)

2 large ripe tomatoes, cut into chunks

2 garlic cloves, crushed

1 teaspoon salt

2 tablespoons fresh breadcrumbs, fried until crisp in a little olive oil

2 tablespoons toasted almonds

1 dried red chilli, deseeded and crumbled

2 tablespoons red wine vinegar

150 ml (¼ pint) olive oil

The salty chewiness of the fish is perfectly balanced by the sweetness and richness of the salsa, a speciality of the Catalan city of Tarragona. The deep red of the sauce comes from roasting the tomatoes as well as the dried red peppers (ñoras).

1 Drain the fish and remove the bones and skin – feel carefully with your fingers. Cook fiercely under a preheated hot grill until the flesh blisters and blackens a little at the edges. Shred into small pieces.

2 Roast the peppers and tomatoes under the grill until they blister and take colour. Scrape the pulp from the skin of the peppers. Skin the tomatoes, scooping out and discarding the seeds. Drop them in a liquidizer or food processor with the garlic, salt, breadcrumbs and almonds and pulverize to a paste, or pound in a mortar with a pestle.

3 Add the crumbled red chilli and the vinegar, then add the oil gradually in a thin stream, as if making a mayonnaise, and process until the sauce is thick and shiny. Fold the shredded salt cod with the salsa and serve with bitter leaves, such as frizzy endive or chicory.

Hot-pickled Tuna
Atún en escabeche

SERVES 4

4 thick tuna steaks, about
  1 kg (2 lb) in total
1 heaped tablespoon
  plain flour
1 tablespoon pimentón
  (Spanish paprika)
2 tablespoons olive oil
1 onion, finely sliced
1 garlic clove, crushed
1 small carrot, sliced
1 tablespoon chopped
  parsley
1 bay leaf, torn
6 peppercorns, roughly
  crushed
1 teaspoon crumbled
  dried oregano
4 tablespoons sherry
  vinegar (or any other
  good vinegar)
salt

Tuna takes particularly well to a spice bath, a valuable method of preservation in pre-refrigeration days. For those who lived in the uplands well back from the long sea coast, it was not only useful but also added variety to the diet. Mackerel also takes happily to the treatment.

1 Sprinkle the tuna steaks with salt and leave to firm and juice for 30 minutes. Pour off any liquid, pat the fish dry and dust each steak lightly through the flour mixed with the pimentón.

2 Heat a frying pan and add half the oil. Lay the fish in the hot oil and fry for 2–3 minutes, or until the flesh is opaque and the exterior a little browned – take care not to overcook. Transfer to a shallow dish in a single layer.

3 Reheat the pan, add the remaining oil and gently fry the onion for a few minutes until soft – don't let it brown.

4 Add all the remaining ingredients and bubble up to blend the flavours and soften the carrot. Pour this warm scented bath, unstrained, over the fish. Cover with a clean cloth and leave overnight in a cool place.

5 Spoon the pickle over the fish whenever you remember. It's ready to eat in a day, better in two, best in three.

Swordfish Steaks with Garlic Sauce

Pez espada a la plancha con alioli

SERVES 4

4 swordfish steaks, about
  150 g (5 oz) each

1 tablespoon olive oil

salt and freshly milled
  black pepper

ALIOLI

4 large garlic cloves

1 tablespoon fresh white
  breadcrumbs

juice of 1 lemon

½ teaspoon salt

300 ml (½ pint) olive oil

Swordfish and tuna are treated more like steak than fish, and are often served as the main course in a meal. The flavour is robust enough to stand up to an alioli – a garlicky mayonnaise made without eggs. For a thicker, more mayonnaise-like sauce, include a whole egg.

1 Leave the fish to soak in cold salted water for 20 minutes to firm the flesh and drain out any blood.

2 Meanwhile, make the alioli. Put the garlic cloves, breadcrumbs, lemon juice and salt in a liquidizer or food processor and process to a thick paste. Add the oil gradually in a thin stream, as if making a mayonnaise, and process until you have a thick sauce.

3 Drain the fish steaks and pat dry. Rub the cut surfaces with the oil and season with salt and pepper.

4 Heat a griddle or heavy iron frying pan until it is smoking hot. Smack on the swordfish steaks and cook them fast for 2–3 minutes each side, turning once. Serve the fish with the sauce on the side.

Sea Bream Baked with Potatoes

Besugo al horno con patatas

SERVES 4

- 1 sea bream, about 1.5 kg (3 lb), gutted and scaled but with the head left on
- 1–2 bay leaves
- 1 lemon, quartered
- 500 g (1 lb) potatoes, peeled and cut into bite-sized pieces
- 500 g (1 lb) onions, quartered
- 500 g (1 lb) firm tomatoes, cut into chunks
- 500 g (1 lb) green peppers, cored, deseeded and cut into chunks
- about 150 ml (¼ pint) dry white wine
- 4 tablespoons olive oil
- coarse sea salt

A simple way with a fresh fish, and one that makes an expensive luxury go further. The potatoes take the flavour of the fish, and the tomatoes and onions melt to make a rich sauce with the oil.

1 Wipe over the fish with kitchen paper and salt it lightly inside and out. Tuck the bay leaves and lemon quarters into the cavity. Cover and set aside at room temperature.

2 Arrange the vegetables in a roasting tin, pour in the wine, trickle with the oil and cover with foil, shiny-side down. Bake in a preheated oven, 180°C (350°F), Gas Mark 4, for 30 minutes or so until the potatoes are tender.

3 Remove the foil. Lay the fish on the bed of vegetables, replace the foil and bake for a further 10 minutes until the fish is cooked right through. It's ready when the thickest part feels firm to your finger.

4 Remove and leave to rest for 10 minutes to allow the heat to reach right through to the bone.

Fish Hotpot
Guiso de pescado

SERVES 4

1 kg (2 lb) white fish
   fillets

150 ml (¼ pint) olive oil

2 large onions, sliced

3–4 garlic cloves, sliced

1 tablespoon chopped
   serrano ham

1 litre (1¾ pints) fish
   stock (made with heads
   and bones, but be
   careful to remove the
   gills or the stock will
   become bitter)

300 ml (½ pint) white wine

1 bay leaf

1 kg (2 lb) yellow-fleshed
   potatoes, peeled and
   sliced lengthways

500 g (1 lb) chard or
   spinach, roughly
   shredded

salt

Homely but classic, this is a fish stew that has no need of fancy sauces. Ask the fishmonger for the heads and bones to make a stock. Salt-cured cod, bacalao, can be used instead of fresh fish: soak for 48 hours in several changes of water.

1 Skin the fish fillets if necessary and remove any whiskery bones. Chop into bite-sized pieces. Salt lightly and set aside.

2 Heat the oil gently in a roomy saucepan. Add the onions and garlic, salt lightly and fry very gently for 20 minutes or so until soft and golden – don't let them brown.

3 Add the serrano ham and the stock, wine and bay leaf and boil rapidly until the volume has reduced by half.

4 Add the potatoes and simmer gently for 15–20 minutes until just tender. Add the chard or spinach and bubble up until the leaves wilt.

5 Lay in the fish, return the broth to the boil and cook for another 4–5 minutes – just long enough for the fish to turn opaque. Serve in deep bowls and eat with a spoon and fork.

Vegetables & Accompaniments

Tomatoes with a Pine Nut Stuffing

Tomates rellenos con piñones

SERVES 4

4–8 ripe firm tomatoes

4 tablespoons olive oil, plus extra for oiling

2 garlic cloves, finely chopped

2 tablespoons pine nuts

1 tablespoon finely chopped serrano ham (optional)

1 tablespoon chopped parsley

4 heaped tablespoons fresh breadcrumbs

salt and freshly milled black pepper

Pine nuts – the stone-pine's oily little seeds extracted with difficulty from their rock-hard shells – give a deliciously resiny flavour to this simple stuffing.

1 Wipe each tomato, then slice a little lid off the stem end and reserve. Scoop out the seeds and discard. Hollow out the tomatoes, reserving the pulp. Arrange the hollowed-out tomatoes in an oiled baking dish.

2 Warm half the oil in a small pan and fry the garlic. Add the pine nuts and let them take on a little colour. Then add the reserved tomato flesh and bubble up to make a little sauce. Stir in the ham, if using, parsley and breadcrumbs. Season with salt and pepper.

3 Stuff the tomatoes with the breadcrumb mixture. Top with the reserved lids and trickle with the remainder of the olive oil.

4 Place the tomatoes in a preheated oven, 220°C (425°F), Gas Mark 7, for 25–30 minutes. Larger tomatoes need a slightly lower temperature and a longer cooking time. Serve at room temperature.

Mixed Salad with Tuna and Egg
Ensalada mixta

SERVES 4

1 cos lettuce, thickly sliced

1 green pepper, cored, deseeded and finely sliced

2 large tomatoes, cut into chunks

2 small or ½ large cucumber, cut into chunks

½ mild Spanish onion, finely slivered

1–2 tablespoons green olives

200 g (7 oz) can tuna, drained and flaked (optional)

1–2 hard-boiled free-range eggs, shelled and quartered (optional)

6 tablespoons olive oil

2 tablespoons red or white wine vinegar or lemon juice

coarse sea salt

Salads of chunky raw vegetables and crisp cos lettuce leaves are preferred to soft-leaf salads – which are, in any event, too delicate to stand up to the heat of a Spanish summer.

1 Arrange all the salad ingredients in layers on a large flat plate, finishing with the onion rings and olives. Arrange the optional extras, if using, over the top.

2 Dress with the oil, vinegar or lemon juice and a generous pinch of coarse sea salt – don't blend into a vinaigrette first; Spain likes the taste of its olive oil. That's all.

Broad Beans with Serrano Ham
Habas con jamón

SERVES 4

1 kg (2 lb) young broad beans in their pods (or 350 g/11½ oz mature podded beans)

4 tablespoons olive oil

1 onion, diced

2–3 garlic cloves, thinly sliced

2 tablespoons diced serrano ham

about 150 ml (¼ pint) dry sherry or white wine

1 tablespoon fresh breadcrumbs

1 tablespoon chopped parsley

salt and freshly milled black pepper

Young broad beans, picked while the pods are still soft and furry, are used whole for this dish, which have a delicate flavour rather like okra and retain their fragrance during the cooking. Later in the season, discard the pods and make it with the beans alone.

1 Top, tail and string the young beans in their pods and then chop them into short lengths following the swell of each bean.

2 Warm the oil in a flameproof casserole or heavy saucepan. Fry the onion and garlic for a moment without allowing them to take any colour.

3 Add the beans, ham, sherry or wine and enough water to cover. Add salt and pepper, and bring all to the boil. Cover and stew gently for 1½ hours – this can be done on the hob or in a preheated oven, 160°C (325°F), Gas Mark 3. Check intermittently and add water if necessary.

4 When the beans are tender, allow to bubble up, uncovered, for a moment to evaporate the liquid - the beans should be juicy but not swimming. Stir in the breadcrumbs and parsley. Reheat, taste and add more salt and pepper if necessary.

Fried Green Peppers with Garlic
Pimientos fritos con ajo

SERVES 4

750 g (1½ lb) green frying peppers

about 4 tablespoons olive oil

3–4 garlic cloves, unpeeled and roughly chopped

salt

sherry vinegar, to serve (optional)

Frying peppers in Spain come in two kinds: the long, thin, torpedo-shaped dark green pods with very thin flesh and a gentle, grassy flavour; and pimientos de Padrón *which are small, triangular and equally thin-fleshed: though chilli-like in shape they are mostly mild but with a few fiery ones in every batch.*

1 Rinse the peppers and shake them dry. Don't core or deseed them but leave them whole.

2 Heat the oil in a frying pan until a faint blue haze rises. Add the peppers and fry over a high heat, turning them until all sides take a little colour. Turn the heat right down, add the garlic and salt lightly and cover the pan. Cook over a gentle heat for about 10 minutes until the peppers are soft.

3 Remove the lid and bubble up for 1–2 minutes until the oil loses its moisture and begins to clear. Allow to cool to room temperature and serve sauced with their own oily juices. Sprinkle with a few drops of sherry vinegar – or not, as you please.

VEGETABLES & ACCOMPANIMENTS

Lentils with Rice
Moros y cristianos

SERVES 4

MOORS

500 g (1 lb) lentils

½ large mild onion, finely chopped

2 tablespoons olive oil

salt and freshly milled black pepper

CHRISTIANS

250 g (8 oz) white long-grain rice, boiled and drained

2 garlic cloves, chopped

1 tablespoon olive oil

TO FINISH

2 hard-boiled free-range eggs, shelled and chopped

2 tablespoons toasted almonds

This dish's name – Moors and Christians – commemorates the epic encounter at the gates of Granada when the Moors of Al-Andaluz were chased from their last stronghold by the combined might of Ferdinand of Aragón and Isabella of Castile. The combination delivers a nutritionally-perfect balance of pulses and grains.

1 For the Moors, cook the lentils in enough water to cover to a depth of 2 fingers – they'll take 40–50 minutes to soften. Season with salt and pepper and stir in the onion and oil. Bring back to the boil, allow one big bubble to let the oil form an emulsion with the lentil juices and remove from the heat and reserve.

2 Meanwhile, for the Christians, turn the rice and garlic in the oil in a roomy frying pan, then add water to cover to a depth of 2 fingers. Bubble up, turn down the heat and simmer gently for about 20 minutes until tender.

3 Pile the lentils in the middle of a hot serving dish and surround with the rice: the Moors are encircled by the Christian battalions. Finish the lentils with the chopped hard-boiled egg and the rice with the toasted almonds. Propaganda on a plate.

Artichokes with Broad Beans
Alcachofas con habas

SERVES 4–6

8–12 artichokes (depending on size)

squeeze of lemon juice or 1 teaspoon vinegar

1 large onion, finely chopped

2–3 garlic cloves, finely chopped

4 tablespoons olive oil

about 150 ml (¼ pint) white wine

250 g (8 oz) shelled broad beans (skinned, if old and leathery)

1 tablespoon chopped parsley

1 tablespoon chopped mint

1 tablespoon fresh breadcrumbs

1 tablespoon toasted flaked almonds, to garnish

salt and freshly milled black pepper

This is a classic combination from Granada's fertile market garden, the vega, known since Roman days for its succulent broad beans and fine fat artichokes. When preparing the hearts, remember that the artichoke is a member of the daisy family and that you're dealing with a flower head.

1 Prepare the artichoke hearts first: trim off the stalks close to the base. Scrape the stalks to remove the hard exterior fibres – the tender centre can be eaten – and drop into cold water with the lemon juice or vinegar. Snap off the tough outer leaves, then, with a sharp knife, cut off the tops of the remaining leaves close to the base, exposing the small leaves that protect the choke. Nick out the inner leaves and carve out the choke. Drop the prepared hearts into the water.

2 In a roomy flameproof casserole, gently fry the onion and garlic in the oil until they soften. Add the artichoke hearts and stalks. Cover and let everything fry over a low heat for 15 minutes, shaking regularly, until the artichoke begins to take a little colour.

3 Add the wine and let it all bubble up until the liquid has reduced by half. Add the shelled beans and a glass of water. Season with salt and pepper. Allow to bubble up, turn down the heat and leave to cook gently for about 15 minutes until the vegetables are tender, adding a little boiling water if necessary.

4 Stir in the chopped parsley and mint, and a handful of breadcrumbs to thicken the juices. Heap on a warm serving dish and sprinkle over the toasted almonds.

Chard with Ham and Garlic
Acelgas con jamón y ajo

*Chard, also known as Swiss chard, is a robust, spinach-like
vegetable with dark green leaves and pale, juicy stalks. An all-year
crop, in summer it's less vulnerable to heat than spinach, and in
winter it grows faster than cabbage (which, in any event, likes a
touch of frost).*

1 Rinse the chard (it grows in sandy soil and may be
gritty) and separate the stalks from the leaves. Shred
thickly and keep the leaves and stalks separate.

2 Cook the shredded leaves in a lidded pan with
a little salt and the minimum of water for about
5 minutes or so until they wilt and soften. Drain
thoroughly. Toss with half the oil, and the
lemon juice and rind. Season and reserve.

3 Meanwhile, rinse the stalks and slice into
lengths about as fat as your finger. Heat the
remaining oil in the pan and add the garlic.
Add the chopped stalks and cook for a minute,
then add the water and bubble up. Cover
tightly and cook for about 10 minutes until
perfectly tender, then stir in the ham and parsley.

4 Add pepper (no salt) and serve. You could also
arrange the leaves on one side of the serving dish
and the stalks on the other.

SERVES 4–6

1 large bunch of chard
(8–12 stalks)

4 tablespoons olive oil

juice and finely grated
rind of 1 lemon

4 garlic cloves, finely
sliced

1 tablespoon water

1 tablespoon chopped
serrano ham

1 tablespoon chopped
flat leaf parsley

salt and freshly milled
black pepper

Potatoes with Almonds and Saffron
Patatas en ajopollo

SERVES 4

500 g (1 lb) potatoes, scrubbed or peeled and cut into chunks

2 tablespoons olive oil

2 tablespoons whole blanched almonds

1 garlic clove, finely chopped

1 tablespoon fresh breadcrumbs

1 tablespoon chopped parsley

12 saffron threads, soaked in 1 tablespoon boiling water

salt and freshly milled black pepper

The almond and saffron sauce, a Valencian combination, is particularly good with tender-skinned baby new potatoes. Main-crop potatoes should be peeled and cut into bite-sized chunks.

1 Drop the potatoes into salted water and set them aside.

2 Heat the oil in a small frying pan and fry the almonds until golden, then stir in the garlic and breadcrumbs. Stir over the heat until light golden brown. Add the parsley and saffron and its soaking water and allow to bubble up.

3 Tip the contents of the pan into the food processor and process with a couple of spoonfuls of water to a thick paste, or pound in a mortar with a pestle.

4 Drain the potatoes and transfer them to a heavy pan. Add the almond and saffron paste and pour in enough water to come halfway up the potatoes. Season with salt and pepper. Bring to the boil, cover and cook gently for about 15 minutes until the potatoes are nearly tender, turning them halfway through the cooking to allow the top potatoes to come into contact with the heat at the bottom.

5 Remove the lid and boil rapidly until the cooking broth is reduced to a thick sauce and the potatoes are perfectly soft. Serve at room temperature.

Braised Aubergines

Pisto de berejenas

SERVES 4

4 tablespoons olive oil

4 firm aubergines, diced

1 teaspoon cumin seeds

2 large onions, finely
  sliced

salt

Gentle cooking enhances the sweetness of the onions, which contrasts with the smooth flesh and earthy flavour of the aubergines. Large, firm, meaty and purple-skinned in its Mediterranean incarnation, the aubergine cooks to a satisfying richness when paired, as here, with olive oil.

1 Heat half the oil in a heavy frying pan and gently fry the aubergines, sprinkled with the cumin seeds and a little salt, until they soften and take colour. Be patient – first they will soak up oil like a sponge and then they will release it again, which is when they begin to fry a second time. Transfer to a sieve placed over a bowl to catch the drippings.

2 Return the drippings to the pan and fry the onions until soft and lightly golden. Take your time – allow at least 20 minutes. Stir in the aubergine and cook for another 5 minutes.

3 Leave to cool to room temperature. Eat with thick slices of country bread toasted over a direct flame and rubbed with garlic, if you like; perfect with a few slivers of Manchego cheese.

Cauliflower with Garlic
Coliflor con ajo

SERVES 4

1 cauliflower

2 tablespoons olive oil, plus extra if necessary

2 garlic cloves, chopped

1 tablespoon black olives, pitted and chopped

1 teaspoon cumin seeds

1 teaspoon hot pimentón (Spanish chilli powder)

salt

This, in my experience, is just about the only way to make cauliflower taste exotic. For a touch of luxury, stir in a handful of diced serrano ham.

1 Divide the cauliflower into bite-sized florets. Cook in salted boiling water until tender, then drain.

2 Heat the oil in a roomy frying pan and fry the garlic until it softens and takes on a little colour. Add the drained cauliflower and fry for a few minutes, or until it begins to sizzle and colour slightly.

3 Add the olives, sprinkle with the cumin seeds and season with salt and the hot pimentón. Fry gently for 10 minutes or so, turning the cauliflower until it browns evenly a little all over and takes on the flavours of all the spices. Serve at room temperature.

Broad Beans with Chestnuts

Habas con castañas

SERVES 6–8

350 g (11½ oz) dried skinned broad beans, soaked overnight in cold water

1 short length of serrano ham bone or a bacon knuckle

1 free-range chicken quarter

350 g (11½ oz) dried chestnuts, soaked overnight in cold water (or 500 g/1 lb fresh ones, skinned)

2 tablespoons olive oil

1 onion, roughly chopped

1 large carrot, chopped

1 bay leaf

1 thyme sprig

½ teaspoon crushed black peppercorns

1 short cinnamon stick

about 250 g (8 oz) pumpkin, deseeded, peeled and diced

about 2 tablespoons chopped fresh coriander

1–2 links of fresh (soft) chorizo, crumbled and fried (optional)

salt

In this dish from the sierras of Seville, dried broad beans are combined with dried chestnuts. The finishing flavouring of coriander leaves is found nowhere else in Spain, a result of trade with the pig herdsmen of Portugal, who acquired the taste from trade with the Orient.

1 Drain the beans and put them in a roomy flameproof stew pot with the ham bone or bacon knuckle and the chicken quarter. Add enough water to cover all to a depth of 2 fingers. Bring to the boil and skim off any grey foam that rises to the surface.

2 Add the drained dried (or skinned fresh) chestnuts, oil, onion, carrot, herbs and spices and bring back to the boil. Turn down the heat, cover loosely and leave to bubble gently for 1–1½ hours, or until the beans and chestnuts are perfectly soft. Add the pumpkin, return to the boil and bubble up for 15 minutes or so until the pumpkin is perfectly tender. Taste and adjust the seasoning if necessary and finish with the chopped coriander, along with crumbled fresh chorizo fried in its own oily juices, if you like.

3 Serve in deep soup plates, with red wine for the digestion and country bread for mopping.

Grilled Asparagus with Parsley Salsa

Asparagos a la parilla con salsa verde

SERVES 4

1 kg (2 lb) green asparagus spears

oil, for brushing

salt

SALSA

4 heaped tablespoons chopped flat leaf parsley, leaves only

2 garlic cloves, roughly chopped

yolk of 1 hard-boiled free-range egg

2 tablespoons lemon juice

150 ml (¼ pint) olive oil

salt

Once you've tasted grilled asparagus, you'll never want to cook them any other way. The flavour comes through clear and clean and the asparagus remains juicy and lightly blistered with caramelized juices. For grilling, you need green asparagus as thick as your thumb.

1 Wash and trim the asparagus, discarding the woody bits and peeling off any hard skin.

2 Put all the salsa ingredients except the oil into a liquidizer or food processor and process to a smooth purée. Add the oil gradually in a thin stream, as if making a mayonnaise, and process until you have a thick sauce.

3 Arrange the asparagus on a grill pan in a single layer. Brush with oil and sprinkle with salt. Cook under a preheated hot grill for about 4–5 minutes, turning to cook all sides, until they steam and blister black a little in patches. Hand round the salsa separately.

Flageolets with Chorizo

Habas verdes con longaniza y gachas de maíz

SERVES 4–6

350 g (11½ oz) green flageolet beans, soaked for 2–3 hours in cold water

100 g (3½ oz) serrano ham or lean bacon, diced

2–3 garlic cloves, peeled

1 bay leaf

1 small thyme sprig

½ teaspoon peppercorns, crushed

1 longaniza or 150 g (5 oz) fresh (soft) chorizo, sliced or crumbled

1 tablespoon pure pork lard or olive oil

250 g (8 oz) ready-cooked polenta

4 tablespoons chopped parsley

1 tablespoon chopped mint

salt (optional)

In northern Spain, the dried green beans the French call flageolets – dried haricots picked green – are esteemed for their delicate flavour and slightly gluey texture. In this dish from Catalonia, they're combined with the long, thin lightly smoked chorizo known as longaniza, and served with crisp cubes of polenta.

1 Drain the beans and put them with the ham or bacon in a roomy flameproof pot with the garlic, bay leaf, thyme sprig, crushed peppercorns and enough cold water to cover; beans need plenty of room to swell. Bring to the boil and skim off any grey foam that rises. Turn down the heat and simmer for about an hour until they're perfectly soft. You may need to add a little boiling water during the cooking: the beans should be juicy but not quite soupy.

2 Meanwhile, fry the longaniza or chorizo in the lard or oil until browned at the edges, then remove and set aside. Chop the polenta into dice and turn them in the pan drippings until they acquire a crisp little crust on all sides.

3 Stir the parsley and mint into the beans. Taste and add salt if necessary. Top the beans with the longaniza or chorizo and serve the crisp polenta cubes on the side.

Lentil Soup with Pork and Greens
Potage de lentejas

SERVES 4

500 g (1 lb) pork belly

500 g (1 lb) greeny-brown lentils

½ head of garlic (about 6 fat cloves), unpeeled

2–3 links of chorizo, or 100 g (3½ oz) shoulder pork, diced, and 1 tablespoon pimentón (Spanish paprika)

500 g (1 lb) canned or fresh tomatoes, roughly chopped

½ teaspoon cumin seeds

2 litres (3½ pints) water

1 large potato, peeled and cubed

250 g (8 oz) spring greens or spinach, shredded

2 tablespoons extra-virgin olive oil

salt and freshly milled black pepper

2–3 hard-boiled free-range eggs, shelled and quartered, to garnish (optional)

Lentils, floury and nutty, are the fast food of the pulses, since they don't need soaking. For a soup, choose the large, greeny-brown Spanish lentils, which collapse in the pot and drink up the flavour of whatever else goes into the stew.

1 Trim the pork belly without discarding any fat – it adds flavour and the lentils will drink it all up – and then dice. Pick over the lentils, checking for any tiny stones. Spear the garlic head on a knife and hold it over a gas or candle flame until the papery skin singes and blackens a little and the flesh is lightly caramelized.

2 Put everything except the finishing ingredients into a roomy saucepan. Salt lightly and bring to the boil. Turn down the heat, cover loosely and leave to simmer gently for 40–50 minutes until the lentils are perfectly soft and beginning to collapse into the broth. Stir occasionally to avoid sticking and add a splash of boiling water if it looks like drying out.

3 When the lentils are tender, add the cubed potato. Return to the boil and turn down the heat. Cover again and cook for another 10 minutes until the potato is nearly soft – test for doneness with a knife. Stir in the spring greens or spinach and bubble for another 5 minutes. Stir in the oil and bubble up again to amalgamate it with the broth – it disappears like magic, leaving a silky smoothness without a trace of oiliness. Taste and adjust the seasoning.

4 Ladle the soup into deep bowls and finish with the hard-boiled egg quarters, if you like. Accompany with a young red wine, nothing grand – a little acidity aids the digestion.

Desserts & Cakes

Peaches in Red Wine with Cinnamon

Melocotones en vino con canela

4 large, firm yellow-fleshed peaches

1 bottle strong Spanish red wine

5 cm (2 inch) cinnamon stick

2 cloves

8 peppercorns

1 bay leaf

about 4 heaped tablespoons caster sugar

juice of 1 lemon

Visually as well as gastronomically dramatic, the peaches acquire a rich burgundy velvet jacket, which, when cut open, reveals the golden flesh. Good with mantecados, *the soft, powdery almond biscuits Spanish children hope to find in their shoes on Twelfth Night, when all good Catholics receive their Christmas presents.*

1 Scald the peaches and remove their skins. Set them in a heavy saucepan that will just accommodate them.

2 Add the rest of the ingredients – the wine should just about cover the fruit. Bring to the boil, then turn down the heat to low, cover and let the pears poach very gently for about 30–40 minutes until tender. Transfer the fruit to a serving dish.

3 Bring the poaching liquid to the boil and bubble up fiercely until thick, shiny and reduced by half. Strain the syrup over the peaches.

Custard Fritters
Leche frita

SERVES 4-6

CUSTARD

6 free-range eggs

about 125 g (4 oz) plain flour

150 ml (¼ pint) milk

grated rind of ½ lemon

1 short cinnamon stick

1 teaspoon orange flower water or orange juice

125 g (4 oz) vanilla sugar

COATING

2 free-range eggs

2 tablespoons milk

about 100 g (3½ oz) finely crushed toasted breadcrumbs

oil, for deep-frying

TO DUST

ground cinnamon

caster sugar

This is Catalonia's sweet version of Andalusia's savoury croqueta. Instead of vanilla sugar, perfume the custard with scrapings from a piece of vanilla pod or a drop of real vanilla extract, or ring the changes with cinnamon, grated orange rind or a splash of your favourite liqueur.

1 Whisk 2 of the eggs to blend. Mix in as much of the flour as the liquid will accept to make a stiff paste. Whisk another 4 eggs separately, then beat them into the paste, working until smooth.

2 Bring the milk to the boil in a heavy saucepan with the lemon rind and cinnamon stick. Remove from the heat and leave to cool.

3 Whisk in the egg mixture, beating until smooth, and bring gently towards the boil, stirring continuously. Just before it boils, cool it down with the orange flower water or orange juice. Stir in the vanilla sugar. Continue to cook gently, but without allowing it to boil, until thick enough to set when you drop a blob on a cold saucer.

4 Line a baking tray with clingfilm and pour in a layer of the custard as thick as your thumb. Leave to cool, cover with another sheet of clingfilm and transfer to the refrigerator to firm for a few hours, or overnight if possible.

5 Cut the custard into bite-sized fingers, squares or triangles for coating. Beat the remaining 2 eggs on one plate with the milk and spread the breadcrumbs on another plate. Pass the custard shapes first through the egg and milk mixture to coat thoroughly, then press gently into the breadcrumbs, making sure all sides are covered. Check that there are no gaps – if so, repair them with a dab of egg and a sprinkle of crumbs. Set them back in the refrigerator for another hour or so to set the jackets – or freeze until you're ready to cook.

6 Heat a saucepan of oil for deep-frying until a faint blue haze rises. Slip in the custard fritters straight from the refrigerator, a few at a time so that the oil temperature remains high, and fry, turning them once, until crisp and brown.

7 Remove carefully with a draining spoon and transfer to kitchen paper to drain. Dust with cinnamon and sugar, and serve piping hot, before they lose their crispness. Delicious with a salad of sliced oranges dressed with honey, or fresh strawberries in season.

Chocolate and Cinnamon Ice Cream
Helado de chocolate con canela

SERVES 4

50 g (2 oz) best-quality dark chocolate (at least 70% cocoa solids)

150 ml (¼ pint) plus 450 ml (¾ pint) hot (not boiling) water

1 teaspoon ground cinnamon

2 free-range egg yolks

4 tablespoons condensed milk or double cream plus 4 tablespoons caster sugar

The ladies of the Spanish court were the first to taste the addictive joys of drinking chocolate, unknown in the Old World before Columbus made landfall in the New. In Spain, where it's a pick-me-up after a night on the tiles, it's usually spiced with cinnamon.

1 Break the chocolate into small pieces and soften it very gently over a low heat in a small saucepan with the 150 ml (¼ pint) hot water. As soon as it liquefies, whisk in the larger quantity of hot water. Add the cinnamon and whisk until perfectly smooth. Remove from the heat.

2 Beat the egg yolks with the condensed milk or cream and sugar and whisk the mixture into the hot liquid. Stir it over a gentle heat until the mixture thickens enough to coat the back of a wooden spoon.

3 Freeze in an ice cream maker according to the manufacturer's instructions. Alternatively, put in a lidded freezerproof container in the freezer until almost solid. Tip it into a liquidizer or food processor and process briefly to break up the ice crystals, then freeze again until firm.

4 Remove from the freezer about 20 minutes or so before you're ready to serve to allow it to soften. If you like, finish each portion with a trickle of Pedro Ximenes, the thick, black maple-syrupy sherry made from the grapes of the same name, and a sprinkle of toasted almonds.

Orange Caramel Custard
Flan de naranja

SERVES 4–6
CARAMEL

4 tablespoons caster
sugar

2–3 tablespoons water

CUSTARD

450 ml (¾ pint) freshly-
squeezed orange juice

3 whole free-range eggs,
plus 3 yolks

2–3 tablespoons caster
sugar

The everyday version of a popular dessert loved by all Spanish children, found on every restaurant menu from Bilbao to Cádiz. It is usually made with milk and a packet mix but in this sophisticated Valencian version, it is made with freshly-squeezed orange juice – packet orange juice won't do. If you prefer a dairy version, simply replace the juice with full-cream milk.

1 Make the caramel in a small saucepan. Melt the dry sugar, stirring all the time with a wooden spoon, over a steady heat until the sugar caramelizes a rich chestnut brown. This will take only a moment or two.

2 Add the water off the heat – be careful, as it will splutter. Stir over a low heat until you have thick, dark syrup. Divide this caramel into 4–6 individual cocottes or mini soufflé dishes if that's your preference. Tip to coat the base.

3 Heat the oven to 150°C (300°F), Gas Mark 2. For the custard, beat together the orange juice, whole eggs, egg yolks and sugar until well blended. Divide the mixture among the cocottes or mini soufflé dishes.

4 Transfer the cocottes to a roasting tin and pour in enough boiling water to come halfway up the cocottes. Cover the whole thing in foil and transfer to the preheated oven. Cook for 25–30 minutes or until the custard is just set. The set is delicate but it will firm a little more as it cools.

5 Serve at room temperature in their cooking dishes, with a crisp biscuit to dip in the caramel sauce which forms beneath the custard.

Spiced Almond Shortbreads
Mantecados

MAKES ABOUT 24

500 g (1 lb) pure pork lard, plus extra for greasing

500 g (1 lb) caster sugar

4 free-range egg yolks

finely grated rind and juice of 1 lemon

1 kg (2 lb) plain flour

500 g (1 lb) ground almonds

1 tablespoon ground cinnamon

These melt-in-the-mouth Christmas cookies – also known as polverones *(dusty biscuits) – are a treat for good children when the Three Wise Men come to visit the Christ child on 6 January. The rich, powdery shortbread is shortened with lard rather than butter.*

1 In a large bowl, beat the lard until it softens, then beat in the sugar and whisk until fluffy. Beat in the egg yolks and lemon rind.

2 Sift in the flour and beat it a little more. Then fold in the ground almonds and cinnamon. Add a tablespoonful of lemon juice and work it some more until you have a soft dough.

3 Roll out the dough to the thickness of the width of your thumb and cut out rounds with a small wine glass.

4 Transfer the cookies to a lightly greased baking tray. Place in a preheated oven, 190°C (375°F), Gas Mark 5, for 20 minutes, and then reduce the oven to 180°C (350°F), Gas Mark 4, and bake for another 15–20 minutes, or until the cookies are pale gold.

5 Transfer the cookies carefully to a wire rack to cool – they're very crumbly. Wrap each cookie in a scrap of tissue paper and store in an airtight tin.

St James's Almond Tart
Pastel de santiago

SERVES 6−8

PASTRY

100 g (3½ oz) **pure pork lard or unsalted butter**

100 g (3½ oz) **caster sugar**

1 **free-range egg**

1 **teaspoon ground cinnamon**

about 200 g (7 oz) **plain flour, plus extra for dusting**

FILLING

8 **free-range eggs**

500 g (1 lb) **caster sugar**

500 g (1 lb) **ground almonds**

juice and finely grated rind of 1 lemon

icing sugar, for dusting

This rich, lemony tart was baked to fortify pilgrims on the long walk to Santiago de Compostela, the shrine of St James. The lemon is for the sorrow of Good Friday and the almonds, grown from stock from the Jordan Valley, serve as a reminder of the Holy Land.

1 Make the pastry first. Beat the lard or butter with the sugar until light and fluffy. Beat in the egg and cinnamon. Using your hand or a food processor, work in enough flour to make a smooth, softish paste. Work the paste into a ball, cover with clingfilm and leave to firm for 30 minutes. Roll it out very thinly on a floured surface and use to line a tart tin 22 cm (8½ inches) in diameter and no less than 5 cm (2 inches) deep. Save any pastry scraps to bake as biscuits.

2 Now make the filling. Whisk the eggs until light and fluffy, then sprinkle in the sugar spoonful by spoonful and continue to beat until white and doubled in volume. Keep going – even with machinery the process takes longer than you think. Gently fold in the ground almonds and lemon juice and rind. Spoon the mixture into the tart base – it can come right up to the edge because it shrinks as it sets. Don't overfill: if you have any left over, bake it in little madeleine tins or as cupcakes.

3 Place in a preheated oven, 200°C (400°F), Gas Mark 6, for 45–50 minutes, or until the pastry is crisp and the topping firm and beautifully browned.

4 Unmould. When cool, finish with a dusting of icing sugar with a scallop shell on the surface. You can, if you wish, spread a layer of Quince Paste (see page 155) or damson jam on the tart base before you top it with the almond mixture – if so, give the pastry base 10 minutes in a hot oven first, just long enough to set the surface.

Yeast Cakes with Almonds and Fruit
Cocas con almendras y frutas confitadas

SERVES 6–8

1 kg (2 lb) strong bread
  flour, plus extra for
  dusting

½ teaspoon salt

1 tablespoon easy-blend
  dried yeast

1 teaspoon finely grated
  lemon rind

4 free-range eggs

100 ml (3½ fl oz) mild
  olive oil, plus extra for
  oiling

250 g (8 oz) caster sugar

about 500 ml (17 fl oz)
  warm milk

MARZIPAN

150 g (5 oz) ground
  almonds

150 g (5 oz) caster sugar

1 free-range egg yolk

TO FINISH

1 free-range egg, beaten
  with 1 tablespoon
  water

2 tablespoons chopped
  crystallized fruit

Purists will tell you that the true coca, *as prepared in the Levant and on the Balearic islands, is a primitive flat bread. Pay no attention; this festive version topped with marzipan and crystallized fruit is much more delicious.*

1 Sift the flour with the salt into a warm bowl. Mix in the yeast and lemon rind. Make a well in the flour mixture and add the eggs, oil and sugar. Work in enough warm milk to make a soft dough. Knead well until the dough forms a ball that leaves the side of the bowl clean. Cover with clingfilm – stretch it over the top so that it makes a little warm hothouse with plenty of room for the dough to expand – and leave in a warm place until doubled in size. It will take at least 2 hours: this is a very rich dough that takes longer to rise than a plain dough.

2 Meanwhile, make the marzipan. Work the ground almonds and sugar with the egg yolk until you have a soft, spreadable paste – you may need a little water.

3 When the dough has doubled in size, knock it back and knead it vigorously to distribute the air bubbles, then form the dough into a ball. Cut the ball into 6–8 equal-sized pieces, knead again and pat or roll out each piece into a rectangle no thicker than the width of your thumb. Transfer the rectangles to an oiled and flour-dusted baking sheet. Spread each piece with the marzipan, leaving a narrow margin around the edges.

4 To finish, prick the breads in a few places with a fork, brush with the egg and water mixture and sprinkle with the crystallized fruit. Cover with clingfilm and leave to rise again for another 20–30 minutes.

5 Place the breads in a preheated oven, 180°C (350°F), Gas Mark 4, for 30–40 minutes until well risen and light. The marzipan will toast and firm – if it looks like burning before the dough has risen, cover with foil. Transfer to a wire rack to cool. Perfect served with a chilled glass of agua de Valencia – cava on ice with orange juice.

Madeira Cake with Olive Oil
Biscocho de aceite

SERVES 6–8

200 g (7 oz) plain flour

50 g (2 oz) ground almonds

2 level teaspoons baking powder

250 ml (8 fl oz) light olive oil (not extra-virgin), plus extra for oiling

4 free-range eggs, lightly whisked

250 g (5 oz) caster sugar

juice and finely grated rind of 1 small Seville orange or lemon

This is a basic four-quarter cake made with olive oil rather than butter; anyone with a nut allergy can replace the ground almonds with the same weight of flour. Pick a mild rectified olive oil rather than extra-virgin – but if virgin is all you have, bring it up to frying-temperature and then allow to cool before using.

1 Mix the dry ingredients together first, then tip everything into a food processor and beat until the mixture is smooth and free of lumps. Easy, isn't it?

2 Oil a 1 kg (2 lb) loaf tin and line the base with greaseproof paper. Drop in the cake mixture (soft dropping consistency is what you're looking for), and spread it into the corners.

3 Place in a preheated oven, 180°C (350°F), Gas Mark 4, for 45–50 minutes until the cake is well risen, firm to the finger and has shrunk from the sides. Wait until it cools a little before you tip it out and transfer it to a wire rack to cool completely. If you store it in an airtight tin it will keep for at least a month.

Nut Milk Granita
Granita de horchata

MAKES ABOUT
1.5 LITRES
(2½ PINTS)

**250 g (8 oz) whole
blanched almonds**

**about 2 tablespoons
caster sugar (more
if you like)**

1 short cinnamon stick

Horchata, a legacy of the Moorish presence in Andalusia, is an infusion of crushed nuts and water flavoured with cinnamon and lightly sweetened with sugar. As a thirst-quencher, it's served in a long glass, well iced, and is sold in refreshment bars in southern Spain throughout the summer.

1 Put the almonds into a liquidizer with about 300 ml (½ pint) water and process to a thick cream. Add enough water to make the volume up to 1 litre (1¾ pints) and leave to infuse overnight.

2 Next day, strain the milky liquid into a saucepan, stir in the sugar and add the cinnamon stick. Bring to the boil and then leave to cool. Remove the cinnamon stick.

3 Freeze in an ice cream maker according to the manufacturer's instructions. Alternatively, put in a lidded freezerproof container in the freezer until almost solid. Tip it into the liquidizer or a food processor and process to break up the ice crystals, then freeze again until firm.

4 Remove from the freezer about 10 minutes before you need it, and crush the mixture again before you serve it.

Quince Paste
Dulce de membrillo

MAKES ABOUT
1 KG (2 LB)

2 kg (4 lb) ripe quinces

1.5 litres (2½ pints) water

about 1 kg (2 lb) preserving sugar

oil, for oiling

Quinces ripen and soften in store, and are ready when you can smell their perfume. This fine preserve is a traditional Christmas treat, usually eaten with a slice of mature Manchego cheese.

1 Wipe and roughly chop the quinces – don't core or peel them – then put them in a preserving pan with the water.

2 Bring to the boil, then turn down to a steady simmer and cook until the quince flesh is soft – don't boil them too long or they will turn red and the colour of the paste will be too dark.

3 Push the flesh, juice and all, through a sieve. Weigh the pulp and stir in 500 g (1 lb) sugar for each 500 g (1 lb) fruit.

4 Put into a saucepan and bring very gently back to the boil, stirring until all the sugar has completely dissolved. Spread the paste in a very lightly oiled baking tray and leave in a preheated oven, 110°C (225°F), Gas Mark ¼, to dry out overnight. Alternatively, simmer, stirring throughout, for about 30–35 minutes until the pulp pulls away from the side of the pan and then spread it in the baking tray to set.

5 When cool, cut the paste into squares, wrap in greaseproof paper and store in a tin in a dry cupboard. It darkens and firms as it matures.

Index

Acknowledgements

Executive Editor: Eleanor Maxfield
Senior Editor: Sybella Stephens
Art Direction and Design: Tracy Killick
Design Concept: Smith & Gilmour
Photographer: Noel Murphy
Home Economist: Sue Henderson
Home Economist's Assistants: Rachel Wood and Paul Jackman
Stylist: Wei Tang
Production: Caroline Alberti

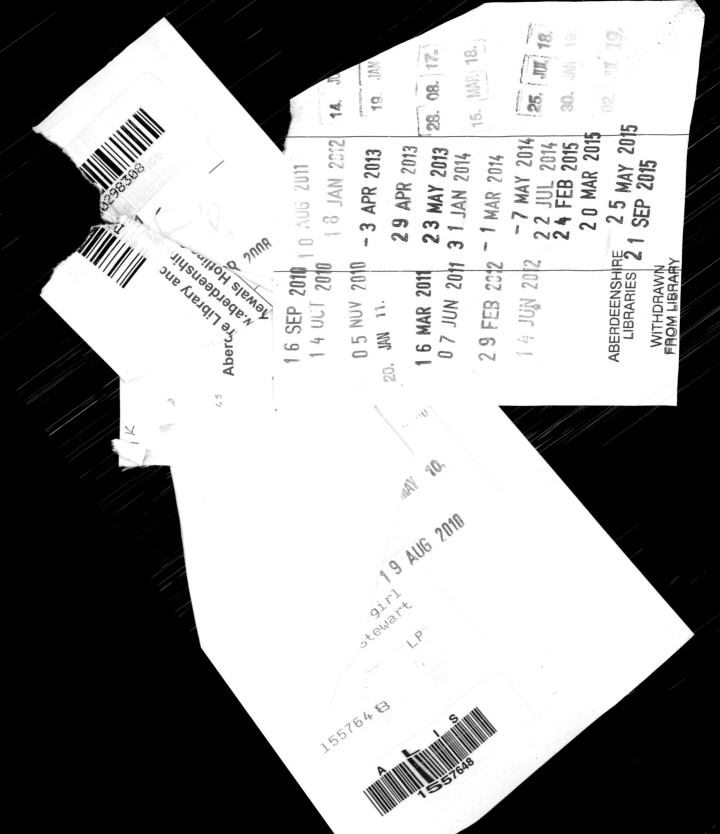

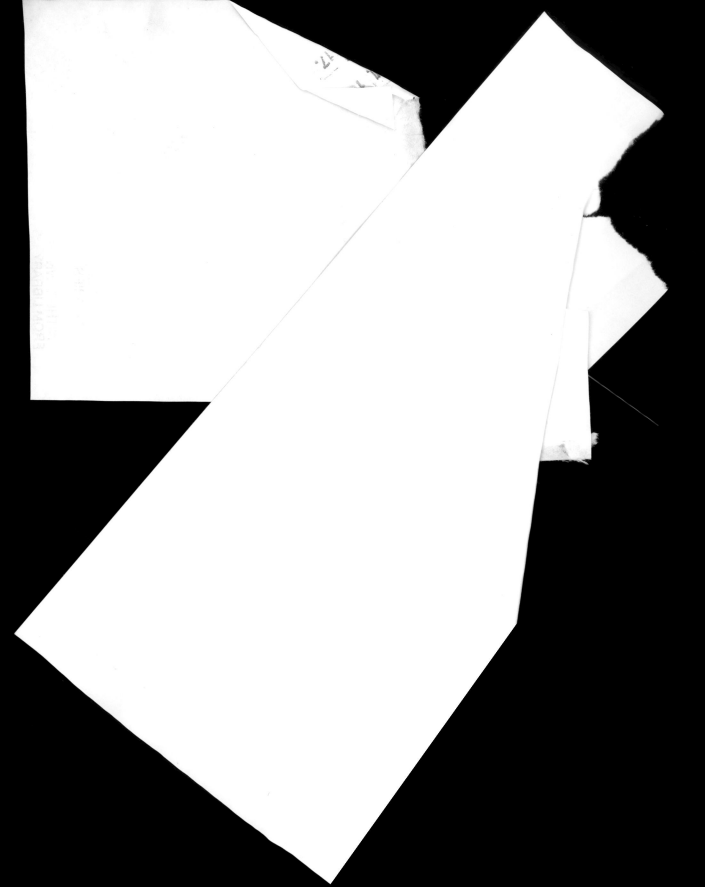

TRAVELLING GIRL

TRAVELLING GIRL

Sally Stewart

Severn House Large Print
London & New York

This first large print edition published in Great Britain 2003 by
SEVERN HOUSE LARGE PRINT BOOKS LTD of
9-15 High Street, Sutton, Surrey, SM1 1DF.
First world regular print edition published 2002 by
Severn House Publishers, London and New York.
This first large print edition published in the USA 2004 by
SEVERN HOUSE PUBLISHERS INC., of
595 Madison Avenue, New York, NY 10022.

Copyright © 2002 by Sally Stewart.

British Library Cataloguing in Publication Data

Stewart, Sally
    Travelling girl. - Large print ed.
    1. Tour guides (Persons) - Fiction
    2. Russia (Federation) - Social conditions - Fiction
    3. Love stories
    4. Large type books
    I. Title
    823.9'14 [F]

    ISBN 0-7278-7328-8

Except where actual historical events and characters are being described for
the storyline of this novel, all situations in this publication are fictitious and
any resemblance to living persons is purely coincidental.

Printed and bound in Great Britain by
MPG Books Ltd, Bodmin, Cornwall.

To my dear Fellow Traveller

One

Kate got out of bed wondering why March was such a disagreeable month – still always winter, when it ought to be spring. Rain hurled itself at her window, and she thought reluctantly of a wet and miserable drive to Gatwick. It was just the morning *not* to be going anywhere, least of all to be going to Russia. She broke a fingernail getting dressed and immediately snagged a new pair of tights on it. Worse still was the discomfort left in her mind by a nightmare she couldn't precisely recall. The omens hardened into a conviction that her best course was to crawl back into bed and stay there. But her uniform hung ready on the wardrobe door, and there was no real alternative to getting into it: brown jacket and skirt, and a cream silk shirt striped in shades of brown and coral – no hardship to wear for a girl with russet hair and eyes the colour of ripe chestnuts. The telephone rang as she was about to hurry out of the door – her boss at Three Cs, no doubt, with a last-minute change to the group she was shepherding this morning.

'Kate, darling...' Definitely *not* her boss, nor any adjustment to the tour. It was dear Andrew Carmichael instead, and her private grievance against *him* was that he never changed at all. She could predict what he would say as accurately as she could visualize him in her mind's eye, his unvarying bachelor breakfast spread out all round him while he telephoned.

'You sound cross,' he said plaintively. 'Did I wake you?'

'Hardly! I was on my way out of the flat – a morning departure, Russia again.'

'It sounds horrible, but it serves you right for not agreeing to marry me instead. Thank God that wretched company of yours keeps sending you to the frozen north – you'll get sick to death of it before long. I'd have more of a problem if you were always going somewhere beautiful and warm.'

She gently shooed him back to his breakfast without agreeing with what he'd said; but, driving through the freezing rain and almost midwinter darkness, she didn't regret not being comfortably wedded to a man whose chief ambition in life was to keep her in a state of idle luxury. He was a kind, reliable companion, reckoned brilliant in his own, actuarial line. He could work out

8

a company pension plan on the back of an envelope, but still failed to understand her fascination with a country he thought of as cold, primitive and violent.

Ahead of her the lights of Gatwick airport shone through the murk and, once inside the warmth and bustle of the building, she tucked Andrew back into a corner of her mind. With him went the flicker of unease that she'd begun the day with: there was nothing to worry about; whatever problems *might* crop up she was trained to deal with.

'Hi, Kate; poor old you – Russia again!'

'I know – sickening, isn't it?' She grinned at a colleague who was trying not to look too pleased at the thought of flying to Tangiers. 'Seen any of my people yet?'

'Little huddle over there, I think – can't miss the moth-eaten fur coats and snow-boots!'

'Mine for a certainty! See you, Allie.'

She headed in the direction of the little group, thinking that they looked typical of the people Three Cs specialized in conveying about the globe. In return for what was offered to them – Culture, Comfort and Courtesy – they usually gave the minimum of fuss. This morning's intake had the well-groomed faces and quiet orderliness she had come to expect: thirty conventional souls from the home counties, all aware of doing something a little less conventional than their neighbours, who played things safe with a fortnight in Florence or Baden-Baden. Kate wondered, as she always did, what they expected. Life amid the cosiness of gymkhanas and harvest-festival suppers wouldn't have done much to prepare them for the decaying magnificence of St Petersburg, once the capital of Russia and, as Leningrad, scene of one of the epic sieges of Russia's Great Patriotic War. Moscow would probably unsettle them even more, with its mixture of primitive beauty and modern brutal ugliness.

'Miss Kirkby – we seem to have been brought here *much* too early.'

Kate recognized in the voice tones of gentle complaint that had been honed by years of pointing out the failings of the local parish council. She guessed who the speaker was from the list in her hand: Mrs Phyllis Newcombe, widow; dressed for a cold climate in a good but slightly old-fashioned moleskin coat and hat. Her mouth smiled, but her pale-blue eyes were cold and measuring.

'I'm sorry that you have to wait, but the security checks nowadays are time-consuming,' Kate explained cheerfully. 'It's all done for our own good, but it slows things down rather.'

Mrs Newcombe rescued an elegant travelling case from the clutch of a small black child who'd earmarked it as something to sit down on at a convenient level. He stared at her with huge reproachful brown eyes, but she remained unmoved, and he trailed off in the wake of a caravan of brothers and sisters.

'Airports are *so* squalid now that everybody travels,' Mrs Newcombe said fretfully. 'Time was when one's fellow-passengers were...' She fumbled for an acceptable phrase, and Kate finished the sentence for her with a sweet smile: '...people like oneself?'

The lady's smile became more fixed, and it was time for a Three Cs courier to make a desperate grab at fast disappearing Courtesy.

'Let me introduce you to some other members of the party – it might help to while away the delay.'

'Thank you, no ... there'll be time enough to get to know them.' She sounded unenthusiastic about the prospect, but indicated the thick paperback clutched to her moleskinned bosom. 'I've all the company I need here.'

Having won a bet with herself that Mrs Newcombe's travelling companion would be *Anna Karenina*, Kate gave a smiling nod

11

and felt free to get on with the job of identifying the people on her list still not ticked off and welcomed: Ranald McEwan, for one. It was too good a name not to conjure with, even though she'd been embarrassed before by a tendency to imagine people wrongly before she met them in the flesh. Not much like a native of Midhurst or Petworth, surely? Her guess was an elderly Scots engineer, now retired to the softer life of Sussex after a lifetime spent festooning dams across the face of the Third World. It was a sweeping conception, grounded in legends of Kipling and the British Raj, and on the equally uncertain fact that all expatriate Scots were engineers. She liked this heroic picture of Mr McEwan, but it was tiresome of him not to have announced himself, because she must now go looking for him.

In the event she didn't so much find him as fall over him. Having stepped out of the path of a very large trolley under the uncertain control of a very small Indian, she collided with the back of a man bending over a cabin bag. She knocked him off balance as well, and the two of them landed in a heap on the low cushioned seat. Immediately in front of her eyes dangled the tag attached to the bag: R. A. McEwan, c/o St Petersburg Hotel. Here, for certain, was the missing Mr McEwan, but where was the mellowed, tropic-wizened warrior of her imagining?

She was put on her feet again with a speed that suggested he couldn't wait to get her off his lap. When he had uncoiled himself and was standing at his full height, she found that she was being frowned at by a Caledonian giant whose straight black eyebrows almost met over the bridge of a commanding nose. He was weatherbeaten but not wizened, and mellowness didn't stand a chance. If Mrs Newcombe had hinted at problems ahead, this member of the party announced the same message like a trumpet blast.

'Don't apologize,' he said morosely. 'I dare say it comes of my being on the small side.'

For a moment she was tempted to smile, thinking that the remark was intended to be humorous; but a cold, grey glance flicked over her, freezing the idea to death. Kate adjusted her uniform cap – becoming, when perched at the right angle, but silly, she thought, when not – and bit back the first unconsidered answer that came to mind.

'Indeed I *must* apologize, but I was caught between you and the tea trolley ... Scylla and Charybdis, you might say!' Still no flicker of a smile, but she persevered. 'If I've inflicted any damage, I could always whistle up a wheelchair.' At a rough guess he weighed fourteen stone to her eight, and seemed constructed out of Highland granite rather than the more usual flesh and blood. A sparrow landing on an Aberdeen Angus steer would have had as much chance of doing damage.

'No wheelchair will be necessary, I believe. I shall limp bravely to the aeroplane, assuming that it ever materializes.'

He spoke with such dead-pan gravity that she was almost certain that he was amused after all, but McEwan didn't seem to be a sharing man, which was a pity. It would add considerably to her normal courier's problems if she was never going to know whether he was laughing or not.

'We shall be late leaving, but our aircraft is waiting on the tarmac. Have faith in us, please!'

His eyes examined her with so little pleasure that she feared her cap must still be askew.

'You're our shepherdess, I take it?'

'Yes ... I was coming to look for you. The rest of our group are sitting in the next aisle, near the departure gate.'

'I know ... I've seen them; that's why I'm sitting here.'

He and Mrs Newcombe were made for each other, it seemed. Courtesy prevented

14

her from saying so, but at least she could stick up for the rest of them.

'They're all very nice people. If you don't enjoy group travel, why do it? You must surely have realized what you were joining?'

'What *have* I joined, in your view?'

'A group of civilized and charming citizens who are appreciative of all that Russia has to offer.'

'Well said, Miss Kirkby! No devoted representative of Three Cs could have done better than that, but I detected the sting hidden in the honey: you're afraid your charming civilized group has been infiltrated by an unmannerly Scottish oaf better suited to plodding barefoot across Patagonia with a rucksack on his back.'

Hard put to it not to agree, she shook her head instead, suddenly remembering something that caused her eyes to gleam with laughter. 'I'm specially delighted to have you in the party, Mr McEwan,' she assured him gently.

'Hope springing eternal? You're thinking a little sweetness and light might rub off on me from the rest of your group?'

'That's possible, but I was really thinking how useful you're going to be at St Petersburg station when we catch the train to Moscow. No porters visible there, you see; we're left to manhandle all the luggage

15

ourselves.'

His eyes wandered thoughtfully over the frail ladies clustered in the next aisle and then came back to Kate's expectant face.

'Your trick, I'm afraid, Miss Kirkby.'

She bowed and walked away, leaving him to return to the company of his own thoughts. Kate Kirkby obviously wondered what he was doing among this flock of elderly culture-hungry sheep, and no doubt the same question would occur to other people as well. He rearranged his bag so that a book prominently advertising his interest in fourteenth-century Russian ikons couldn't be missed, and adjusted a pair of horn-rimmed spectacles on his beaky nose. If the picture of an earnest student of art was still improbable, it was the best he could do. An amused grin at himself lightened his face for a moment, but Kate was too busy to see it, having already been button-holed by another member of the party.

'Oh ... Miss Kirkby ... have you a moment, I wonder?'

'As many moments as you need. What can I do for you?' She wanted to pat the agitated little lady on the head, but contented herself with a friendly smile instead.

'My name's Livingston-Smith – Lucy Livingston-Smith. I've been talking to Mrs Newcombe. She seems very knowledgeable about Russia, and she assures me that the water there is *most* unreliable. Of course, I knew it wasn't going to be like dear England, but she says we shall get nothing but borsch soup. I don't wish to be difficult, but beetroot always upsets me.' Her gentle face grew agonized as she contemplated the ordeal ahead. 'I think I've made a dreadful mistake in coming. I did *so* want to see the Winter Palace, but ... no bath for a fortnight, and beetroot for every meal ... I don't think I can, Miss Kirkby, not even for the Winter Palace!'

Kate wondered if she was going to make Three Cs history – the first courier to lose a client before they'd even left Gatwick's departure lounge. She found herself patting Miss Livingston-Smith tenderly on the shoulder after all.

'Mrs Newcombe's alarming you unnecessarily. It's not advisable to *drink* the water in St Petersburg, but nothing terrible will happen if you bath in it, and for drinking and brushing your teeth you can easily buy bottled water. You won't be offered French cuisine, but the food's much better than it was, and at the end of the winter you probably won't be offered beetroot soup at all. On the other hand, I can promise you that the Winter Palace *will* live up to everything you've ever heard of it.'

She was rewarded with a tremulous smile. 'How *kind* you are ... I can see that in your hands we have nothing to fear.'

Kate decided against pointing out that she would soon be sharing her responsibilities with an Intourist guide. It would be like telling Lucy that they were about to be fed immediately to the KGB or handed over to the manager of a salt mine in Siberia.

'Russia is changing very rapidly; perhaps that's partly why you've chosen to come now. But there's nothing to fear except a little mental indigestion from seeing so many strange and beautiful things.'

Lucy smiled more confidently. 'That doesn't worry me. I have to make up for all the wasted years when I didn't see anything at all. I *gulp* down beauty now, Miss Kirkby.'

She was God's gift to a conscientious courier: undemanding, appreciative, and genuinely interested. Damn Phyllis Newcombe for trying to spoil her pleasure. Kate looked at the departure board and saw that at last it was showing a take-off time and gate number for their flight. She need only keep Lucy's nose pointing in the direction of the Russia of the Tsars for another ten minutes to have her safely past the point of no return.

'We shall be off quite soon now. There'll be things you won't like about Russia – it's got a lot of catching up to do – but think of this trip as being a great adventure.'

Lucy nodded her neat mouse-coloured head. 'You're right! I shall try to be as bold as a lion from now on,' she promised earnestly.

Still smiling at the thought, Kate moved along the row, suggesting to people that they should begin to collect their books and cabin bags. Some of them had already formed themselves into two little groups of close friends who would stay together throughout the trip. It left the half-dozen or so outsiders she'd already indentified, and a final couple not yet spoken to who were in front of her now. The Hon. Nigel Faringdon, fiftyish and of vaguely military bearing, looked fit enough to help cope with the luggage of unaccompanied ladies at the railway station. His daughter Linette – eighteen, Kate judged – made no attempt to smile. Instead, a cool stare registered the courier's luminous eyes, freckled, tip-tilted nose, and auburn hair tucked under her pillbox hat.

'I'm sorry about the delay,' Kate apologized to both of them. 'You've been kept waiting far too long, but we shall soon be airborne now.'

Mr Faringdon's pale eyes warmed into a shy smile. 'Not your fault, Miss Kirkby ... or are we allowed to call you Kate?'

'Certainly – in fact I answer to "Hi" or any loud cry!'

He smiled so politely that she knew he hadn't recognized the absurd quotation. Perhaps not too much humour to be expected of him, but at least he looked amiable, which was more than could be said for the sullen-faced girl beside him. Kate looked directly at her and tried again.

'I hope you're going to enjoy the trip, Miss Faringdon.'

Linette's bored glance considered the people around her for a moment, then returned to her magazine. 'Enjoy it? You must be joking.'

The courier resisted the temptation to dash the magazine out of her hand, and the Hon. Nigel looked uncomfortable at his daughter's rudeness.

'Linette hates crowds, I'm afraid ... not at her best when hugger-mugger with a lot of other people!'

If other enjoyment failed, Kate thought, she and Mrs Newcombe could console each other, bemoaning the days when riff-raff knew their place and the upper crust weren't expected to rub shoulders with them; but a glance at the beautiful, discontented face in front of her was enough to melt irritation into pity. It was a sad achievement, to be bored with life at eighteen.

All the same, the party could have done without Linette Faringdon. Apart from Ranald McEwan, she was younger than any of the others by at least thirty years, visibly reluctant to be there at all, and at no pains to conceal the fact from the rest of her fellow-travellers. Kate liked her clients to be happy, but she could see no hope of making this girl happy. Just *one* admiring male under the age of fifty might have helped, but for the life of her she couldn't fit the Caledonian giant into this category. He would either take fright at Linette Faringdon's facade of bored sophistication or ignore her completely. A different sort of man might have seen her as a challenge, but Kate exempted him from that sort of male vanity.

'We shall be out of the crowds any moment now,' she said cheerfully to Linette, 'and I shall be surprised if you don't find the trip more interesting than you bargain for.'

Miss Faringdon looked as if she'd be not so much surprised as astonished, but at least she consented to put her magazine away.

'Lead on ... I can't wait for the excitement to begin!' The exaggerated drawl should have been ridiculous, but there was a glimpse in her face of something heartsick and sad as she shrugged herself into a pale-cream sheepskin coat.

'Just the thing for a girl with black hair,'

said Kate warmly, but Linette was used to compliments apparently. She shrugged it aside, and drifted towards the departure gate, where a small commotion seemed to be centred round the massive figure of Ranald McEwan.

'Problem, Miss Kirkby,' he said, sounding pleased, she thought. 'Professor Dirk Engelsman here will explain.'

The Dutchman smiled winningly, but it was his wife – as large and pink and cheerful as himself – who acted as spokesman for them both.

'We have our boardink passes lost,' she confessed with an air of surprise.

After a fevered search the passes were eventually found acting as bookmarks in the volume Ellie Engelsman had been reading. Kate also retrieved the camera that Mynheer the Professor had absent-mindedly hidden under his chair, and fielded stray possessions that dropped from her charges' grasp as they bounded along the passageway to the waiting aeroplane.

'They're doomed, you realize,' McEwan murmured beside her. 'They'll lose every essential document you give them, be late for every carefully timed arrangement, and play havoc with us generally; but through it all they'll smile, confident of being rescued and loved!'

'Why not?' Kate asked. 'It's my job, rescuing people like the Engelsmans.'

'Odd sort of job for a girl,' McEwan suggested morosely. His grey glance swept over her again, indicating that she was probably an odd sort of girl; but they were at the door of the aircraft now, and he was content to wave her on board in front of him.

For the next four hours she could draw breath, with nothing more arduous to do than sort out thirty entry visas, and help those who couldn't make head or tail of the complicated customs forms – standard tasks for the journey out. She found it hard to concentrate on them, all the same. The faint sense of apprehension with which the day had begun had returned to worry her. It had something to do with Linette Faringdon, prowling down the aisle to the rear of the aeroplane, because her white, set face spoke of some trouble worse than spoiled adolescence. Perhaps it had even more to do with the sombre-faced man sitting across the aisle, who now sported a scholarly-looking pair of spectacles but hadn't turned a page of his book for at least a quarter of an hour. Kate hadn't the slightest idea what was taking him to Russia, but if it was a passionate interest in fourteenth-century painted ikons or the treasures of the Winter Palace, she'd eat her uniform hat. It was ridiculous to worry, of course. Linette was travelling with her father, and whatever fears a conscientious courier might entertain about McEwan, anxiety about his ability to take care of himself surely needn't be one of them.

She was still frowning over the thought when he turned his head to catch her eyes fixed on him. A dark eyebrow lifted slightly, and she cursed herself for the blush that seemed to reveal an interest in him. It was professional only, but she could scarcely shout the fact across the aisle. She returned instead to the list she was checking, and only looked in his direction again half an hour later, when he vacated his seat to allow someone beside him to get out. His horn-rimmed spectacles slipped down unnoticed to the floor and she leaned over to rescue them. A glance through them as she picked them up confirmed the suspicion that had occurred to her: impressive frames, but the lenses were of completely ordinary glass!

She handed them back to him with a smile. 'You must be very lost without them … unable to see a thing!'

His eyes gleamed acknowledgement of the hit, but he settled them back on his nose with no visible trace of shame. 'Oh, I can manage well enough, but I don't feel quite dressed without them!'

Two

With their late departure, and watches adjusted to take account of a three-hour advance in time, it was beginning to grow dark when they landed at Pulkhovo 11 airport. Snow was falling outside, and inside the building the welcome on offer seemed equally frigid. Kate looked over her flock, seeing its lust for adventure dwindling in the face of the surly fur-hatted officials in charge of Immigration. One of them rapped on the counter at Lucy when she got nervous and tried to look anywhere but at them, and group enthusiasm faded altogether in the slow crawl through Customs control. A plane-load of French tourists had followed them into the hall and showed a regrettable tendency to jump the chaotic queue, but McEwan's great bulk suddenly barred the way in a gesture that couldn't be misunderstood, and Kate acknowledged to herself that there were times when he was undoubtedly going to be useful.

It was, of course, Ellie Engelsman's

customs form that held them all up. For fear of making mistakes, she'd written it first in pencil, then gone over it with the required black ink – a proceeding that the wall-eyed official who detected it seemed to think highly suspicious. Kate was brusquely forbidden to help her, and there was nothing to do but wait while Ellie laboured over another form by herself. She rolled her eyes at Dirk, separated from her behind a barrier and muttering a piteous *'Mein Gott'* from time to time, but Russian officialdom remained unmoved.

At last she was allowed through, and they straggled outside behind Kate into the evening's bitter cold. She could see the Intourist bus waiting for them, but the girl she expected wasn't visible. Instead, it was Sergei Ivanov who stood there, hunched inside his old dark-blue quilted jacket. The assorted irritations of the past few hours seemed trifling now. Sergei was the real blow that the day had finally delivered. They had worked together fairly regularly the previous year, and the collaboration had begun badly because he'd soon discovered that his colleague's command of Russian was better than his of English. He'd disapproved of her altogether, in fact, but russet hair and beautiful legs and a smile that came from Kate's friendly heart hadn't made it easy to go on disliking her. He'd soon given up trying and leaped instead to the most opposite extreme that a volatile Slav was capable of. Fending him off without hurting him was going to be a complication now that she'd have preferred to do without.

He clasped her hands tightly, but released her as the others arrived to climb into the bus; then he introduced himself, after pointing out severely that they were late. 'I am Sergei, and I shall remain with you throughout your stay in Russia.'

He made it sound so like a threat that Linette murmured from the seat behind Kate, 'Delightful, I'm sure – all the party needed, in fact!'

The interruption went unheard, and Sergei proceeded with his instructions. 'Dinner will be waiting for you at the hotel, in the restaurant on the third floor. Kindly go straight there when you arrive, because your meal will be ready.'

He spoke English competently but always repeated everything he said, on the assumption that the people he was required to steer round the Motherland were not only bourgeois but half-witted or deaf as well. Kate had almost ceased to notice the habit, but she could see Mrs Newcombe bristling to be told all over again to go *straight* to the third floor. Still attuned to English time, she couldn't understand how dinner at four in the afternoon could possibly be considered reasonable, much less late. Kate looked round at the wan faces in the bus, recognizing the signs that her flock were feeling discouraged by cold, fatigue and their first bruising encounter with the Russian system. Their own firesides in Sussex had never seemed more desirable, and their Florence-bound neighbours had been right after all. She knew that morale would rise again after a night's sleep, but for the moment their spirit of adventure had sunk out of sight.

Next morning she breakfasted ahead of them as usual, so as to be free to deal with the complaints they'd have stored up over-night. She was still alone in the restaurant when Nigel Faringdon wandered in, trying not to look as if he hoped to find her there. She gestured to a chair, smiling at the expression on his face as he gazed at the selection of food in front of her: sliced garlic sausage, hot rice pudding, hard-boiled eggs, and black bread!

'I must remember to tell Lucy Livingston-Smith that she's not obliged to eat *all* of it,' she said cheerfully. 'The bread's very good, by the way, when you get used to the colour!'

28

She glanced at his face, thinking that he looked pale and worried for a man who was supposed to be on holiday. 'I hope Linette slept well,' she said gently. 'She seemed tired last night.' It was a generous description, because his daughter had retired to bed surly and unapproachable.

'I suppose you're wondering what she's doing here,' he burst out abruptly.

'I don't have the impression that she's very interested in fine art, or in this country's ongoing social revolution,' Kate conceded cautiously.

'It was intended as a kind of shock treatment ... but God knows whether it will work or not.' He sounded like a man ravaged by anxiety and Kate turned a deaf ear to Rule 22 of Three Cs policy, which said that couriers should *not* get embroiled in their clients' personal affairs. Being interested in people, she would have found it a maddening rule anyway, but it was an article of faith with her that people who needed help couldn't be brushed aside.

'What was the shock treatment meant to do?' she asked tentatively.

'Make her forget the ruinous life she's been allowed to lead in Paris. Her French mother went back there when our marriage ended. I managed to keep Linette at school in England, but as soon as she left,

Marianne invited her over there. My ex-wife sees nothing wrong in introducing her to the kind of life she lives herself – experiments with sex and drugs among people like herself with too much money and no desire for anything but self-destructive pleasure. There's a kind of spurious glamour about it, of course, for a child of eighteen. This is probably a hopeless attempt to get her interested in something else.'

'What made you bring her *here*? It's fascinating, of course, but still alien in some ways. Wouldn't something more obviously exciting and attractive have been a better idea? Our clients aren't usually found among her age-group, I'm afraid.'

'I didn't want the obviously attractive. I was looking for an experience as far removed as possible from her mother's messy life. This country also had something that I hoped *might* appeal: she loved Russian stories and ballet as a little girl – used to dream dreams of herself as a snow-maiden or swan princess.'

He spoke so wistfully that Kate thought he was probably touched by the same northern romanticism himself – imagined fur-swathed princesses being drawn through snow-lit forests to the jingle of harness and sleigh bells. Alas for dreams ... it wasn't much like present-day Russia, if it had ever been

Russia at all.

'Well, I hope the shock treatment works,' she said eventually. 'There's a chance it may, because this isn't a place quite like any other. People *do* find themselves reacting to something so different from their normal experience that it leaves them different from when they arrived. At the very least they have to make comparisons with what they've come *from*.'

Nigel Faringdon smiled at her, relieved to have made a confession that had seemed necessary.

'I wanted you to know about us, Kate. Don't be hurt, please, if my mixed-up daughter should happen to be rude to you; she pretends that she doesn't need help.'

He walked away in search of Linette and Kate returned thoughtfully to the black bread and jam she'd managed to isolate from all the other items in front of her. She'd been right in thinking something was seriously amiss with the Faringdons, but she couldn't help feeling that the anxious father looked for more benefit than a couple of weeks could possibly provide.

She was just thanking a waiter for the coffee he'd been persuaded to bring instead of the inevitable tea when another early riser ambled into the room – Ranald McEwan this time, looking even more enormous than

31

usual beside the stocky Russian waiters. She expected him to settle on a chair as far removed from her as possible, but for once he seemed minded to be sociable.

'Good morning, Miss Kirkby ... you're favoured, I see. The rest of us were commanded to be *in-the-restaurant-on-the-third-floor* at eight o'clock. God help us, apparently, if we're a minute early or late. I'm early, as you see.'

'God help you indeed,' Kate agreed. 'Meal times are rigid here. The food, hot or cold, will be put on the tables for you whether you're here or not. So, at lunchtime, you can eat the ice cream before the soup, if you've a mind to.'

Unlike Nigel Faringdon, he didn't content himself with staring at her breakfast. He sat down, helped himself to a slice of black bread and covered it with garlic sausage.

'You've forgotten to steal some of my butter,' she pointed out cordially.

'So I have – I thought there was something missing.' He rearranged his sandwich and bit into it with gusto. 'What's on the programme for this morning?'

'What we always start with: a visit to the cemetery.'

He swallowed incautiously and was seized by a violent attack of coughing. The noise brought a waiter hurrying up with more coffee.

Ranald smiled his thanks, wiped streaming eyes, and looked pleased with himself. 'I was afraid it was going to be difficult to get you to part with some of *your* coffee; but now I've got my own.' He sipped in silence for a moment. 'You weren't serious about the cemetery, of course. That was just Miss Kirkby forgetting herself to the extent of mocking a poor credulous customer.'

'Miss Kirkby wouldn't dream of doing such a thing,' she said virtuously.

Amusement touched his face like a shaft of winter sunlight. Smiling, he *was* personable, she realized.

'I'm used to it now, but I suppose it does seem like an odd beginning,' she said thoughtfully. 'Intourist insist that the Piskarev-skoye Memorial Cemetery should be the first stop on a tour of the city. You'll understand when Sergei tells you about it.'

'The legend of the "heroic" city, I suppose?'

'Yes ... and although the legend has probably become embroidered over the years, the truth is remarkable enough. Half a million citizens died in the siege, most of them from starvation; but after nearly three years the Germans were *still* denied the prize. That's heroic by any standards.'

'I wasn't knocking the legend,' he said,

mildly for once. A little silence fell, and then he changed the subject abruptly. 'This *is* a strange job – I think I said so once before, but you didn't tell me why you do it.'

She surprised him by answering seriously. 'I'm a courier because I like travelling and I like people. I came *here* because I'm deeply interested in this country – its terrible past, its rather chaotic present, and its incalculable future.' In case she'd been too serious she suddenly changed tack. 'My guess is that you're a latter-day Victorian: you disapprove of women gallivanting about the globe. We should all settle down to cosy domesticity, keeping the children out of the way and ministering to our lords and masters!'

'It sounds an excellent arrangement.' He spoke with unblinking gravity, and she distrusted him deeply. Seeing no reason to enlarge, he helped himself to another morsel of garlic sausage.

'Why did *you* join this tour?' she found herself suddenly asking. 'You more or less admitted that conducted holidays aren't something you normally enjoy.'

There was a little pause. 'I wanted some protective colouring,' he said with slow deliberation. 'I needed to look more inoffensive than I actually am.'

It was Kate's turn to choke. 'If I – I

understand you correctly, you're not here to look at objets d'art at all ... you've got some n-nefarious purpose of your own!'

The indignation in her voice tried him severely, but he managed not to smile. 'Not at all n-nefarious, but otherwise you're substantially correct!'

She was too genuinely worried to consider whether he was serious or not; even if he wasn't, she didn't trust him not to try to tease Sergei. If he *was*, her mind boggled at the complications they might all get into.

'You should never have been allowed to come,' she said with real feeling. 'It's taken years of hard work for the company to build up the trust of the authorities, but its reputation could be wrecked in a moment. Things aren't nearly as tough as they were even ten years ago, but we must still be careful ... discreet. I think I should warn Sergei about you.'

His hand, brown against the white tablecloth it was resting on, suddenly clamped itself round her own, upsetting her heartbeats.

'I hope you won't do anything of the kind. I told you because it seemed distasteful to be sailing under false colours; and, in any case, you ought to know the truth, just in case something goes wrong.'

'*What* might go wrong?' she enquired

coldly. 'I suppose you'll get pinched for selling a suitcase full of jeans – or are you peddling something worse? Hard currency, maybe; or have you got a profitable line in drugs? I hope something *does* go wrong.'

The tirade rather amused him, apparently. 'You're forgetting: "Courtesy at all times",' he chided her gently. 'In any case, you didn't listen; I said *not* nefarious.'

She was still struggling with the contradictions raging inside her – distrust of a man who was an oddity among them fighting a conviction that he wasn't someone to dislike – when the familiar sight of Sergei's blue anorak materialized from the huddle of people now drifting into the restaurant. A moment later he was standing by her chair, and McEwan's gaze was fixed intently on her face. She didn't know why it should be so impossible to denounce him when she'd intended to do exactly that.

'Good morning, Sergei,' she said with difficulty. 'Sorry I wasn't downstairs to meet you – there seem to have been a lot of interruptions this morning. Did you meet Mr McEwan last night?'

The men nodded at each other but didn't shake hands, and it was a relief when McEwan said unblushingly, 'Time I began my breakfast, I suppose.' He smiled wholeheartedly at her for the first time – a reward, she decided, for not telling Sergei that he wasn't what he seemed. Then he wandered over to enquire of Miss Livingston-Smith how she'd survived her first night on Russian soil.

Mrs Newcombe's problem created a diversion. 'The plug in the bathroom basin, Kate, lets out more water than it keeps in. *How* is one expected to wash?'

'A universal plug's the answer. I've got some spares upstairs. Any other problems?'

Phyllis Newcombe surveyed the breakfast table. 'Rice pudding and chocolate-covered buns? It's worse even than the horrors remembered from one's schooldays.'

'Well, maybe! But please eat something, at least. It's extremely cold outside, and you'll soon feel tired if you go without breakfast.'

'Think of it as an adventure, Phyllis,' said Lucy Livingston-Smith, now smiling bravely over a forkful of garlic sausage.

Mrs Newcombe sniffed but, not to be outdone, sat down and helped herself to a chunk of black bread. If the timid spinster next to her was bent on coming to terms with Russia, Phyllis Newcombe was not going to be found wanting either.

Three

An hour later they were all outside, got up in heavy coats, boots and a strange variety of headgear. Sergei's brisk instruction to 'follow, please' sent them trailing after him towards the Intourist bus parked outside the hotel. The snow had stopped for the moment, but it lay everywhere, and the River Neva and the city's network of canals were still completely frozen. Kate wished their first glimpse of St Petersburg could have been different. The morning was grey and misty, but clear, winter sunlight was needed to reveal the pastel-coloured, classical beauty of the city that Peter the Great had brought into being three hundred years ago.

In today's bitter cold there was something undeniably chastening about the cemetery, when Sergei recounted the story of the siege and pointed out the mass communal graves watched over by Piskarevskoye's Eternal Flame. It was a shivering and subdued group that he eventually led back to the relative warmth of the bus.

Kate watched their faces, aware that the visit had affected them all. There was none of the usual chatter in the bus, and she suspected that Sergei's next onslaught of statistics fell on completely deaf ears. Linette, especially, seemed at last to be in the grip of something other than her own discontents.

'I didn't believe what he was saying on the way there,' she muttered to Kate. 'All that stuff about men chaining themselves to their benches so that they could go on working without falling down – frankly, it was just too much!' She stopped talking and her eyes, blue like her father's but dramatically fringed with dark lashes, stared at some inward vision of horror that had taken hold of her.

'Are you believing it now?' Kate asked gently.

Linette nodded. 'You can't help it after seeing that place. It's not even over and done with – Sergei talks about it as if it's just happened.'

The actuality of a war that had ravaged Europe but meant nothing to her because it had been fought before she was born, was suddenly all around her; for the moment, at least, her mother's Paris seemed a long way away.

The afternoon was less traumatic – spent 'following, please' – as they were conducted round the picture crammed acres of the Hermitage. At the end of it Lucy turned for another glimpse of the green-and-white-painted facade of the Winter Palace. She admitted to feeling tired, but her gentle face shone with remembered delight.

'You were right, Kate,' she said gratefully. 'Never have I seen so many wonderful things. But for you I might have missed coming!'

They were herded straight into the restaurant when they got back, but for once Sergei disappeared, leaving Kate to apologize for the fact that Russian meal times were something to be got used to.

'I know that dinner at half past five seems outrageous,' she said ruefully, 'but there's nothing we can do about it, and in any case the theatres here start so early that you'd never get to them otherwise. This evening, at least, you don't have to go out into the cold again; the performance of folk dancing is just next door, and there's a corridor connecting the theatre with the hotel.'

'*Folk* dancing?' Mrs Newcombe sounded outraged. 'My dear Kate, we came here to see classical ballet, not a troupe of Siberian peasants built like carthorses cavorting about the stage.'

40

Her displeasure was such that everyone else seemed obliged to disown the peasants as well. They were all tired, and disgruntled at being deprived of what they craved – a relaxing bath, followed by a civilized drink and dinner at a reasonable hour. They were jaded, and she couldn't really blame them. The performance ahead would almost certainly restore them, but she couldn't drag them bodily along the corridor.

'I know how much you want to see the Kirov Ballet, but there's no performance this evening,' she explained patiently. 'I won't try to persuade you if you're feeling tired, but the folk dancing *is* worth seeing, and the evening's going to seem rather long otherwise.'

McEwan's deep voice suddenly boomed from the table where he was sitting with the Engelsmans. 'The folk dancing sounds just my cup of tea; I'm sick of those silly little cygnets prancing around.'

Lucy plucked up the courage to make herself heard in public. 'I shall come with you, if I may, Mr McEwan.'

The Engelsmans followed suit and so, after a glance at his daughter, did Nigel Faringdon. With the tide now flowing strongly against her, Phyllis reluctantly withdrew her objection, and the whole party eventually headed for the corridor leading to the theatre.

McEwan caught up with Kate and loped along beside her. 'You might look grateful to me for saving your bacon,' he murmured.

'A quid pro quo because I held my tongue with Sergei this morning?' she asked straightly.

'No ... I just thought you seemed as if you needed a little help.'

She felt slightly ashamed of herself, but didn't say so. 'I may need more help yet if the dancers are not as marvellous as I remember them. Mrs Newcombe, for one, will rend me into pieces!'

'Fear not; if the proceedings look like flagging I'll invite Ellie to take the floor with me – we're well matched for an elephantine pas de deux. Is that a good enough offer?'

'Irresistible,' she agreed, smiling at him.

In the event it wasn't needed. A couple of joyous hours later even Phyllis was smiling, and Lucy had so far thrown caution to the winds as to follow the rest of them into one of the cafés still open in the hotel. She accepted the glass of Russian tea and cream bun that Nigel Faringdon brought to her, and forgot that her digestion was not normally asked to cope with anything after a light supper at seven o'clock.

'Oh, Kate – how delightful it was,' she said happily. 'The day's been a tremendous rush, but for some reason I don't feel tired at all. For two pins I'd have got up and danced with those boys and girls myself! Thank you for insisting that we shouldn't miss all that colour and gaiety.'

Nigel patted her hand, bringing a faint flush to her cheeks. She was a pretty woman, Kate realized for the first time, but it had taken the small excitement of being in a late-night café in the company of a pleasant man for the inhibitions of a lifetime to be laid aside. There was a slightly wondering air about her, like a baby chick wiggling out of its shell for the first time.

'Kate won't let you miss anything she knows you'll enjoy,' said Nigel Faringdon, smiling at her.

'We're so lucky to have her,' Lucy agreed. 'Sergei is wonderful, but just a little intimidating. I feel as if I ought to apologize for the comfortable life we've always known at home.'

Kate wondered about Lucy's life: it might have been comfortable, but had almost certainly been devoted for years to an aged and demanding parent. Lucy was on her own at last, but she probably still filled her days with a round of small services to the community she lived in.

'Why apologise? I doubt if you have the *slightest* reason to feel guilty,' said her new-found friend firmly. 'All we *are* obliged to do is acknowledge that we're lucky. Life's been kinder to us than it has been to the people of this tortured country. They've yet to know what it means to live in free, peaceful and secure conditions – though at last perhaps they're getting there.'

Lucy looked comforted by this authoritative male view. She'd begun by feeling shy of someone as worldly-looking as Mr Faringdon, but he was easy to talk to after all, and took care of her so beautifully.

Kate's glance wandered from her animated face to the sight of Linette, silky black hair brushing McEwan's hand as he sat drawing something for her on a scrap of paper. She looked up to ask him a question and, for the moment at least, sulkiness and sadness had disappeared. Kate told herself that she'd been wrong not to earmark him straightaway for the job of salvaging an unhappy teenager. It was true – she'd even noticed it herself – that when he smiled, his craggy face became unexpectedly attractive; but she suspected that there was more to it than that. Linette, rootless and muddled as she was, sensed in McEwan some strength that was worth holding on to.

Kate acknowledged the fact to herself with a faint sense of resentment; she would have preferred *not* to have to think well of Ranald

McEwan. It was safer to admit that the day had been a strain, and that she was extremely tired. She said a general goodnight and trailed up three floors to her own room – too hot, of course, and demanding the usual nightly struggle to get the window open.

The snow-covered city was quiet except for the occasional clatter of a tram going past far below. A golden spire or dome glinted here and there, floodlit in the cold darkness, reminding her that she was far from home. Perhaps that was her trouble: a simple attack of homesickness. If Andrew had materialized in the doorway at that moment, she'd have fallen into his arms. McEwan had said hers was a 'strange' job; perhaps it was, and the time had come to give it up and settle down after all. For once she even felt too tired to read the chapter of Jane Austen she allowed herself each night as a corrective to too much Russianness. But even with the light switched off, sleep refused to come. Memories of a long day floated to the surface of her thoughts, clear-cut cameos in her mind's eye: the large Scot quietly insisting that he needed protective colouring; Linette staring white-faced at whatever vision Piskarevskoye had held for her, and even Lucy beginning to abandon the conviction that life had somehow passed her by. Kate remembered her feeling – only yesterday it had been – that this wasn't a trip quite like any other. She didn't know why the instinct had been so strong, but it had certainly been right. Again Rule 22 of Three Cs' guide for the health and sanity of their couriers came forcibly to mind: they were on no account to get involved in the private lives of their customers. Somehow she must keep sight of that for as long as the tour lasted. When it was over and her charges were safely back at Gatwick, she'd consider whether it was time to agree with what Andrew had said; she might by then have finally had enough of Russia.

Life looked more normal in the morning. The temperature had dropped still further during the night but the sun was shining. They were to visit Pushkin – once *Tsarskoye selo*, or the Tsar's village – summer home of the Imperial family from the time of Peter the Great until the last tsar. It had been used by the Germans as their headquarters during the siege of the city, and they'd gutted it before being forced to leave; now it had been restored in every magnificent detail. Kate had visited the palace many times before but still looked forward to going, especially when they could also enjoy a ramble in the snow-covered park in the sunshine.

Her breakfast was undisturbed – sure sign that her flock were beginning to get the hang of things. They were learning their way about the hotel, growing confident enough to smile at waiters they couldn't talk to, and getting accustomed to the feel of a society still very different from their own. Cheered by the sunshine, they assembled for breakfast with the endearingly blasé air of old hands; she could safely leave them to begin the first of the day's battles. Her immediate objective was a little co-operation from the staff behind the money-exchange counter. Like the people in the post-office section next to it – in fact like any member of Russian officialdom – they never functioned at the times advertised; in fact, they showed a strong inclination never to function at all except when the whim took them. With her mind on the confrontation ahead, she stepped out of the lift and collided once more with the unyielding stuff of which McEwan was made.

'You seem determined to do me an injury,' he pointed out, reminding her of their first ridiculous encounter at the airport.

But the complaint was made without his usual forcefulness, and she had the feeling that McEwan's mind was on other things – the real reason for his being there at all, perhaps. About to suggest this, Kate suddenly found herself questioned instead.

'Something wrong, shepherdess? You're looking rather grim on this bright and sunny morning.'

'Mental effort! I'm working out my battle-plan with the awkward creatures who man the bureau de change!'

'Stand no nonsense from them is my advice. I had an invigorating tussle earlier on with the thug who calls himself the commissionaire at the front door. He seemed reluctant to accept the idea that I was going out for a pre-breakfast stroll.'

Kate's face relaxed into a smile, but she felt obliged to put in a word for their hosts. 'It's hoped that tour groups stay together – they don't get into difficulties that way. But you obviously won your tussle – you've brought the cold, fresh air in with you!'

He nodded, then spoke of something else. 'It was enjoyable last night; even our little Linette cheered up. She's a nice child when she's not pretending to be a world-weary femme fatale – also very pretty!'

Kate remembered Linette's face as she'd smiled at McEwan in the café the night before, and was suddenly beset by a fresh anxiety. The man himself was very taking when he set out to be, but he was older in years than Linette and in – probably sinful – experience, very much older indeed.

'She's going through a difficult patch at the moment,' Kate explained carefully. 'It wouldn't take much to unbalance her still more than she is already.'

'And I'm just the man to do it, you reckon,' Ranald McEwan suddenly all but shouted at her. 'Credit me with a grain of common sense, woman. Can I not see that she's an impressionable, unhappy child?'

'I wasn't suggesting that you're about to seduce her,' Kate protested faintly.

'Only because you didn't quite have the nerve, and that in itself is something to marvel at.'

He stalked into the lift and left her standing there remembering that the road to hell was said to be paved with good intentions. She prudently kept out of his way after that, sitting next to Mrs Newcombe in the bus and reloading her camera for her. Phyllis insisted on photographing everything in sight, but liked to be assured that, if her films weren't correctly loaded, she could blame someone else for the mistake.

They discarded coats and bags as usual in the cloakroom at the Palace, and then queued up at the slipper box to equip themselves with the overshoes that were insisted upon as a protection against damage to the fine parquet floors. Ready for the fray at last, they trailed up the magnificent marble staircase, admired the ornately beautiful white plasterwork, which looked as if it had been carved out of wedding-cake icing, and followed Sergei into the first of a series of gorgeously decorated rooms. They began to straggle in the way that always irritated him, determined to go at their own pace, in order to stop and stare, and photograph. McEwan was still at the bottom of the staircase, fiddling with a light meter, when a scream from above just preceded the sight of one of the party, Elspeth Grant, hurtling towards him. There was a split second in which to brace himself, open his arms, and gather her safely as she arrived at the bottom of the staircase. The impact made even him reel backwards, but he managed to keep his feet and finally deposit her on the ground unharmed. The entire episode took no more than a moment or two, but, flying down the stairs to reach her, Kate imagined what the outcome could have been. Elspeth's ashen-faced husband, Dr Grant, followed Kate down.

'So sorry,' Mrs Grant murmured distractedly. 'Such a fuss to cause ... but I stumbled because my slipper came off, and then I lost my balance. I'm perfectly all right, thanks to Mr McEwan.'

Ranald smiled at her kindly. 'Elspeth and I are thinking of rehearsing a circus act together!'

It made her laugh, and she said more confidently that she intended going on with the tour because there wasn't the slightest thing wrong with her. Alexander Grant took her firmly by the hand and led her up the staircase again, leaving Kate staring at McEwan.

'I don't know how to thank you – she might have killed herself.'

'She didn't, so we'll forget about it, if you please. Let us ascend this damned vulgar staircase instead; we're keeping everybody else waiting.'

Rebuffed by his sharpness, Kate gave a little shrug and 'ascended' as she'd been bidden.

The rest of the morning went by without any more alarms, and when they'd been sated with the treasures inside the palace they were turned loose outside to photograph the blue-and-white facade, which looked dazzling in the sunlight. It was time for a conscientious courier to relax and wander by herself through the snow-covered park. The statues were still hidden inside the wooden boxes that protected them during the winter, and she liked to imagine them in the darkness, talking to themselves and longing for the moment when spring released them into daylight again.

51

'Shuffled off your Intourist admirer?' It was McEwan's voice behind her.

'If you mean Sergei, he's simply a colleague and friend.'

'Less than honest, I'm afraid. It's obvious even to me that the poor chap's in a state about you.' The Scotsman's grey glance was fixed on her face more intently than she liked. 'It isn't a problem now, surely? He's not about to be hauled off to Siberia for falling in love with a foreign infidel?'

'It's only a small problem for me,' Kate admitted, 'but not one that need bother anyone else. I'm more concerned to know what you're up to, Mr McEwan. *Why* are you here?'

For a moment she thought he wasn't going to reply; then he said slowly, 'I've come looking for an old friend ... the sister of an even older friend. If he didn't work for the government in a sensitive area, he'd be here himself; as it is, I've come instead.'

'Why look for her here?'

'Because it's where she came on a student exchange visit that should have finished by now. She was expected home for Christmas, but, instead of Jenny herself, the Maitlands got a letter saying that she thought of going on to Moscow – she wasn't ready to leave Russia yet.'

'If she wanted to come at all, why

shouldn't she be interested enough to stay?' Kate suggested. 'Surely the choice is hers?'

'She's only interested in finding a man called Nikolai Kemanska,' McEwan said bluntly. 'He came as a fellow scientist to visit Robin Maitland in Edinburgh a long time ago. Being all of fourteen at the time, and very impressionable, Jenny fell in love with him. We used to tease her about a schoolgirl infatuation she was certain to grow out of. No such thing, it now turns out; instead, we know that she's been waiting ever since to come and look for him.'

'I assume you've got addresses for Jenny or the scientist friend?'

'I tried them both this morning, when I was supposed to be taking my stroll. Thank God I found a taxi driver who could speak a little English. Jenny had left here, to go to Moscow. There was no sign of Nikolai, and the couple at that address said they'd never heard of him.'

'So her search and yours are now transferred to Moscow.' Kate thought of adding that Jenny Maitland was old enough to do as she pleased, but the expression on McEwan's face prevented her. Instead, she was reminded of another headstrong girl and suddenly spoke of *her*.

'I'm sorry if I offended you this morning – I didn't mean to. It's just that Nigel Faringdon explained about Linette's recent disastrous time in Paris with her mother; *this* trip is supposed to calm her down again.'

McEwan stared at her, then asked a question of his own. 'Do you get involved to this extent with all your customers?'

She shook her head, unable to explain that in all sorts of ways it didn't seem to be a typical tour at all. 'What are you in real life, if *not* a scientist in a sensitive area?'

'A scientist of sorts: I'm an agronomist, trying to stop people starving in odd parts of the world by advising them what crops to grow.'

Kate's glance wandered over his sheer size. 'I suppose you intimidate the poor souls – bully them into growing alfalfa when they'd rather be paddling about in a rice-field, or some such thing.'

'More or less,' he agreed, but was prevented from saying any more by the sound of a horn summoning everyone back to the bus. Their belated arrival together earned Kate Linette's usual scowl, and a look of burning reproach from Sergei, but they weren't the last to return.

Ellie and Dirk climbed aboard to an ironic chorus of cheers from everyone else. It was behaviour that Kate knew her Russian colleague couldn't understand. Sergei felt irritation – anger even – for this large, disorganized couple who kept failing to follow his instructions, and the amused tolerance that seemed to be the English way of dealing with them simply defeated him.

It was Ellie who rebelled when told on the journey back to the hotel to look at a remaining statue of Lenin.

'More of Lenin I do not wish to see,' she bellowed confidentially to her husband.

Nigel Faringdon turned round in his seat to smile at her. 'Not quite as fashionable as he was, Ellie, but don't forget he took the place of God for many Russian people.'

'For them, I doubt; for me, certainly not,' the Dutch lady said emphatically. 'He was just a man, with a face like a – Dirk, what is *weisel* in English?'

'Weasel, of course, my darlink.'

The word meant nothing to Sergei, but he got the drift of the argument and reacted to it at once. 'Lenin was the father of our socialist revolution. We must always revere him for freeing the Russian people from the slavery of the Tsars.'

A respectful silence followed – born, Kate realized, of the sheer politeness of her flock; but over lunch, when Sergei had left them, the conversation revealed the extent to which they were in a ferment about the country they were visiting.

'It's disgraceful – those poor women

shovelling snow in the street.' This was Mrs Newcombe, incensed by the discovery that any lowly, boring or arduous job in Russia seemed to be given to women to do. 'Don't tell me that a country capable of exploring space can't work out some mechanized way of clearing the streets, if it wants to; it *doesn't* want to. Women are second-class citizens here.'

Gentle Dr Grant, a neighbour of Mrs Newcombe's at home, decided, with what Ranald thought was lunatic bravery, to play the part of devil's advocate.

'The women don't look precisely unhappy to me,' he pointed out. 'I'm not sure they aren't even enjoying the work they share – a sort of street camaraderie over the broom and shovel.'

Even before Phyllis could recover from the effrontery of this suggestion, Lucy turned on him, eyes positively flashing. 'And I suppose they enjoy queuing up for hours afterwards, to buy food at prices they can just about afford – *queue* camaraderie, Dr Grant?'

'Better perhaps than the loneliness of living by themselves in one room; there's still a shortage of men here,' Ranald pointed out quietly. 'The terrible losses of the war can't have been made good yet.'

Kate watched them all while the battle

raged, aware that they were finding it hard to come to terms with the contrasts that Russia presented. Lucy had wanted to marvel at the treasures of the Tsars. Exotic and beautiful as they were, she was now more concerned with the babushkas who guarded them – tight-faced old women in whom joy or even cheerfulness had apparently dried up for ever. Ranald McEwan was, like the rest of them, thankful to see Russian Orthodox churches no longer reduced to the status of mere museums, but the austerities of a Calvinist upbringing made him disapprove of the painted ikons, coloured marbles, and pillars completely sheathed in gold leaf that seemed to glorify a God different from his own. She feared that, sooner or later, he would get into an argument with Sergei about them. Eventually, of course, he did, though not quite in the way that she had expected.

Four

They had spent the afternoon on the island in the Neva where the city of St Petersburg had begun – the Peter and Paul fortress. The cathedral there was crowded as usual, and Ranald commented on the fact when they were walking back across the causeway. Sergei overheard him.

'The dying remnants of an old superstition,' he said contemptuously. 'Our people shouldn't need such things any more.' Kate saw Ranald's dark eyebrow climb, but he let Sergei go on. 'People, especially old people, are obstinate in clinging to old ways. The new generations know what they have to feel proud of, and believe in.'

Then the quiet answer came: 'People, old or new, don't find much to lift their hearts in outworn slogans and statistics about gas turbine production. They go into the churches looking for what everyday life doesn't offer them: beauty and colour and a mysterious belief in something beyond themselves. You and your leaders might

58

consider that "decadent", but it's human nature and you're stuck with it, my friend.'

Sergei was tall for a Russian, but even so McEwan towered over him. The two of them confronted one another, instinctive hostility finally acknowledged between them.

'I'm sorry that you don't like what you find in Russia, Mr McEwan,' the Intourist guide said stiffly.

'I find Russia fascinating!' was the reply; then he strolled on, leaving Sergei staring after him.

'The Scots are an argumentative race – not like the placid English!' Kate pointed out, trying to pour oil on troubled waters.

'I'm sorry that man is in the group; he is not welcome here,' Sergei insisted. 'I do my best – try very hard to make him see the truth about Russia – but all the time I think he is laughing at me inside.'

That was likely to be true, she knew. An occasional ill-concealed snort from the back of the bus indicated that McEwan was growing restive under the daily shower of statistics reminding them of the Motherland's heroic past and her continued greatness, despite the inconvenient fact that the old Soviet Union was now no more.

It would have helped to be able to explain to Sergei that the Scotsman had anxieties of his own and a purpose in being there different from that of the rest of them. Unable to mention that, she smiled at the Russian more warmly than she meant to, and saw his taut face relax.

'Dear Kate,' he whispered, 'what does a stupid man like him matter when *you* understand what we've achieved? Let him laugh if he wants to.'

That evening they set off for the Kirov Theatre – the opera lovers among them anticipating a treat, the rest prepared to endure several hours' boredom relieved by looking round a theatre restored to all its pre-war splendour. The opera was *Prince Igor*, and even Kate had to admit by the second interval that, as operas went, it wasn't memorable.

'One good tune, and the Polotsvian Dances,' McEwan said sourly in her ear. 'Moreover, the staging is fifty years out of date and the soprano's a stone overweight.'

'Cheer up – only one more act to go. Admit, at least, that the theatre's beautiful.'

He looked around with a jaundiced eye at the exquisite blue-and-gold décor. 'Pretty ... but the chairs are damned uncomfortable!'

It was to be concluded that Mr McEwan was not enjoying himself, and she was surprised to be told by Lucy in a whisper while the scene was changing that their friend was utterly absorbed in the performance. She glanced along the row at him: head sunk on his chest, hand shielding his eyes – the picture of earnest concentration. Regrettably, their friend was sound asleep, but she didn't tell Lucy so.

Linette, dressed to kill in velvet pants and a silk top the colour of her eyes, spent the evening sitting next to Sergei. Kate saw them deep in conversation several times, and was curious to know what they made of each other. When he'd left them back at the hotel, and they'd settled in the rouble café that had now become a late-evening ritual, Linette unburdened herself.

'Kate, you seem to get on with our Intourist man, but he baffles me. I don't know whether to be mad at him for despising us, or feel sorry for the ghastly life he leads. What I'd like to do is just be friends, but how can you get to know someone who refuses to believe that we're all part of the same human race?'

Kate registered a change in the girl in front of her; a week ago Linette would have ignored the courier completely.

'Things aren't nearly as bad as they were,' she tried hard to explain, 'but still difficult enough for someone like Sergei. He lives with a widowed mother and sister – probably reasonably well by Russian standards; but he must protect his job, and always be careful.'

Linette nodded thoughtfully. 'I don't buy half what he says, but there's something ... compelling ... about him, isn't there? If he knew about the life I was leading in Paris, he'd think he was justified in calling us decadent.' She stared at Kate. 'Pa told you about that, didn't he?'

'A little ... just enough to explain why you looked unhappy.'

'I suppose it *was* decadent, though it seemed madly grown-up fun at the time! It isn't only Sergei who makes me stop and think. Ranald's an eye-opener too. Among my mother's circle of friends the only thing people worry about is having a good time; *his* idea of a good time is teaching Ethiopian peasants the best way to grow Indian corn!'

Kate smiled in spite of herself at the note of wonder in Linette's voice. 'It's his job – perfectly chosen, I'd say. He has a natural talent for telling other people what to do.'

'*Not* the nice kind Kate we know!' Linette said with a rare grin. 'What's he done to upset you?'

'Nothing at all ... blame it on chemistry! We spark a little.' For no reason that she could think of she felt obliged, all the same,

62

to apologize for her snide remark. 'I suspect he's a man with a mission in life; he can't bear to see people making a mess of things when a little help from him would set them right!'

She hoped it sounded rational to a girl who turned an unexpectedly sharp eye on other people when she stopped looking inwards at herself. The truth was, of course, that chemistry – good or bad – had nothing to do with her snappiness about McEwan. She was simply in a state of anxiety for what she knew about him, and for what would happen when they got to Moscow.

Over breakfast the next morning she explained the arrangements for their departure from St Petersburg. Picnic lunch packets would be waiting for them, and the Intourist bus would take them and their luggage to the railway station. There, orderly planning usually broke down, and extemporization had to take over.

'It will look like a mad free-for-all,' she confessed, 'and since no whistles are ever blown, we don't exactly know when the train is going to start moving! But if you'll stay together and hang on to your hand-luggage, we'll get you and everything else safely on board. Sergei will be there to stow the cases in our reserved coach, but if hale and hearty members of the party can lend a hand as well, the job will get done more quickly.'

She was careful not to catch McEwan's eye, but found him behind her when she walked out of the restaurant.

'Neatly put, Kate! Anyone who doesn't fall over himself to enrol in your chain gang will feel ashamed of himself. I hope the more elderly members of the party don't all have heart attacks trying to live up to your expectations.'

'We shall dissuade the more elderly ones,' she said quickly, 'but I don't feel any great anxiety about you.'

'No need to tell me that. I doubt if your withers would be wrung if I expired on the spot.'

'Inconvenient,' she said after a moment's thought. 'Think of the problems you'd cause.'

'Vixen,' he said sadly, and walked away.

It wouldn't last long, but just for the moment she had the feeling of having managed to get the better of him.

Thanks largely to McEwan's enormous strength and ruthless ability to organize other people into doing what he wanted of them, nothing and no one got left behind when the high-speed train – the *Avrora* –

pulled out of Moskovsky station, destination the capital, four hundred miles away across the great Central European plain. Relieved to have got over the hurdle of getting themselves and their belongings safely installed, everyone began by enjoying the journey. It was a relief to sit still after a week spent keeping up with the pace set by Sergei, and it was pleasant to be spared any more of his statistics for a while. For the first hour or so, relief was enjoyment enough, coupled with the novelty of looking at the landscape outside the train window – flat land covered with snow and bare silver birch trees. At the end of the second hour the view was exactly the same – more flat land, more silver birch trees – and, when asked, Kate had to confess that the view would be much the same all the way to Moscow. It was time to investigate the lunch boxes.

Afterwards, food and boredom induced snatches of sleep, broken by the excitement of an occasional stop. At one of these Ellie tried to disembark, to photograph the train standing in the station. To do either was not permitted; Kate hauled her back on board to a chorus of 'Nyets' screamed at her by a posse of large female train guards, and then politely insisted on the return of Ellie's camera, which they had confiscated.

'I should have been watching,' Sergei said

wretchedly, woken by the commotion. 'It's always *her*; I think she *tries* to be a nuisance.'

'It isn't deliberate; she's just naturally prone to small disasters.' Kate smiled at his worried face. 'Go back to sleep, please – you look tired still, and short of falling off the train Ellie can't come to any more harm!'

He looked more than tired, she thought – a care-worn thirty-two instead of the age she knew he was: a year older than her own twenty-four. He was an eager, clever man, but she'd rarely heard him laugh, and never known him to make a joke of any kind. A decade of Glasnost had released the Russian people from the straitjacket of state control, but they still weren't entirely sure that it might not suddenly come back again. Petty, pointless restrictions remained, like a woman not being allowed to photograph a train, and there was still some echo in the Russian air of past terror and suffering not yet forgotten.

Kate watched Sergei's eyes close again and then surveyed the rest of them. A few were reading, most snoozed, except for McEwan and Dr Grant quietly playing chess together at the far end of the coach – everyone safely present ... No – Linette was missing. Kate remembered her walking past, presumably on the way to the lavatory outside in the corridor, but that had been some time ago.

She'd been looking bored again, because her father had moved to sit beside Lucy and McEwan had deserted her for Dr Grant.

Five more minutes ticked by before Kate obeyed the insistent pricking in her thumbs and slipped out of her seat beside the sleeping Sergei. The long train took some negotiating and she got held up several times along the way, but she finally arrived at last at the end coach, made up of separate, small compartments. Being nowhere else, Linette had to be here – and so she was, hemmed in by three Russian soldiers, whose tedious journey had been whiled away in drinking a considerable amount of vodka until Fate supplied them with even better entertainment. One of them held her by the wrist, and she looked white-faced and desperately frightened – uncertain whether to shout for help or risk getting into even worse trouble if she didn't make a scene.

The men were drunk but not incapably so, and the arrival of a second girl – unlooked-for good fortune – distracted them into an argument among themselves as to which of them was going to be unlucky. It was something to be grateful for that Linette couldn't understand the conversation, but Kate realized that what happened next depended on their degree of drunkenness: open opposition might inflame them into sudden brutality; friendliness might be taken as an encouragement. She had to get Linette safely out of the compartment, but for the sake of Three Cs and Sergei's reputation with Intourist it must be done without a public scene. She began to explain that her English friend had got lost and that her father and the Intourist guide were looking for her further along the train. No doubt they would soon arrive themselves. The words registered sufficiently for the man to release his grip on Linette, and Kate nodded in the direction of the corridor. 'Get out,' she ordered in English. 'Don't wait – I'll follow you in a moment.'

Linette hesitated, but Kate's expression said, 'Go,' and she pulled herself together sufficiently to make for the door. The men didn't attempt to follow her and when she was safely out of the way Kate dredged up another casual sentence about it being time to rejoin her friend. She was immediately grabbed by a soldier drunker and larger than the other two.

'Fools,' he said scornfully, 'we might have had both of them. This one's mine, though. You can get out and mind the door.'

The situation had darkened into something horribly threatening. The other two, perhaps not sorry to quit a scene they feared was getting out of control, lurched out and at once Kate was pushed down along the seat, with the third man sprawled on top of her. With her hat on the floor and the pins fastening her hair lost in the struggle, she knew the full extent of her danger. The man's hands tore at the neck of her shirt, and his wet mouth fastened disgustingly on her own. Terror made her mind go blank, but instinct told her not to struggle. She must pray to God that the moment would come when, forgetting discretion, she could draw enough breath to scream.

The moment came, but not as she imagined it. Instead, the door was flung open, and the drunken soldier on top of her was dragged upright and flung on to the opposite seat. The huge figure of Ranald McEwan towered over both of them; the wrath of God himself, she thought, quite enough to reduce her assailant to the cowering wreck he'd suddenly become. McEwan pointed to her cap, still lying on the floor, and the gesture told the soldier to pick it up. He bent down, even tried to rub some dust off it, and handed it back to Kate.

'Now get out of here,' McEwan said briefly. She did as she was told, surprised to find that her trembling legs would support her at all. The other two men outside were backed into the corner of the corridor, watching like mesmerized rabbits the giant who followed her out. She struggled as far as the restaurant car, then collapsed in a seat – just sufficiently herself to register that none of the Three Cs group were there drinking tea. McEwan signalled to the waitress, then sat down opposite her, while she tried to bundle up disordered hair under her cap.

'Yes, hide it, for God's sake,' he murmured. 'It obviously inflames the licentious soldiery like that.' His expression mirrored the cold contempt in his voice. 'Your shirt is also still undone, but perhaps that's to inflame Sergei or me.'

Her face whitened still more, but she said nothing while her unsteady fingers buttoned up the shirt again; then she clamped her hands round the glass of tea that had been put in front of her. It felt hot and comforting against her cold hands, and it was something to hold on to while she dealt with the shock of what he'd just said.

He took a gulp of scalding tea himself, and forced his mind to relinquish a sickening mental picture of Kate passed on to each of those drunken soldiers in turn. The thought was unbearable, and so was the fear that flirting with danger was a game she enjoyed.

'If you make a habit of teasing men, here or anywhere else, you'll get more excitement than you bargain for one of these days.'

Anger restored some colour to her sheet-white face, but she forced herself not to shout at him. 'I'm grateful to you for the rescue, but there's no need for you to share a table with me a moment longer – in fact, I'd much rather you didn't, Mr McEwan.'

'Call me Ranald, or McEwan, or any damn thing you like, as long as it's not *Mr McEwan*!'

'I should have said McEwan of McEwan, I suppose?'

'Yes, as it happens. Now drink your tea so that I can see you safely back to your seat.'

She picked up her glass again and sat sipping at it, apparently composed, but he could see a pulse still beating in the white skin of her throat and he had to resist the temptation to touch it, to still its agitated throbbing.

'How did you know I was there?' she asked, more or less calmly.

'I went looking for Linette because Nigel said she'd been gone a long time. She was running back along the corridor in a state of panic – she thought *you* might be in difficulties.' He stopped abruptly, then spoke again in a different tone of voice. 'Should we do something – report those men?'

'No, please don't. They'd be severely disciplined, and so might Sergei as well. It wasn't his fault, and the men were drunk; it

71

wouldn't have happened otherwise.'

Reaction was setting in and she struggled with the strong desire to burst into tears. She was tired of the job she was doing, tired of living among people she didn't really understand. The thought of Andrew Carmichael was suddenly in her mind – dear, dependable Andrew. So vivid was the image that she wasn't even surprised when McEwan's train of thought echoed her own.

'Isn't there some nice, respectable man at home ready to keep you out of trouble and make you settle down?'

She could almost manage a smile. 'There is, as it happens, but he's been very patient so far.'

She supposed that it would make McEwan look pleased, but his grim expression remained unchanged, and it was a relief to see Ellie's cheerful pink face smiling at them as she walked into the restaurant car.

'This journey is too lonk, dear Kate ... why did we not the aeroplane take?'

'Because a courier's life the Russians like to make difficult,' she said, unable not to copy the Dutchwoman's way of talking. 'Thirty seats booked on an aeroplane are apt to be countermanded at the last moment, if they decide they want to move a group of officials or military around. The train may be tedious' – she managed to say it calmly without looking at McEwan – 'but at least this way I know we'll all arrive together.' She stood up to leave, grateful for the fact that he was now hemmed in by Ellie. 'Time I saw how the others are getting on, if you'll excuse me.'

Linette was waiting for her at the door of their own coach, looking tense and white-faced still. 'Kate ... you've been gone ages. I wanted to come back with Ranald, but he swore he'd throw me off the train if I didn't do as I was told. Is ... is everything all right?'

'Everything's fine. No harm done, so let's forget about it.'

Linette shook her head. 'I've had quite a lot of practice at handling lecherous men, and I don't normally panic, but that was something I didn't know how to handle.'

The dreadfulness of it was, thought Kate, that she wasn't even boasting. 'If that's really what your life in Paris was like, I think you could do better,' she suggested gently.

'That's what my father says, and I'm beginning to think you may both be right.' Her face brightened suddenly in a tremulous grin. 'Maybe I'll turn over a new leaf – grow like dear Lucy, with whom my father's rather taken! I expect it's because she's just about as different from my mother as a woman could be.'

'I'm rather taken with her, too,' said Kate.

'In her own quiet way, she's something special.'

'I wasn't laughing at her,' Linette surprisingly explained. 'It's just that I've never met anyone quite like *her* before, either.'

'That's travel for you – it broadens the mind!'

Linette smiled again, more easily, then grew serious again. 'Kate … it was not being able to talk to those soldiers that made them so frightening. I couldn't explain to them that I hadn't come looking for – for a man.' She shivered at the memory of it. 'I suppose the truth is that this whole country frightens me. Sergei makes it *sound* like paradise – everybody getting a fair share, no unemployment, housing that even the poorest people can afford – but it's his job to gloss over the truth and hide away what they'd rather we didn't know.'

'You're right, of course,' Kate agreed slowly. 'It's far from being paradise even now, but it's an immeasurably better place than it was. At least people no longer live in fear of being hauled off to infamous labour camps just for daring to oppose the system. *We* can't properly understand what that means.'

'I'm like this country – all mixed up,' Linette admitted finally, 'impressed by what is true … The people here have suffered so much and worked such miracles. But a lot more of what Sergei says *isn't* true, and I don't understand how someone as intelligent as he is can't tell the difference.'

Kate stared at her puzzled face; impossible to see in it now any trace of the petulant teenager who'd slouched on to the aeroplane at Gatwick so reluctantly. If northern magic wasn't working on her, Russian reality certainly was.

'We don't know for certain that Sergei *can't* tell truth from fiction,' Kate said finally. 'All we do know is that at the moment he does his job, and looks after us very well. Don't forget that his father and grandfather were given no choice – they *had* to believe in the Communist Party and the system. Some of that still rubs off on him.'

Linette nodded. 'Poor Sergei – torn between his upbringing and you!'

'Nonsense! My only appeal is that I'm a bit different from what he's used to. Come on, I'll buy you a glass of delicious Russian tea. I've had some already, but I could drink some more.'

They walked along the corridor together, but at the door of the restaurant car Linette stopped suddenly; there was still a confession to make. 'I didn't want to come on this trip – you probably got that impression at Gatwick! But Kate, I'm very glad I did.'

Five

It was dark by the time they finally drew into the station at Moscow. A biting wind drove a mixture of snow and sleet into their faces while they waited for the tedious process of getting their luggage on board the train to be put into reverse. The Intourist bus was slow to arrive; when it did, the driver was surly, and Sergei took charge again with the more autocratic manner that Kate had noticed in him before when a tour reached Moscow. She supposed that it had something to do with nearness to Intourist headquarters and the centre of power; in St Petersburg he felt less watched. He announced that they were going to be late for dinner again and must go *straight* to the restaurant when they arrived.

'I *won't* do it,' Mrs Newcombe called firmly from halfway down the bus. 'Dinner can wait for *me* for once. After all day in a train I insist on washing first.'

She'd said no more than they were all feeling; tolerance of being hectored was wearing thin and it was most likely to give way completely, Kate knew, when they were cold and tired and hungry. She walked along the aisle to Sergei, sitting beside the driver, and explained quietly in his own language that, even if they were late already, dinner must wait a bit longer. He looked reluctant, but thirty pairs of eyes trained on him were repeating Mrs Newcombe's message; the blood of the Home Counties was up. He finally shrugged and conceded that they might go quickly to their rooms, and then to the restaurant. Kate returned to her seat at the back of the bus, and Nigel leaned across to give her hand a little pat.

'Well done, Kate. Our friend nearly had a revolt on his hands just now.'

'It's not his fault; his job is to keep to the timetable that's been fixed, and it's understandable that he should get nervous when we fall behind schedule.'

'Yes, but he must learn when to slacken the reins, especially for the English. We tend to get bloody-minded when we think we're being pushed around!'

'I had noticed! It's an important difference between us. The Russians, poor things, are conditioned to being pushed around.'

McEwan was sitting next to Nigel, apparently listening to the conversation, but she had the impression that his thoughts were elsewhere. She imagined him trying by sheer will-power to conjure up his friend Jenny, hidden somewhere in the city that surrounded them in the darkness.

'You still have your ... quest ... in mind?' she asked quietly, not sure whether they were now on speaking terms or not after the train episode.

'Of course; it's what I came for.' He sounded surprised that she'd even bothered to ask the question. 'I'll make a start at the British Embassy tomorrow, just in case Jenny's been in touch with anyone there. If our Intourist watchdog wants to know where I am, perhaps you'll explain that the reek of these bloody diesel fumes has driven me to walk in the fresh air.'

'It even has the merit of sounding true!' she agreed.

She was about to move away when he suddenly spoke again. 'Linette has confirmed what I should have been able to guess for myself. It was *she* who went looking for excitement on the train, not you.'

'It doesn't matter.'

'In fact, it does. I was presumptuous and inexcusably rude. Forgive me, please.'

'Apology handsomely made, and accepted,' she said. 'Now it certainly doesn't matter.'

She saw his face relax into the first

wholehearted smile he'd offered her, but had to turn away from him because Lucy was trying to attract her attention.

'Kate, dear ... what about the water *here*?'

Her mind, still fixed on the thought of unknown Jenny, found it hard to grapple with the question. 'It's ... it's better than in St Petersburg,' she said after a moment. 'Drinkable, in fact, even though it doesn't taste very nice.'

'Then I shall risk it,' Lucy decided firmly. 'One must try not to be *too* craven when one is abroad.'

Kate smiled at her with affection, thinking that she'd already taken quite a lot in her gentle stride. All the same, she was almost certainly going to find Moscow harder to accept than the city they'd just left behind. Kate herself found it so, even though numerous visits had now made her familiar with the capital. At this point in the tour she was always getting tired and beginning to look forward to the end of it, but there was more to her reaction to Moscow than that; for all the fairy-tale beauty of the Kremlin, she found it an uncongenial city. This time matters were further complicated – by a growing anxiety about Sergei and her relations with him, and by her knowledge of McEwan's search for a girl who might not want to be found. Without help he had almost no hope of tracking her down, but Kate knew that by abetting him she risked implicating not only Three Cs but Sergei as well. She stared out of the snow-speckled window, trying not to think of her cosy flat at home. Perhaps Andrew was right and it *was* time she gave up travelling; but for the moment she was in this cold, alien city and there was still a job of work to do.

Their hotel, the Kosmos, was comparatively new – a great curving mass of glass and concrete overlooking the open spaces of the Park of Economic Achievement.

'Small is not beautiful in Russia,' Dr Grant murmured wryly, squinting up at the twenty-six storeys towering above them.

'No, but hang on to your sense of proportion,' said Ranald, minded to be fair. 'What looks right at home would seem ridiculously miniature here, but there's more to it than that. The Russians are obsessed by size, which is why they discount *us* completely and feel a national need to go one better than the Americans. Anything the USA can do, the Motherland can do bigger!'

What he said was even more unarguable inside the hotel. Everything was on a vast scale, and it had the cosy, personal charm of an international airport. But if the Hotel Kosmos couldn't be called homey, at least its windows gave them a remarkable panoramic view of the city. On the twenty-fifth floor they were almost on a level with the monument commemorating Russian exploits in space. For once it wasn't the usual massive sculpture of a man and woman striding off a triumphal arch lugging an outsize sheaf of corn; instead, the silver rocket, poised on top of its curving steel vapour trail, seemed on the point of soaring into flight. It was both genuinely imaginative and beautiful.

The Intourist bus waited for them as usual after breakfast next morning. Sergei counted heads and found one missing, and Kate duly explained that Mr McEwan had preferred to go wandering on his own instead of joining the organized tour. It was a show of independence that Sergei disapproved of, even though he couldn't forbid it. This man *would* be the culprit, of course; he'd been an unsettling influence for the past week, and Sergei was aware of not knowing how to deal with him. But when they got back at lunchtime, it was to find him virtuously waiting for them in the restaurant. Sergei relaxed a little, but couldn't resist pointing out that the Scotsman's absence from the tour had been noticed.

'You missed our visit this morning ... you

would have found it interesting,' he said stiffly.

'My morning *was* interesting.' It was polite, as usual, but utterly uninformative, and confirmed Sergei's impression that his and this man's conversations were never about the same thing. Watching the two of them, Kate was put in mind of a Great Dane allowing a belligerent terrier to snap at him. All the same, she must tell McEwan that he would draw attention to himself if he missed the afternoon tour as well.

'Fear not, I shall be there,' he murmured when she slipped into a chair beside him. 'You worry too much, by the way. I hope Three Cs realize what a paragon of an employee they've got.'

'I'm beginning to think it will be a miracle if I'm still an employee at all by the time we get home. Did you get any news at the embassy? I assume that's where you were this morning.'

McEwan frowned at the tablecloth in front of him. 'No news at all. Jenny's not normally one for remaining unnoticed – if she's anywhere around, you're liable to know about it. But here she seems to have gone completely to ground.' He spoke calmly, but not even immense self control could conceal from her the anxiety that consumed him inside. Jenny was the long-known sister of a friend, but Kate felt certain that she was more than that to McEwan. He loved this girl he was looking for.

'What did they say at the embassy?' she asked quietly.

'Very little, but, as you might expect, they said it very politely! If she were to ask for help, they'd try to give it. But if an adult British national chooses to stay here, they're not in a position to ship her out against her will.'

'You didn't mention the man she's looking for – Nikolai?'

'No; what would be the point? But he has no listing in the telephone directory. I asked the concierge to check.'

'What happens next?'

'I shall present myself at the university – an old friend who happens to be passing through Moscow.'

'You need help,' Kate said suddenly, 'Russian-speaking help. Without knowing the Cyrillic alphabet, you won't even be able to make head or tail of street names.'

'I don't need *your* help, if that's what you're offering,' he said bluntly.

'I was joking about losing my job ... let me help, please.'

'Nothing doing, though I'm touched by the offer. I've got the name of the university written down in Russian. All I have to do is find a taxi driver who can read.'

'Pig-headed as *well* as bossy,' she said bitterly, and saw the smile that occasionally softened his face so charmingly. But, before he could reply, Phyllis Newcombe plonked herself in the chair on the other side of him and private conversation was over.

They spent the afternoon in the Kremlin and there was the usual queue to get into the citadel. They inched their way forward among a line of other tourists, mainly Russian, and finally got inside the red-brick battlemented walls. They were inside the ancient heart of the city – walls, watch-towers and massive gateways enclosing Moscow's past history as well as all its present power. There was another queue to get into their first port of call, the Armoury, and nothing to entertain them while they waited in the cold except glimpses of official black limousines that ferried high-ranking officials to and from the Kremlin Palace. One, curtained as usual but larger than most, hurled itself down the icy hill towards the gateway, didn't check at the traffic lights showing red, and rocked to a skidding halt when its bumpers entwined with those of a much smaller car making its lawful way up the hill. There was a deafening bang and a tinkle of breaking glass, but no one seemed to be hurt.

Lucy said so with relief, but Ranald, standing just behind her, snorted. 'Don't you believe it. Someone *will* get hurt! The driver of the little car will certainly be found to be at fault.'

'But it wasn't his blame,' Lucy insisted, looking horrified. 'The lights were clearly in his favour. Should we insist on saying so to someone?' Justice was involved, and for this she was even prepared to take on what the infamous old KGB now called itself – the Federal Bureau of Security.

'We can say so, but it won't do a particle of good. The big car had more important officials inside, for a certainty. Might is still right over here, Lucy, even though democracy's golden day is supposed to have dawned.'

He spoke to her, but the taunt was aimed at Sergei, and Kate's heart bled for a man obliged to defend what was indefensible. Before she could think of some way of turning the conversation, Ellie blundered in, making matters worse. 'All men – are they not equal here, Sergei? Wasn't that what the socialist revolution claimed?'

He was aware that the rest of them waited for him to answer, and that some corporate sense of fairness in them was outraged by a system still so weighted in favour of those in power.

'The driver of the large car was at fault,' he acknowledged stiffly. 'The driver of the small car may well be ... reprimanded; but no doubt your own officials are equally as much looked after at home.'

'Sergei is right,' Kate said quickly. 'However unfairly, people in power *anywhere* always benefit.' Her eyes accused them of the different unfairness of baiting *him*, and it was a relief when the next intake of visitors allowed them to shuffle through the doorway into the Armoury.

Like so much else they'd seen, the succession of halls and galleries had been lavishly repaired and redecorated. Beautiful in themselves, they housed treasures unimaginably rich, even for people who regularly trailed round the stately homes of England. The accumulated wealth of centuries of tsarism were displayed in a profusion that was simply staggering. Despite Sergei's exhortations to them to 'follow, please', they tended to fragment, the men lingering over carriages and weapons, while the women in the party gasped over costumes and jewels. Silk, satin and velvet, sumptuous in themselves, had been re-embroidered with gold or silver thread, sometimes almost resurfaced with a layer of precious stones. They were jewelled carapaces, rather than clothes.

Kate found Lucy lingering over smaller treasures, fascinated by the things the great Fabergés had made for the Imperial family, such as the silver egg that opened to reveal a perfect minuscule gold train inside, with windows of crystal and a minute ruby serving as a headlamp.

She stepped back from the case to let Lucy take a closer look and found McEwan close behind her. She would have walked away from him, but his hand enclosed her wrist suddenly.

'I suppose I'm in disgrace for teasing Sergei?' he murmured. 'Still, you fly to his defence so charmingly that he ought to be grateful to me.'

'Leaving aside Sergei's feelings, why draw attention to yourself? I should have thought that was unwise.'

'It was unwise, but irresistible.' He waved an arm round the room, changing the subject abruptly. 'I suppose you've seen all this umpteen times before? It's indigestible, isn't it? I find I'm easily surfeited with gold plate and cabochon emeralds the size of pigeons' eggs. Even the poor carriage horses, apparently, had to be decked out in diamonds and gold thread.'

Reluctantly Kate agreed. 'I grant you it all gets to be a bit too much. I can never make up my mind what the Russian people think about it – all this unimaginable wealth lying here, and their own lives for the most part still desperately lacking any comfort or colour. But I've never detected resentment in them; it's almost as if they don't expect the good life to come their way.'

'How should they, when they've had nothing but starvation and slaughter for as long as any of them can remember? They can't even see the madness of spending millions of roubles on restoring the relics of a regime they were taught to hate!'

'You really loathe it here, don't you?' Kate said suddenly.

'I loathe what has been done; I don't loathe the people.'

She found herself wanting to ask him not to make his dislike so obvious, but Sergei was signalling to her across the room and it was time to gather the stragglers together.

Six

Dinner was rushed through again that evening, because they were to attend a concert given by the State Symphony Orchestra. Ranald explained loudly to Nigel Faringdon, for everybody's benefit, that he would clap in the wrong places, being tone-deaf, and was therefore better left behind. Linette threatened to embarrass him by offering to stay and keep him company, but eventually he saw them all safely into the bus and, as soon as it had passed out of sight, signalled to a waiting taxi.

The university, grandly sited on the Lenin Hills overlooking the city, would have fascinated him at any other time – a collection of gothic skyscrapers that might have been designed by a Victorian ahead of his time. At the moment, only Jenny filled his mind. Clutching in his hand a piece of paper on which he'd copied from a phrase-book the sentence: 'Please take me to someone who speaks English,' he found that it wasn't necessary after all. A formidable-looking woman behind the reception desk in the enormous entrance hall spoke a heavily accented but understandable kind of English. Better still, she understood *him* without any difficulty.

'Miss Jenny Maitland is a student on an exchange visit from England – here now, I think, after being in St Petersburg. I should very much like to get in touch with her.'

The monolith behind the counter shrugged massive shoulders. 'No good – vacation time,' she said briefly.

'She must be somewhere, even in vacation time. Where can I find her?'

Another shrug, and a lack of interest in the subject barely concealed. 'The course is finished now ... everybody go home.'

Ranald mastered a strong desire to shout at her and tried again. 'There must be other English students here, with nowhere else to go in vacation time. Could you tell me where to find *them*?'

He thought she was going to refuse, but her pale-blue eyes lighted on someone loping across the hall. 'There – English over there – ask *him*.'

Ranald pursued his quarry to a row of lifts set in the far wall of the lobby and flung himself inside just as the door was closing. 'Sorry – my name's McEwan – I'm looking for an old friend called Jenny Maitland. Is she known to you, by any chance?'

'Aye, she's known to me.' Curtness was catching, apparently, but at least in one respect the woman at the desk had misled him; the young man beside him was another Scot, with an accent that unmistakably placed him as a Glaswegian.

'The charming receptionist implied that Jenny was no longer here.'

Glaswegians didn't thaw easily, but even this one couldn't help grinning at the choice of adjective. 'You'll have enjoyed meeting Olga. Why are you looking for Jenny?'

'Her kith and kin expected her home by now; she's a rotten correspondent and they're anxious about her.'

'She doesn't have to write if she doesn't want to.'

'True, but it would be nice to make sure she's all right ... help me, if you can.'

The appeal was direct enough to register, but Jenny's fellow-student shook his head. 'Not sure I can ... She moved out of here to live with a family she seemed hooked on. I had an address, but people like that tend to move on. Even now, if they've been dissidents, they aren't popular.'

'I'd be grateful for what you have,' Ranald said steadily. 'If you'll write it down for me, I can shove it under the nose of a taxi driver.'

Five minutes later he crossed the hall again, bowed to the impassive Olga, and climbed back into his taxi. Optimism lasted for the ten minutes it took the driver to find the address on his piece of paper.

The small apartment house was shabby to the point of dilapidation, and a low-powered bulb barely showed him the numbers on the door. The building smelled of poverty, and he felt sick at the thought of Jenny living in such surroundings. No one answered his knock for so long that he was almost on the point of turning away when the door suddenly opened and a sombre-faced woman threw a question in Russian at him.

Appalled by his own impotence, Ranald embarked on a 'me Tarzan, you Jane' kind of dialogue, mouthing the few key words that he could manage: 'English girl, Jenny, here? Me English friend...' He repeated the word 'English' desperately, but drew not the slightest response from the hostile face watching him. She was about to close the door when he offered the only Russian he knew – the name of Nikolai Kemanska. It drew a response, though not the one he'd hoped for: a stream of agitated words and gestures was followed by the slam of the door. Nothing gained after all, and even if desperation had suddenly lent him the gift of tongues, he felt sure she wouldn't have opened the door to him again. He went back to the waiting taxi and the Hotel Kosmos, feeling foolish, frustrated, and on the verge of despair.

By the time the others returned from the concert he'd come to the conclusion that he must ask Kate to translate into Russian for him a few basic sentences explaining why he was there; with this and the request that she should write down the present address of the Kemanskas, if she knew it, he would try his luck with the lady at the apartment house again tomorrow. He knew he should look for Kate early next morning at breakfast, but the fear that she might not be free of other people, or might need time to compose the message he required, fretted him unbearably. Her room number had been given to them in case of need; his need now was great, and he must make use of it.

He found her room, knocked, and waited in the corridor, aware that he felt vulnerable standing there, and uncomfortably liable to be misunderstood. It only needed Phyllis Newcombe, for example, to walk past for the fat to be well and truly in the fire. The whole of the long frustrating evening seemed to have been spent in front of closed doors, waiting for them to open; but suddenly this one did. Kate stood there, dressed in a green robe, with fluffy mules on her bare feet. Her hair was loose, reminding him of those few terrible moments in the train when he'd seen it like that. Tense and tired as he was, he couldn't fail to register how lovely she was. The all-too-patient man at home must have been out of his mind to allow her to roam about the world, distracting even unimpressionable males like himself from more important matters.

'My apologies for disturbing you, Kate, but I need a little help. May I come in?'

She hesitated a moment, then nodded, and closed the door behind him. He should have been relieved, but found himself angry instead. She was too generous, too unsuspicious by half, and even at the risk of making her angry he'd end by telling her so. First, though, he must explain what he'd come for.

'I went to the university this evening, but my lead turned into a dead end because the woman I was told to talk to thought the safest thing she could do was get rid of me. If you could translate these sentences into Russian for me, I'd try again tomorrow.'

She glanced over the sheet he held out to her and nodded. 'I'll bring it down to breakfast.'

It concluded the conversation, apart from delivering his warning that she should open her door in future to no one but himself. He

94

was on the verge of taking the risk of doing so, when another knock came at the door. This time it was pushed open the moment she released the catch and Sergei Ivanov launched himself into the room.

'Kate, forgive me, but I had to come. I can't help it ... I need you so...' The words came out in a feverish torrent that was cut off in mid-sentence by the sight of McEwan standing outside the circle of lamplight. It was beginning to look like a French bedroom farce, she thought feverishly. Who'd be the next to appear – Dr Grant or Dirk Engelsman?

'What ... what are *you* doing here?' Sergei shouted at McEwan.

'I might ask you the same thing, but I won't – the answer seems to be too obvious! Looks like a busy night, Kate, but if you *can* find time to do my little chore, I should be grateful.'

With a cold smile for her and a courteous bow to the Russian he was gone, leaving her with the sad certainty that this time she'd been more seriously misunderstood. McEwan had apologized for thinking she'd deserved embroilment with a bunch of drunken soldiers, but nothing would convince him now that she hadn't made a habit of enticing Sergei to visit her at night. This new contretemps mattered – she knew that as clearly as she knew anything at all – but the damage was done and couldn't be undone; she knew that as well. What she *must* do was deal with the white-faced man who stood watching her.

'McEwan was here because he needed a piece of Russian translation done.' She tried to speak calmly, but the agonized suspicion in Sergei's eyes didn't change.

'He had no right here.'

'He needed help; so he came. It's my job to help people.'

'He needed *you*, Kate, but not nearly as much as I do. Will you let me stay, please?' Fever-bright eyes in his thin, anguished face stared at the picture she made in her soft, green robe – how often had he dreamed of being alone with her, instead of being watched by a herd of fools needing to be waited on.

He saw the sadness in her face and rushed on before she could find some gentle way of refusing him. 'I love you very much ... I need you to be here always. I shall take care of you, Kate.'

Farce was far away now; she wanted to weep instead for the hopelessness of it all – for the pain that life inflicted on people, whether they deserved it or not.

'Sergei, listen to me, please,' she begged him unsteadily. 'I can't stay here; I don't belong in Russia, even though I know what an extraordinary and wonderful place it is. It's not *my* place, and you aren't the man I love – he's waiting for me to go back to England and marry him.'

She no longer knew whether it was true or not that she loved Andrew Carmichael, but she must convince Sergei of it now, and sooner rather than later work out the truth for herself. The sight of Sergei collapsed in a chair with his head buried in his hands made her go to her satchel and pour out a small measure of the brandy she kept for emergencies.

'Drink this, my dear friend,' she insisted quietly. 'Then you must go home. Tomorrow we both have to be on duty again.'

The brandy made him shudder, but he put down the glass and stood up, in control of himself.

'I didn't expect you'd stay, Kate. What do I have to offer you except myself and my faith in Russia, that fools like the man who was here just now can only sneer at?'

'McEwan and the rest of us were brought up under a different system,' she said steadily. 'We find it hard to forget or forgive what the communist system did to your people, but *none* of us sneers at you, Sergei, or at the faith you have in the future. Now you must go, please, because I'm very tired.'

He caught hold of both her hands and kissed them, and then almost ran to the door. A moment later she was alone at last, clutching McEwan's piece of paper without being aware that she had picked it up. All that the endless day still required of her was that she should flog her exhausted brain into translating the sentences he'd scribbled there; when that was done, she could fall into bed.

McEwan was accustomed to enjoying nights of unbroken slumber – the reward of virtue, he liked to think. But throughout the hours that followed his visit to Kate he remained stubbornly wide-awake. He was angry with her, of course, but more so with himself. How she spent her off-duty hours was no concern of his; she could entertain a dozen Russians in her room. But there was no comfort in the thought and he was thankful to see the faint beginning of dawn in the sky outside his window and the first trams swaying along far below, taking early workers into the centre of the city. Down in the restaurant much too soon, his drawn face inspired a waiter kinder than most to bring him tea, and he was sitting there hunched over it when Kate arrived. She sat down at his table without saying good-morning, but handed him back his piece of paper with a Russian translation written neatly at the bottom.

'It's probably not a hundred per cent grammatical,' she said quietly, 'but it can't be misunderstood. I've only one thing to add, which is that I shall certainly choke you with it if you're about to refer again to my busy night.'

'No such thing, Miss Kirkby,' he said with deliberate formality. 'You're free, white and over twenty-one, as we used to be allowed to say, and I am *not* your keeper.'

She would have answered him in kind, too angry to remember courtesy at all times, but the waiter who always watched out for her was already bringing coffee and the freshest bread he could find. She smiled her thanks at him, then delivered the question to McEwan that she *was* entitled to ask.

'What will you do next – go back to the woman you saw yesterday?'

'I'll call this evening. For all I know, there may still be some stigma attached to anyone receiving an obviously foreign visitor. I'll be less noticeable in the dark.'

'Dark or light, you stick out like a sore thumb, being a head taller than everyone else around,' Kate told him crisply. 'I hope Jenny's family are suitably grateful for all the trouble you're taking.'

It was a leading question and she expected

to be snubbed for asking it; instead he gave a quiet, slow answer.

'Jenny's father and mother took me in when my own parents were killed – I was ten at the time – and James Maitland's son, Robin, became my brother in all but name. When his wife died, James remarried, and Jenny is the child of that marriage. She's much loved. She's something special, is Jenny Maitland.'

He said it simply, but his own love for her couldn't be missed, and it made no difference, Kate realized, that Jenny seemed to imagine herself devoted to Nikolai Kemanska. This man would still go through fire and water to rescue her, if she needed rescuing.

'I hope you find her,' Kate said gently, because her battles with him now seemed trivial. It didn't even matter, except to her own foolish pride, that he seemed determined to misjudge her. Their paths had briefly crossed and would diverge again when the fortnight's tour was over – end of story, as far as they were concerned. The only important thing was to help him find Jenny Maitland.

McEwan finally broke the silence. 'What's today's programme – more "culture" to delight the soul of Phyllis Newcombe?'

'Some light relief first – a ride in one of

Moscow's beautiful underground trains. After that you can choose between a visit to Lenin's tomb, or a dawdle in GUM, the famous department store. I'm usually shamed by my clients opting with one voice for GUM!'

'Thereby confirming Sergei's low opinion of decadent Westerners, I suppose?'

'He expects it now, I'm afraid, even though I've tried to explain that we don't make a habit of embalming our national leaders, or even mind very much when they die.'

'I feel rather sorry for him,' McEwan said unexpectedly. 'Tiresome though he is, repeating this tour again and again is enough in itself to drive him mad – apart from the torment he's in over you.'

It brought them back to dangerous ground again, and she was thankful to see Nigel Faringdon walking towards them.

The morning's expedition was disarranged by the fact that what Kate had feared from the outset of the tour finally happened: they lost Ellie Engelsman. With long legs, boundless energy, and a passion for investigation, she was often briefly mislaid; but this time Dirk gave a cry of anguish as she disappeared behind the closing doors of a train that wasn't theirs. There was uproar for a moment until Kate pushed Sergei and Dirk into the following train, and then corralled the rest of the group into a corner, from which they were besought not to stray. The wanderer was brought back ten minutes later, gathered up from the next station along the line and now tied securely to Dirk's hand by her long woollen scarf.

Kate's prediction was proved right: no one wanted to visit Vladimir Ilyich Lenin in his tomb, and on the whole she was grateful. There was no telling what Ellie might have felt moved to say out aloud there; she was safer striding round the arcaded halls of GUM, which she rightly decided seemed more like an eastern souk than a modern department store. But this opinion, though delivered in a loud voice, was not understood and gave no offence at all.

Seven

The evening's entertainment was to be, for most of them, the highlight of the tour: a visit to *Swan Lake* at the Bolshoi Theatre. With tickets always hard to obtain, Kate and Sergei took it in turns to accompany the parties: tonight it was Sergei's evening to go. Kate had nothing to do but admire the turn-out of her flock – Lucy especially charming in lilac wool, Linette irked by McEwan's refusal to go but decked out in black velvet pants and beaded top nevertheless, and Ellie splendidly upholstered in peacock-coloured brocade.

Having waved them away, Kate changed from her Three Cs uniform, put on a heavy coat and fur-lined hood, and then stationed herself just outside the front doors. McEwan's figure coming out wasn't hard to spot, and she followed him to the line of waiting taxis.

'What the hell are *you* doing here?' He almost forgot not to shout.

'Slowly freezing to death, waiting for you,'

she said cheerfully. 'Do try to look pleased to see me or the commissionaire over there will think I'm accosting you.'

'I thought I made it clear—'

'You did,' she interrupted, 'but be sensible instead of stubborn. You've very little time in Moscow; why not accept some help?' She climbed into the taxi, uninvited, and after a moment's argument with himself he got in and slammed the door. The journey was made in a silence that she thought it better to leave undisturbed, but she couldn't help a murmur of dismay at the cheerless apartment-house the driver pulled up at.

'Charming, isn't it?' McEwan asked sardonically. 'Now that you're here, perhaps you'd be kind enough to explain to this man that we need him to wait for us.'

He marched up the steps ahead of her, but had the good sense to know that Kate must conduct the conversation with the hostile woman who finally opened the door. She agreed reluctantly that the Kemanska family had lived there – bad people – the neighbourhood had been glad to see the back of them.

Kate pinned a friendly smile to her mouth and soldiered on. 'Madam, we believe an English friend of ours might be staying with them. If you *could* possibly recall where they went, we would be so very grateful.'

For a moment matters hung in the balance; then, perhaps to get rid of them, the woman muttered, 'I know very little, but I think they went from here to Kalynka Prospekt – Building 12, Number 81. It's all I can tell you.' The door was closed, and they were left staring at each other, their breath freezing on the bitter air.

'By "bad people" I suppose she meant dissidents, not criminals,' Kate suggested, forgetting that McEwan hadn't followed the brief conversation.

'Call them what you like,' he said impatiently, 'do we know where they *are*?'

'We know where they went from here – that's all,' she answered just as shortly. She repeated the address to the waiting driver and they set off again in a frigid silence, which McEwan suddenly broke.

'Forgive me, please. I should have got nowhere with that poor woman but for you. I'm immensely grateful even though I can't help feeling you shouldn't be here at all.' He spoke in his normal tone of voice at last, and she supposed she was meant to understand that another truce had now been called; the scene in her room the previous night was to be forgotten.

'Just worry about finding the place,' she suggested. 'If the driver knows that Kalynka Prospekt is where "bad people" live, he'll want to dump us as soon as he can.'

At least he took them as far as its beginning, and pointed to a line of concrete tower blocks whose brutal ugliness was barely softened by a veil of falling snow. Its fresh whiteness lay like a reproach over the patches of rough ground and piles of rubbish left between the blocks. Each one resembled its neighbour, and probably contained a hundred apartments. No one but themselves walked the street, and only the faint glow from a curtained window here and there reassured them that these *were* places where people lived.

Building 12 was almost the last one in the line. Its hallway was scruffy and ill-lit, and the staircase leading out of it uncarpeted. The corridors above were all painted the same depressing shade of grey.

'If only *one* of them had stepped out of line,' Kate whispered as they studied the numbers at each level. 'Think what a bright-yellow door would have done for everybody's spirits!'

McEwan's strained face broke into a smile. 'I'm afraid you're just an unredeemed deviationist! Lead on, shepherdess.'

Then the number they were looking for was suddenly in front of them. He hesitated, lifted the knocker, and the too-loud sound echoed along the empty corridor. Kate listened to it gradually die away, wondering what they could possibly do next if the Kemanskas had moved on yet again. They might even be there but refuse to open the door to strange night-time callers. But the door *did* open slightly, and a tall, thin man stood looking at them.

'Mr Kemanska?' Kate asked quietly, and saw him nod. 'Forgive us for disturbing you, but we're friends of an English girl – Jenny Maitland. We were told that you might know where she is.'

'Your names? Some proof of your identity?'

She passed over the card McEwan handed her; then the door was closed again.

'What's happening? Tell me, please,' McEwan insisted.

'I don't know yet, but at least he didn't say that Jenny's name meant nothing to him. I have a feeling that she *is* here and that he's gone to talk to her.'

They waited in the unnerving silence. The corridor looked as empty as a rifled tomb, but Kate couldn't rid herself of the impression that they were being watched. At last the door opened again and the same man beckoned them in.

'Be pleased to come inside,' he said in slow, careful English.

There was no hall; they were in the

family's only living room, as cheerless and shabby as the rest of the building that they'd seen. The ugly wallpaper was streaked with damp, and the furniture was made from cheap wood stained a hideous yellowish-brown. It was all totally at variance with the gentle, refined face of the man who had let them in. But there *were* books overflowing from shelves on to the floor, and something else that improbably gave life to the room: a canary sang in a bright-red cage hanging in one corner.

'Jenny's here,' McEwan murmured to Kate. 'The canary's her contribution, I'll swear.'

There was another human being in the room. A middle-aged woman sat at the table, but she gave no sign that she knew they were there. Her face had been lovely once, but now the skin was drawn too tightly over the fine bones, and her mouth was set in a bitter, suffering line. Too much had had to be endured, but she would endure to the end, her expression said, because that was her only remaining pride.

Her expression registered no change even when an inner door opened and a girl walked into the room: Jenny Maitland, Kate knew without being told. She had long brown hair and hazel eyes that looked over-large in the extreme thinness of her face; but its pallor was flushed with sudden colour as she looked at McEwan, dwarfing the others in the room.

'It *is* you, Ranald – I could scarcely believe it...' The words petered out because she was trying not to weep. She couldn't allow herself to run into his arms, either – it was the woman's basilisk glance, Kate thought, that made it impossible.

'Robin wanted to come himself, but I talked him out of it,' McEwan said unevenly. 'Your last letter rather upset them all at home.'

Her mouth trembled, but she spoke in Russian to the couple, and then introduced them: Anatoly Kemanska and his wife, Ludmilla. The man faintly smiled, but the woman still made no response at all. She was aware of them, but only waiting for them to go away.

McEwan introduced Kate and the formalities, at least, were over.

'I'm here with a group; Kate is our courier,' he said next. 'We fly home on Saturday; come with us, please, Jenny, love. This isn't where you belong.'

Her eyes filled with tears, but she shook her head. 'You're wrong, Ranald. My letter meant what it said. This *is* my home now, with Nikolai and his parents.'

McEwan's glance went round the cheerless room, lingered for a moment on the woman at the table. Then he looked imploringly at Jenny. 'My darling girl, *think*, for God's sake! Can you give up your own family and everything that's been your life for *this*?'

'Just for this, I couldn't. For Nikolai, I can.' A little proud smile touched her mouth. 'He's tried harder even than *you* could to dissuade me, but I've finally convinced him that I'm here to stay. If you aren't leaving until Saturday, you can come to our wedding – it's actually the day after tomorrow!'

Kate looked away from McEwan's stricken face, but knew that she wouldn't be able to forget the pain she'd glimpsed there.

'You went looking for him in St Petersburg, I suppose?' he managed to ask in a level voice.

'He *was* there, but he got the offer of a better job in Moscow; that meant he could live here and look after Anatoly and Ludmilla.'

McEwan stared at the seated woman for a moment. 'It's certain that *we* aren't welcome; what about you?'

Jenny refused to dodge the awkward question. 'Nikolai's mother doesn't want me here. I shall win her round in the end, but when we can afford it, we shall have an apartment of our own. Things are getting easier here all the time.'

Suddenly her eyes shifted to Kate, standing silently by the door, and an enchanting grin broke the gravity of her face. 'Poor you, having to bear-lead Ranald round Russia; he's not known for being a man who likes to be told what to do!'

'We've had our difficult moments,' Kate agreed with an answering smile. She could see easily now what he'd meant about Jenny Maitland: goodness and courage shone out of her. To deserve her as a wife, Nikolai Kemanska needed to be something special himself, even setting aside the appalling mother-in-law he'd be offering her. Then it was Anatoly's turn to enter a conversation that he'd been struggling to understand.

'Jenny has told you about the wedding. Come, please – she should have English friends there.' His smile was sweet and it was clear that he, at least, felt for her all the affection his wife lacked. 'Look – I have the address written down.'

Kate stared from him to Jenny. 'It's our last afternoon that we always leave free, but *should* we come? Might it not make difficulties for you?'

'Not now; it would have done years ago, of course. Nikolai's grandfather died in a Siberian gulag, and Anatoly became a dissident in his turn. He and Nikolai are both trained physicists, but their family history isn't the reason we're poor; their research institute was closed down for lack of funds. Nikolai's got a teaching job now, and I can give private English lessons; so we shall be able to manage quite well from now on.'

'Expect us on Friday,' Kate said firmly. 'I'll even be your bridesmaid, if you'd like one!'

Jenny smiled at her, but shook her head. 'It's not quite that sort of ceremony, but it's a lovely thought.' Then she turned back to McEwan. 'How are my dear ones at home, Ranald?'

'All well, but missing you very much. Don't cut us out of your life, little one.'

She went over to him and put her hands in his. 'I *have* to stay with Nikolai, but it doesn't mean that I love the rest of you any the less. Make *them* understand that ... please, Ranald. There's another thing: promise you won't tell them about the wedding till you get home. Daddy is forbidden to fly now, but he'd come anyway if he knew about it in time.'

McEwan's answer was to wrap her in a hug, while Kate stared at the canary she could no longer see for tears.

It was time to leave; there was nothing

more that could be safely said. Kate held out her hand to Ludmilla Kemanskaya, expecting it to be ignored, but after a moment's hesitation it was taken in a brief clasp.

'Until Friday,' Kate said in Russian. 'What may I bring as a contribution?'

'Nothing; it is scarcely a celebration.'

Jenny had said that she would win Ludmilla round ... when, Kate wondered – in twenty years' time? She shook hands with gentle Anatoly, who *did*, thank God, seem to be looking forward to the wedding, and then kissed Jenny goodbye. McEwan produced one of the few phrases he knew – the Russian for goodnight – and five minutes later they were out in the street again, scuffing through the snow. They walked in silence that she didn't dare to break because the expression on McEwan's face seemed to suggest that he never intended to speak again.

She struggled to keep up with his long stride and to ignore the weariness that now made it an effort to even keep walking at all. The excitement of the search was over; reaction had set in and she felt not only tired but deeply depressed. Jenny Maitland had been found, but lost again as well. Letting concentration waver for a moment, she slipped on the frozen snow underfoot and would have fallen headlong but for McEwan's arm suddenly holding her upright.

'We need a taxi, but God knows how we find one in this benighted spot,' he muttered in a voice frayed by the evening's accumulated strains.

'Meanwhile we must keep walking or freeze to death,' Kate suggested, trying to sound cheerful.

McEwan glanced down at what he could see of her face for the obscuring hood. In the idiom of his own people, she was a mettlesome piece all right; most girls would have been complaining bitterly by now or would just have collapsed altogether in the snow.

'I must continue to hold on to you,' he explained carefully, in case his action was misunderstood. 'They're such damn silly boots you're wearing.'

'They were meant to be decorative. A heavy fall of snow isn't normal in Moscow at the end of March,' Kate was stung into pointing out. 'But then nothing about *this* trip has been normal.'

McEwan heard the slight quaver in her voice, but instead of the comfort he suddenly wanted to offer, he let out a yell instead. There *was* a taxi, at the intersection they were just approaching. Inside it a moment later, she sat huddled in one corner while McEwan stared out at the dismal streets, trying not to think of Jenny with this as her neighbourhood in future.

Back at the hotel Kate expected him to say an abrupt goodnight, but he offered her coffee and brandy instead. 'You need warming up,' he added, seeing her about to refuse.

She followed him into the café, and was shocked by the drawn unhappiness that she could now see in his face. He saw her glance at him, and managed a smile that mocked himself.

'The storybooks don't say what the brave knight does – apart from look a bloody fool – when the maiden refuses to be rescued!'

'At least he needn't blame himself, which is what I think *you* are doing,' Kate insisted. 'It might hurt you still more to have me say so, but what we saw tonight wasn't a girl in thrall to some adolescent hero-worship. Jenny loves Nikolai Kemanska for better or for worse, and nothing you could have done would have changed that. Why not believe that he may even be able to make her happy?'

'A known dissident family, and a miserable home shared with a hostile mother-in-law – are those things liable to make for happiness?'

'You're forgetting Nikolai, and gentle Anatoly ... and, yes, the canary!'

McEwan's taut expression relaxed a little. 'Yes, the canary; I *had* forgotten him. I was carrying a wad of money to give to Jenny, but I suddenly feared she'd say something indiscreet and the whole damn place might be bugged!'

'You'd have no purchases to set against the money. How would you account for *not* having it when you left?'

'I'd forget all about it – just as I did coming in.'

'Infringement of currency regulations,' Kate said thoughtfully. 'It's all we need!'

This time a real grin chased the grimness from his face. 'Something else for you to worry about; a courier's lot is not supposed to be a happy one!'

'I don't normally get to attend a wedding,' she ventured next, reluctant to remind him of it. 'I'd like to go, but not if it would seem like barging in on something that doesn't concern me.'

'Jenny invited you – of course you should go,' he said abruptly. 'I shouldn't have found her at all without your help, and I haven't thanked you nearly enough, I'm afraid. But the evening's been a strain, and you look worn out now. Go to bed, before our ballet-lovers return. Tomorrow will be time

116

enough for them to burble on to you about fouettés and entrechats and the amazing grace and stamina of the premier danseur!'

She agreed with a tired smile and got up to leave. He stood up too, then added an after-thought that she found hard to deal with.

'I'd recommend ignoring *any* knock on your door tonight. It's a piece of well-meant advice, Kate.'

She stared at him uncertainly for a mo-ment, then lifted her hand in a little farewell gesture and walked away. He watched her go, all too aware that the reason for his warning didn't bear investigation. Instead of allowing himself to think of her as she'd been – lovely and infinitely desirable, even in a gloomy hotel bedroom – it was time to put her out of his mind and struggle once more with the complexities of Moscow's telephonic system. James Maitland needed what reassuring news he could be given about his daughter.

Eight

Something was different the following morning, but it took Kate a moment or two to realize what it was. After almost a week of leaden, snow-filled skies, she could see blueness outside her window. Even its coating of winter grime couldn't conceal the brightness of the morning; at last the sun was shining over Moscow.

Downstairs in the restaurant the glory of the previous evening still shone around her flock. Lucy's eyes especially glowed with the memory of it.

'I shall remember it for the rest of my life,' she said simply. 'The theatre itself is beautiful, of course – all that crimson and gold – but the *dancers*, Kate – they *became* swans and princesses; I didn't remember I was watching ballerinas at all.'

Kate smiled at her, thinking that of all the people it had been her job to convey to foreign shores, this little lady had to be one of the nicest and most rewarding. 'So the ordeal of coming to Russia has been worth

118

it?' she asked gently.

Ever truthful, Lucy blushed a little. 'It hasn't been an ordeal at all – instead, nothing but pleasure, thanks to you and to the ... the people I was lucky enough to come with.'

She looked, as she spoke, at Nigel Faringdon walking in to breakfast, and Kate thought she understood the reason for the blush. He was a pleasant, charmingly mannered man who'd been kind enough to offer Lucy small, thoughtful attentions. She wasn't a vain or foolish woman – wouldn't read into them more than he was likely to have meant; but all the same Kate couldn't help feeling anxious about her. Lucy's soft heart would be very easily touched and hurt.

'Linette was with Sergei last night,' Lucy decided to explain, 'so Mr Faringdon was kind enough to look after me.' She smiled at the thought, and then at Kate. 'The evening would have been unforgettable if I'd gone dressed in sackcloth, and sat alone in the gods! Instead of that, looking presentable at least, I was *escorted*, Kate! I had a gentleman to shelter me from the crush, and make *me* feel like a princess. Young and lovely as you are, you probably can't understand what that means to a woman like me. I don't even need to have that treat again – it happened, and no one can take it away from me.'

Throwing the Three Cs rule book to the winds, Kate leaned over and kissed Lucy's cheek. 'Mr Faringdon can think himself lucky: if you ask me, he got a treasure last night!'

They were still smiling at each other when Dirk and Ellie Englesman came loping in, eager to relay *their* impressions of the night before.

'Beautiful, of course, Katey,' said Ellie, 'but Sergei I shall tease about the audience – all those uniforms and medals, and women drippink with sables. A classless society? I don't tink so!'

Dirk smiled forgivingly at his wife, and then explained last night's faux pas. During the interval the strange local habit was for the audience to parade slowly round the outside of the carpet in a large ante-room, always in one direction only. Ellie had caused chaos by deciding to walk first in the wrong direction, and then on the sacred carpet itself.

'There is an English expression, I think,' said Dirk, '...a spanner in the works. That is my dear wife!'

Still laughing, Kate saw the rest of the group straggle in, and remembered that she must go and explain the day's arrangements to them.

★ ★ ★

They spent the cold sunlit morning in the Kremlin again, this time wandering in and out of the churches that ringed Cathedral Square. The starkly white, almost window-less walls of the ancient churches heaved themselves into a brilliantly blue sky, and their forest of gold and silver domes glitter-ed in the sunlight. Kate found herself walk-ing beside a silent Linette, and knew that she was lost in what surrounded her – the setting for a beautiful but barbaric fairy tale.

'Are you trying to remember what grey English cathedrals at home look like?' she asked eventually.

Linette shook her head. 'I wasn't at home at all, but far back in time here ... imagining what the square looked like on some great occasion, when these cathedrals weren't just state museums. Imagine the coronation procession of some tsar in progress, Kate! These incredible buildings, and everyone dressed in the sort of clothes and vestments we saw in the Armoury.'

Kate smiled at her. 'A bit like listening to the music of Mussorgsky played full blast!'

'*Just* like that,' Linette agreed unexpect-edly. 'The odd thing is that I can visualize it so clearly ... I must have been a Tartar prin-cess in some previous incarnation, brought here captive to marry a sprig of the Imperial tree!'

Kate remembered her first conversation with Nigel Faringdon and her own breezy statement that this tour of Russia often made an unusual impact on people. The statement had been truer than she knew for Nigel's daughter.

'I made Sergei talk to me last night,' Linette went on. 'I understand now why he looks so driven all the time. He *knows* the atrocities of Stalin's era, but he still believes in the rightness of the revolution, and the communist system. He *hates* what he thinks they've got now – no system to speak of, just a Mafia-run free-for-all!'

'Transition time?' was all Kate could suggest. 'Russia has survived every kind of upheaval in its long and painful history; I think it will survive this.'

Linette simply nodded and wandered away, still dreaming of a time when misery had at least gone hand in hand with splendour.

That evening the group split up; most of them, guided by Sergei, set off to enjoy a circus performance that he confidently predicted would surpass any they had ever seen before. The few for whom the circus made no appeal were offered instead a concert of Russian music. Kate escorted the Grants,

Lucy and Nigel, surprised to find that Mc-Ewan was also proposing to go with them.

'I'd have guessed you'd be a circus man,' she said as they waited for a taxi.

'I was frightened by a clown at a very tender age,' he explained solemnly, 'and in any case I can't abide the sight of performing animals.'

'Nor I,' she agreed, smiling at him. 'It's a memorable moment: we've discovered something we have in common!'

The concert turned out to be memorable too, despite frail gold-and-white chairs designed deliberately, McEwan said, to discourage any tired member of the audience from inadvertently dropping off. After a blazing performance of Tchaikovsky's *Romeo and Juliet* overture he was moved to admit that Russian music played by Russians was worth everything else they'd been offered in St Petersburg or Moscow.

The soloist in the Rachmaninov piano concerto that came next was a Norwegian, Leif Ove Andsnes, but together he and the Moscow Philharmonic wove a spell that couldn't immediately be broken. Kate, tears glistening on her cheeks, felt a tissue tucked into her hand, and turned to smile gratefully at McEwan.

'It's no good; I *can't* listen to that without weeping.'

'Why try?' he asked unexpectedly. 'Strong men like me go weak at the knees; why shouldn't you?'

She had to turn then to Elspeth Grant, sitting on her other side, but she was aware that he'd spoken seriously for once. It was another insight into the complicated nature of Ranald McEwan, and one that she found surprising.

The following day she went down to lunch with her courier's uniform abandoned for once in favour of a dress of topaz-coloured velvet. It earned her an appraising stare from McEwan, who walked over to sit beside her.

'Festive,' he remarked glumly.

'I should hope so ... I'm going to a wedding; so are you!'

'There's no need to remind me. What a pity I didn't think to bring my kilt.'

She had a mental picture of him in Highland finery – kilt swinging, velvet jacket, and lace jabot at his throat: McEwan of McEwan himself. She blinked the vivid picture away and tried to disown it. 'I think of you less as a Scot than as a citizen of the world!'

'I travel a lot, but I'm a Highlander, first, last and always. When I've done with roaming, I shall retire to the home I've got waiting – a small white house that's tucked into a hill, looking at Skye across the Sound of Sleat.'

She could see it suddenly in her mind's eye – lonely and infinitely desirable. Andrew would choose a mock-Tudor mansion in Virginia Water, as close to the golf course as he could get. Nothing wrong with Virginia Water, she told herself, except that it was a trifle overcrowded.

'It sounds as if you'll have to find a wife who enjoys the simple life.'

'So I shall,' he agreed quietly, and there the conversation languished. Ashamed at her own tactlessness, she remembered too late that the wedding he must go to now was Jenny's.

Half an hour later they were in a taxi heading for the Palace of Weddings.

'What's in there?' he asked, pointing at the parcel on her lap.

'A new set of undies I happened to have with me – precious as gold-dust here. I thought they'd make a wedding present Jenny might appreciate.'

'Nikolai too, presumably!' He sounded sardonic still, but seemed to have decided that the occasion, however trying, would wrest from him nothing but his best behaviour. Suddenly very nervous, Kate hoped she wasn't about to make him change his mind. She hadn't decided when to make the confession that was weighing on her, but perhaps the time was now.

'You'll find one or two other people there when we arrive,' she muttered.

'I dare say. They process wedding couples like sausages, I'm told.'

'One or two of *our* people, I meant.'

He swung round to stare at her. 'Like who?'

'Only the nicest ones – Nigel and Linette, and Lucy – oh, and I asked the Engelsmans too!'

His dark brows drew together in a frown she was now familiar with. Was he going to stop the car and throw her out? Apparently not; self-restraint was achieved after a struggle, and he scarcely raised his voice at all.

'May I ask what you thought you were doing?'

'Giving *them* the chance to see a Russian wedding, for one thing. But I was really doing it for Jenny; it's her wedding day! I couldn't wave a magic wand and produce her family for her, but I *could* produce a little home support.' She couldn't tell from looking at him whether he was blazingly angry, or just moderately enraged.

'You have a nerve, Kate Kirkby,' he ground out finally.

It was true, and she was about to concede

the fact when it occurred to her that his frown might not be for her at all. Then he confirmed it by a sudden gesture that disturbed her heart's regular beat. He lifted her hand and kissed it before restoring it to her lap.

'Inspired, Kate – I should have thought of it myself.'

She didn't answer, being suddenly overwhelmed by the strangeness of the thought that had just occurred to her. A mere two weeks ago she hadn't even known that Ranald McEwan existed. In another day or so she would part company with him at Gatwick airport; but as surely as Linette remembered Russia in future, Kate Kirkby would have to remember *him*. It wasn't something she looked forward to, because she was dimly aware that pain would be attached to the remembering.

The taxi drew up outside a building grandiose or vulgarly pretentious, according to personal view. The others were already there, looking so obviously different from the rest of the crowd milling about that they were being stared at more than Lucy liked. The tall figure of Anatoly Kemanska was immediately recognizable in the middle of a little group of his own, and Ludmilla was there as well, wearing for the occasion the cloth coat and cheap fur hat that she probably went shopping in. Nothing to celebrate, Kate wondered, or were these her only outdoor clothes?

Anatoly nodded to Kate and McEwan, but straight away led his companions up a wide staircase with a gesture that said they should follow suit. The stairs opened out into a kind of ante-room, where Nikolai's supporters ranged themselves in one group, while they formed another one for Jenny. Then the doors at the end of the room opened and Jenny appeared with a thin-faced young man at her side. She wore a simple dress of cream-coloured wool, but held herself with such pride that Kate thought she might have been adorned in satin and a lace veil. Nikolai, in an ill-cut blue suit that looked too big for him, held her hand and smiled at her. The smile was half-tender, half-amused, as if to say that the charade they were about to take part in must be got through and, if possible, enjoyed.

Jenny looked startled to see McEwan and Kate flanked by total strangers, but his comprehensive wave round the little group made her grin in delighted understanding. Then, to the strains of Tchaikovsky's First Piano Concerto, delivered fortissimo from some hidden source, she and Nikolai walked into a chandeliered room and the rest of them fell in behind.

Bride and groom halted in front of a massive woman seated at a desk, with a slightly smaller acolyte beside her. The wedding party was told to dispose itself on chairs behind them, and the ceremony began – brief, businesslike, and sanctified not by God, but by the name of the Motherland. Rings were exchanged and the register signed; then they filed out again, this time to the amplified roar of Borodin. McEwan turned to look at Kate and he saw that her eyes were brilliant with tears again.

'Women! Why is it that they can never attend a wedding without weeping?' he wanted to know. 'Mawkish sentimentality, if you ask me.'

'I'm not asking you, but it's sheer rage, not sentiment, if you want to know,' she muttered furiously. 'How dare they offer this ... this bureaucratic farce as a *wedding* ceremony!'

'Ah, you want a flock of cherubic choirboys and the organ crashing away.'

'I want nothing of the kind, though there's nothing wrong with having either. But the one thing a wedding shouldn't have to do without is the feeling that it's a holy ceremony.'

Her voice trembled with feeling, and she was beyond caring whether she was laughed at or not. Unexpectedly he took hold of her hand. 'Don't be upset. Jenny will have known what she was letting herself in for. It seemed to me that she and Nikolai were enjoying some private joke!'

When they got downstairs, Jenny – now Kemanskaya, the wife of Nikolai – introduced her husband with touching pride, and then shook hands with the strangers who had unaccountably taken the trouble to attend her wedding.

'I heard about your visit,' Nikolai said to McEwan in almost perfect English. 'I'm happy that Jenny had some friends here today. Was it not a dreadful ceremony?'

Kate hesitated about saying so, but Jenny smiled at her. 'Be truthful! It didn't matter anyway – it was only for the officials. A friend of Anatoly's – Father Kolya – gave us God's blessing before we came.'

The charming smile that was reminiscent of Anatoly Kemanska glimmered across Nikolai's thin face. 'Now for the celebration! You must all come, please. Not everyone here speaks English – my mother unfortunately not at all – but we shall manage to understand each other.'

Kate hadn't foreseen such an invitation, but before she could think of a courteous way of explaining that only McEwan was entitled to be called Jenny's friend, Ellie had leapt into the conversation.

'This is most kind, but I fear we are gate-bangers...'

'Gate-crashers, my dearest,' Dirk patiently intervened.

Nikolai looked puzzled, as well he might, but Jenny brushed hesitations aside. 'You're Ranald's friends, and therefore *all* welcome. Please ... we shall be offended if you don't come.'

Lucy and Nigel Faringdon still looked uncertain, but Linette was smiling happily, and Ellie recognized a genuine invitation when she was offered one. The only fault she'd found with the tour was that it had given them no chance to meet Russian people on their own terms; she could see that she was being offered the opportunity now, and she had no intention of turning it down.

'In that case, of course we come,' she said firmly, speaking for them all.

Nine

Kalynka Prospekt looked, if anything, slightly worse in the afternoon sunlight. Snow still covered the rubbish strewn about the ground, but the discoloured concrete blocks themselves were revealed in all their heart-lowering awfulness. Kate could sense the unease in her companions, and wasn't surprised when Lucy whispered sadly to her.

'Does that poor girl really have to live here?'

'For the moment, at least. It gets a bit better once you're inside!'

Apartment Number 81 would still come as a shock, she feared, but she was confident that she could trust her friends to conceal it from their hosts. There was *one* unexpected note of gaiety: someone – surely Jenny – had tied a bow of white ribbon to the canary's cage! But something else had happened as well. For once poverty had been laid aside. The table at which Ludmilla had sat that first evening was now covered with a white cloth and heaped with bottles and food. The

Russian genius for hospitality had taken charge. Ludmilla had been wrong: they *were* attending a celebration after all.

Primed by his son to expect more visitors, Anatoly stood waiting to welcome them. He put a small glass of vodka into Lucy's shrinking hand, downed his own, and then stood smiling at her. What she could see was expected of her was terrible but unavoidable: she must choose to die rather than wound her host's feelings or let down England's good name. She swallowed the dose in one heroic gulp, coughed, and then gave him an astonished smile. Contrary to all the laws of probability she was still alive and once again – as so often on this remarkable journey – life's possibilities had been wondrously enlarged.

'Now you must eat something before you drink again,' Anatoly explained kindly. '*Zakuski*, we call these little things...'

Under his gentle guidance Lucy helped herself to a chaotic mixture of paté, cheese, and the tiny pancakes stuffed with caviar and sour cream that he said were *blini*. She was at a Russian wedding for the first and only time in her life; her English digestion would simply have to cope with the challenge of it.

Watching them, Kate reckoned that Lucy could safely be left in Anatoly's hands. It was time to see how the rest of them were doing. Linette was bravely helping McEwan swop toasts with Ludmilla Kemanskaya. No anxiety need be felt about the Caledonian giant – there was a lot of him for alcohol to make an impression on – but she prayed that he would keep a careful watch on Linette, who stood little chance against a woman reared in a land where the exchange of toasts amounted to an art form.

The change in their hostess, Kate also realized, was astonishing. Some spirit of gaiety, almost submerged by too much misfortune, had suddenly resurfaced in her, and with it had come back vestiges of beauty. She was even getting on terms with Ellie Engelsman, neither of them fazed by the fact that they had no word in common of any known language.

Kate found Nigel Faringdon beside her, looking thoughtful. 'We shan't forget this visit,' he murmured in her ear.

'*This* visit, or Russia in general?'

'All of it, of course, but *this* especially. It's obvious that our friends here have been singled out for ill-treatment and neglect, but they're people whom any right-minded society ought to treasure, *not* crucify. Somewhere along the line I suppose they tried to oppose the system. "To thine own self be true" is all very well, but just look at the price they've had to pay.'

'It was a price they were prepared for,' Kate had to point out.

'I realize that, but how could any regime insane enough to crush its own best people still have the ability to achieve things that fire one's imagination? No wonder we're bemused by Russia's contradictions!'

Kate looked across the room at his daughter, now draping a beautiful silk scarf round the bride's shoulders – one of her own she'd brought as a wedding present.

'Linette said much the same thing,' Kate remembered. 'At least you were right to bring her here: she's not recognizable as the unhappy, resentful girl who left Gatwick.'

Nigel nodded, smiling now. 'Three cheers for Russia, but I think we have to admit that Ranald McEwan's had a hand in the change as well; he's a man who can't help making an impression!' He waited for Kate to agree, but she didn't say anything, and after a moment he went on himself. 'Ranald will move on, of course, but I think Linette is prepared for that. She wants to study languages, she tells me; somehow I'm to get her enrolled in a university for the next academic year.'

Kate could understand the reason for that: she remembered a white-faced girl explaining that she'd been terrified of the soldiers on the train because she couldn't communicate with them. Sensible Linette, to plan to tackle the problem; even more sensible, if she didn't set her sights on a self-sufficient man like Ranald McEwan. He must be enduring this party because it was the thing he had to do, but Kate couldn't help wondering what it cost him to smile at Nikolai Kemanska.

'I must go and hand over my own wedding gift,' she said to Nigel. 'Perhaps it's time *you* rescued Lucy!'

She found Jenny standing alone for a moment, and offered her package. 'Not suitable for opening in public!'

'In that case I can guess,' said Jenny, planting a kiss on her cheek. 'Dear Kate, thank you – you obviously know that pretty things cost the earth here. I shall "keep them for best", as we used to say.' Her smile faded suddenly as she looked at Kate. 'I think Ranald has pinned my husband in the kitchen.'

'To tell him, no doubt, that he must take great care of you.'

'I expect so – my old friend has that sort of look in his eye! Convince him for me, Kate, that he needn't worry ... then he'll be able to convince my parents and Robin as well.'

'I'll do my best, but he's about as tractable

as a lump of Highland granite.'

'Don't I know! I was meant to spend my childhood following in his and Robin's wake. That way they could be sure I wouldn't come to any harm!'

Kate smiled at her. 'I suspect you were greatly loved as well as looked after.'

'Yes,' Jenny agreed gently. 'I hope I still am, despite seeming not to care about *them*.'

'They'll feel better if they can be sure you aren't too proud to admit needing help if things get difficult,' Kate suggested after a moment. 'That's what frightens McEwan, and no doubt your brother as well – the thought that you might need help but won't ask.'

'Tell them not to worry,' Jenny said again. 'I know you'll be gone soon, but will you be coming back?'

'I go where I'm sent,' Kate pointed out, reluctant to admit that she didn't want to return to Russia. 'Right now I think it's time I removed my little flock. Ellie is getting into her outrageous stride, at which point there's no telling *what* will happen. In any case, your Russian friends here need some of your attention.'

'Kate ... thanks for coming. I wanted to be Nikolai's wife more than anything on earth, but we weren't looking forward to today's gruesome ceremony. Having Ranald and the rest of you here transformed it some-how.'

Her eyes lingered on the people in the room and there was a hint of sadness in her face. 'Your friends are nice. Anatoly's been having a lovely time, and even Ludmilla has looked carefree for a little while. I expect she seems rather a dragon, but she adores Nikolai and she's afraid that I'll try to entice him into leaving Russia. I'll convince her in the end that we're all going to stay together.' She saw her husband walk into the room with Ranald and, as she smiled blindingly at him, Kate realized that it would be stupid as well as impertinent to pity her. Jenny Kemanskaya was a woman to be envied, if anything.

It was time to go, and in the confusion of thanking their hosts for such heart-warming hospitality, Kate found it possible to avoid looking at McEwan when he said goodbye to Jenny.

Then they were out in the freezing air again, made impervious to the cold now by a mixture of vodka, Russian champagne, and the conviviality of people who'd been strangers two hours ago. It proved what they all knew: conflicts were engineered by meg-alomaniac leaders. There was no natural law that said the people of East and West must hate each other; Russians and English could be friends.

A quarter of an hour later, back in the hangar-like foyer of the Hotel Kosmos, Linette looked round their little group with a considering eye. 'Reaction's setting in; we need a party of our own. It's our last night; instead of eating in the dreary restaurant here, let's go out to dine.'

'Dine?' Lucy queried faintly, still struggling with the effect of vodka and *blinis.*

'A little sleep and you'll feel fine.' Linette was kind but firm.

'You're *off*,' Ellie agreed joyously.

'*On*, my loved one,' Dirk patiently corrected her.

'Either way, a party!' she insisted, smiling at him.

Half-listening, Kate was also looking round from sheer force of habit, in case anyone from the group should be there needing her. None of *them* waited for her, but the man talking to the concierge she *was* obliged to recognize after a moment of incredulous wonder. It made no sense that Andrew Carmichael, who ought by rights to be toiling away in Threadneedle Street, should be in Moscow; but there he undoubtedly was. A moment later she saw the concierge point in her direction; then Andrew walked towards them, tall, fair-haired, and so unmistakably English that he might have been perfect type-casting for a Hollywood film.

'A dear friend of mine from London,' she said unevenly to the little group still clustered behind her. 'Meet Andrew Carmichael.' Then she smiled at him, holding out her hands. 'Dear Andrew, I'm gobsmacked, as they say, but *very* pleased to see you.'

It was Linette, of course, who assessed the newcomer first and liked what she saw. Her smile flashed, but she was shaking her head. 'You can't have Kate all to yourself, Mr Carmichael – she has to come to *our* party. But we'd love to have you join us as well.'

Watching the little scene, McEwan felt a twinge of respect for the smiling, handsome man. He was too smooth by half, but he was handling the awkward meeting with a good deal of social grace. Kate's lover had obviously lost patience at last, but an evening shared with a gang of strangers couldn't have been what he had in mind. Not that the man was in need of pity! London tailoring and hand-made shoes spoke of a very prosperous City gent who probably drove a Porsche or souped-up BMW; and he held Kate Kirkby's hand in a way that suggested he had a right to it. Still, a residual sense of fairness made McEwan help him fight his corner.

'Dear, sweet child,' he said to Linette,

140

'have a thought for Kate as well as Mr Carmichael. What's left of our party without them will be small, perhaps, but very select!'

Looking at his face, Kate knew that his own choice would have been to have no party at all; he would endure it, as he'd endured the afternoon, but only so as not to spoil Linette's pleasure. It made no difference to him whether she and her Englishman were present or not. Perversely it made her want very much to be there.

'It's our last night together; we leave tomorrow,' she explained quietly. 'We were going to make it a little celebration.'

'Of course,' Andrew agreed after the merest hesitation. He'd abandoned his office on a hectically busy Friday and taken a four-hour flight to be with Kate, not the strange assortment of people she was introducing him to; but he knew it wasn't the moment to say so. He was rewarded by another dazzling smile from Linette, who seemed to have taken charge of the evening.

'We'll meet here in the lobby at seven o'clock,' she announced. 'That ought to give you all time to sleep off the wedding vodka!'

They agreed and walked away, leaving Kate alone with Andrew.

'It's lovely to see you,' she tried to say with real warmth, 'but I can't imagine how you come to be here.'

He smiled a little sadly. 'You don't remember, but I didn't expect you would. We met for the first time a year ago tonight; I've had it planned for weeks – got a Russian visa in case this was where you'd have to be when the time came.'

As gestures went, it was superb, she thought; and it would have to be a lesson to her in future not to write off as dull anyone who was capable of producing it. She smiled at him wholeheartedly at last.

'Thank you, dear Andrew; it was an inspired thing to think of, and you were angelic in agreeing to the sort of evening you can't really have wanted.'

His eyes lingered on her face, noting signs of strain.

'You look tired, my darling. Will you be cross with me if I say yet again that I want you to give up this job? I'm sure the people I've just met are very nice, but *they*'re a strange assortment in themselves and presumably there are others as well.'

'About twenty of them,' she agreed, 'but they're in two groups of close friends who prefer to stick together. Even so, I must go and find them now, and explain tomorrow's departure arrangements while you check in. I'll see you down here just before seven.'

She smiled and was about to turn away when he suddenly caught hold of her hand.

'Kate ... you *are* glad I came? Just for a moment I was afraid I'd made a terrible mistake ... when you first caught sight of me.'

'How could such kindness be a mistake?' she asked gently.

He kissed her hand, released it, and she was free to walk away. It was time to think what it was she had to say to the rest of the flock. But Andrew's gesture had triggered the memory of another man's kiss on her hand and it was vivid enough to bring her to a sudden halt. Instead of the grandiose staircase she was about to climb she saw in her mind's eye a white house glimmering on a lonely headland pointing across the sea to Skye. It was so disorientating that for a moment she couldn't remember where she actually was. But someone brushed against her, and she was back in the Hotel Kosmos again. She pinned a smile on her mouth, and walked into the lounge where the rest of the Three Cs party were blamelessly drinking tea, after spending all their remaining roubles. They were looking forward to a dinner at the hotel that could be leisurely for once. They'd had a wonderful time, they assured Kate, but a fortnight was long enough in Mother Russia; they were very ready to go home.

She explained the following morning's

arrangements to them and said goodnight, but as she left the lounge she had a nagging suspicion that someone was still unaccounted for – surely Phyllis Newcombe had been nowhere in sight? She got back to the lobby again just as Sergei walked in with a cold, tired-looking Mrs Newcombe, the only one of them to have followed his advice to visit the Park of Economic Achievement. All along, Kate reflected, she'd been part of no coterie; perhaps she was always left alone – not because she was a thoroughly unpleasant woman; she just hadn't the knack of making friends.

'A few of us are going out to dine,' Kate said impulsively. 'Won't you come too? A local restaurant's likely to be more fun than the hotel.' It was too late to regret the invitation because Phyllis was already looking pleased. She'd had some faint suspicion of being less than popular, but that couldn't have been the case after all.

'Seven o'clock in the lobby,' Kate said, and saw the lady smile.

'I'm always punctual, as you know – not like some members of the party!' But it was archly said, and then she bustled away, tiredness forgotten.

Kate was left with Sergei, and now there was no question in her mind what else had to be done; a strain had already been put on the evening's gaiety, and she might as well complete its ruin.

'I know you don't normally eat with us at night, but won't you break the habit just this once?'

Neither of them had referred again to the moment when he'd blundered into her room, but the memory of it remained, making the days they'd had to spend together more difficult than any she could remember. Sergei's face looked thinner now than ever, the skin drawn too tightly over his high Slav cheekbones, and her heart ached for an unhappiness that she realized wasn't only about her: he was tormented by other things as well.

'Come and be with us this evening,' she suggested gently, '...not as our Intourist guide, but as Sergei, our friend.'

'As a Russian among English friends?' He considered the strange idea for a moment, and then faintly smiled. 'I think I should like that, Kate.'

He gave his usual little bow and walked away, leaving her only one more thing to do. On the way back to her own room she knocked at Linette's door to warn her that the party had increased by two.

'Not ... not Phyllis?' asked Miss Faringdon, suspecting the worst.

'Yes, and Sergei! Forgive me if I've

145

scuppered the party, but they're both such lonely people. I've scarcely got time to shower as it is, so will you be a love and warn the others? You'll sell it to them better than me!'

Linette's dark eyebrow climbed in a trick surely copied from McEwan. 'Pretty rich coming from Miss Kirkby, who not only winds us all round her little finger, but lures a very dishy man into flying to Moscow just to have dinner with her!'

'Dishy, would you say – Andrew?' She turned away from Linette's confirming grin, thinking that in one way or another it had been a strangely unsettling day. There'd been more emotion than she could handle; *that* accounted for the hallucinatory moment on the stairs a little while ago. She could get through the rest of the evening if she didn't think of Jenny, left behind when they went home tomorrow, or of McEwan's face when he forgot to smile. Something else *did* properly concern her: a growing suspicion that it was time she saw Andrew Carmichael as he really was. Linette had managed it, it seemed, within ten minutes of meeting him.

Ten

Two hours later an evening that had seemed something to be dreaded was becoming unexpectedly successful. They were all tired, Kate realized, of the Hotel Kosmos; this friendly place, with its potted palms and plush seats and gypsy musicians, was suddenly what was needed. Nigel had insisted on treating them to the best beluga caviar, and the authentic chicken Kiev that followed it was equally good – crisp, golden parcels that exploded with melting butter when pierced. The service was leisurely to the point of being downright slow; but that didn't matter – they'd been having to hurry ever since they arrived in Russia.

Kate was watching McEwan gallantly escort Ellie Engelsman on to the dance floor when Linette slipped into the seat beside her.

'I was right about this party,' she commented, '...it *was* just what everyone needed.' She smiled as she spoke, but her blue eyes were fixed on the couple in front of them, and it seemed to Kate that there was sadness in her face when the smile faded.

'Ranald's leave is almost over,' she said abruptly. 'He's off to India next.'

'You wish he weren't going quite so far away, I expect,' Kate ventured, feeling that something was expected of her. 'But I don't suppose his trips last very long.' She smiled to remove any sting from her next remark. 'You're more than capable of keeping tabs on him!'

'I shall do that,' Linette agreed, 'I don't intend to lose touch with him, even though he was kind enough to make things clear early on: he's not a marrying man; nor is domesticity his scene at all. We shall have to see about that.'

She said it calmly enough, but rejection wasn't something she was used to, and Kate felt certain that it would hurt deeply if that was what she got in the end. Whether or not a warning would help, she decided anyway that it ought to be offered.

'I think he'd have changed his mind about domesticity to marry Jenny Maitland, but *her* heart was set on Nikolai.'

'Silly of me,' Linette said after a moment, '...I should have thought of that.' Then she stood up. 'It's time I lured Sergei into some kind of dance that we can both do.'

Kate watched her go, thinking how

unlikely it would have seemed at Gatwick a mere fortnight ago that she should care what became of Linette Faringdon; but she did care, and now found herself offering up a little prayer that disappointment over McEwan wouldn't make a rackety life in Paris seem desirable again.,

'I don't know why our conscientious shepherdess is looking so solemn,' said his voice suddenly in her ear. 'Her lambs all seem to be enjoying themselves. Noble of you, by the way, to let Phyllis monopolize your young man.'

'He's being kind – he *is* kind,' Kate pointed out. 'But *you* don't have to steel yourself to dance with me instead; I feel too tired to do anything but sit and watch.'

'Well that's a relief!' Then he smiled at the spark of indignation in her face. 'I'm not built for a place this size – and nor is Ellie; we damn nearly annihilated the people sitting around the floor!'

'An eightsome reel is more your style, I suppose – all blood-curdling yells and flying skirts.'

'Of course; this mincing about on a pocket handkerchief isn't what we call dancing.'

Kate trod heavily on a small shoot of regret; tired or not, would she have wanted to 'mince' with him and discover what it felt like to be held in Ranald McEwan's arms?

Of course *not*; he'd been a thorn in her flesh since the tour began. But he was still looking gravely at her and, suddenly afraid that he'd guessed what she was thinking, she spoke quickly of something else.

'Linette says you're off to India next.' His unenthusiastic nod made her smile. 'It doesn't seem to appeal.'

'The country appeals very much, but not the interminable round of conferences in store; I prefer to be getting my hands dirty.' Then, with his glance still on her face, he asked a question of his own.

'What about you – another trip to Mother Russia, or has Carmichael's romantic gesture softened your heart?'

'I have some free time due,' she said abruptly. 'My immediate plan is to go home, to the Somerset village where my parents still live. Nice old hamstone houses, nice gentle people. It's where someone like Anatoly Kemanska ought to be; he'd fit in very well.' Then she could have kicked herself for mentioning a name that brought grimness back to McEwan's face; but she'd made the mistake and now might as well go on. 'Have you been in touch with Jenny's family?'

'They know I've seen her, that she's all right but not coming home. I promised the rest would wait until I got up to Edinburgh.'

Kate remembered her own promise and forced herself to say what would rub salt into his wound. 'You must tell them that she's greatly loved by Nikolai and his father. We have to admit that Ludmilla's more of a problem, but Jenny *will* win her over in the end.'

McEwan's dark eyebrow rose. 'And what am I to say about Kalynka Prospekt and the life she'll have to live there?'

'Say the truth,' Kate answered sharply. 'It isn't yet, and may never be, the Maitlands' comfortable, middle-class existence. But we were given true Russian hospitality and warmth this afternoon – you could mention *that* as well.' She heard her voice tremble: emotion was getting the better of her after all; she rushed on before he could speak. 'Now, if the party has gone on long enough, I think we should call it a day. Lucy's beginning to look as tired as I feel.'

He stood up, without answering, but in no time at all, it seemed, he'd seen to it that matters were arranged; the bill was called for and paid, and they were free to leave. Their last and strangest day in Russia was over.

After breakfast the following morning the Intourist bus, still reeking of diesel fumes, awaited them one final time, for the journey to Sheremetyovo airport. In the bus, sitting beside Sergei, Kate attended to her last chore, the filling-in of forms. Then she stared out of the grubby window at row upon row of grey, monolithic apartment blocks, the decaying legacy of the Stalin years. People could find better places to live in now, but only if they belonged to present-day Russia's new rich – young mafioso entrepreneurs, or the *nomenklatura* of old, well placed, when the change of system came, to make sure they could still benefit themselves.

'You're glad to be going home,' Sergei's reproachful voice murmured beside her. 'I'm afraid I shan't see you again. You'll marry that Englishman who came last night – he was the man you told me about. I hated him, Kate.' White-faced and miserable, Sergei turned to look at her. 'Why isn't he here now?'

'He left early to catch the first scheduled flight.' She put out her hand to touch Sergei's cold one in a fleeting gesture. 'I don't know what I'm going to do next – go where I'm sent, I expect, like you. Thank you for taking care of us so beautifully.'

Instead of replying, he sat in mournful silence for the rest of the journey, and Kate was free to acknowledge to herself a failure in the Three Cs' rule book; it included no

152

helpful guidance at all on how to deal with the unhappiness of other people.

At the airport Sergei handed them into the care of British Airways for the homeward flight, then gravely said goodbye. His next task, he explained, was to await the incoming tour and make the complete trip in reverse back to St Peterburg.

'Poor wee sod,' McEwan muttered to Nigel Faringdon as the Russian walked away. 'Can you think of anything worse?'

'Of course, and so can you! But, fascinating though it's been, I have the feeling that we're all ready to go home.' He looked at Lucy as he spoke, and without fuss relieved her of the bulging cabin bag she was carrying.

Invited to join in the conversation, she earnestly agreed. 'I shan't forget a moment of the past two weeks, but oh to see England's small, dear fields again, and little, private houses surrounded by their own patches of garden. How can poor Jenny Kemanskaya not miss such things?'

Nigel smiled at her troubled face. 'You're forgetting something: she's got a husband she obviously adores!'

Lucy nodded, choosing not to say that a middle-aged spinster was the last person able to measure such a blessing. Even that, of course, was no longer true. She'd learned a great deal since leaving home – had even discovered, to her astonished delight, that loving wasn't something that only the young could do – but she'd prepared herself for the moment when Nigel Faringdon would smile and walk out of her life with his beautiful, wayward daughter. Linette had terrified her when they were setting out from Gatwick, but Lucy had made another discovery along the way: as *she*'d got braver, Linette had got more gentle; now the two of them were friends. It was something else to thank dear Kate for: without *her* encouragement Lucy remembered that she might have cried off coming at all.

Their flight left on time, and by mid-afternoon they were back on English soil. Kate went to file her report as usual; Tour 245 safely landed, mission accomplished. She returned to find the group still clustered together, exchanging addresses and the usual promises to keep in touch, reluctant to actually say goodbye now that the moment had come to do so. Only one noticeable figure was missing; Ranald, said Linette, had been in a hurry to catch a connection to Heathrow.

'I was to thank the "shepherdess" on his behalf,' she explained.

'Kind of him to remember me,' Kate said with a bright smile.

She kept on smiling, was hugged and kissed, and heard herself giving Ellie and Dirk a solemn promise that she would visit them in Amsterdam where their main home was. Then at last it was over; she could watch them all go their separate ways, and retrieve her car from the staff car park. Nothing left to do except drive back to London, call at a supermarket on the way, then go home and fall into bed. The headache that she'd begun the day with still troubled her, and she blamed it for the depression that seemed to have settled round her like a miserable grey fog. It was time to remember that she was as free as air for the next two weeks – could go to Somerset and be made much of by her parents, or stay in London and be spoiled by Andrew.

Waiting for the line of traffic she was stuck in to move on, she feared that it was Andrew, not the headache, that most troubled her. Decision time was drawing near, and if she did nothing else with her vacation she must at least make up her mind about *him*. The memory of him guiding Phyllis Newcombe round the dance floor made her smile – such true kindness that had been. Linette's assessment of him was worth remembering, too; her own stupid fault had been to take him far too much for granted.

She thought about it for another mile or

so; but by the time the next traffic hold-up occurred, Andrew's image in her mind had been displaced by that of a different man. He'd been intent, of course, on getting to Jenny's parents in Scotland – she understood that; but he might have waited long enough to say goodbye.

That evening, pretending that she wasn't now feeling downright ill, she was trying to face the idea of a supper of scrambled egg when the telephone rang.

'Darling ... you're safely back.' Andrew Carmichael's voice came along the wire. 'I hope your flight was smoother than my Aeroflot one.'

Kate had scarcely time to say that it had been normal in every way before Andrew was hurrying on again.

'I meant to leave you in peace until tomorrow, but I found a message waiting for me here. There's a meeting in New York on Monday that I feared was in the wind; it means flying out tomorrow. Then I had a brilliant idea: you're on leave now – can I persuade you to come too?'

There was a little silence at Kate's end, and after a moment he went on himself. 'I'm not trying to rush you into anything, Kate ... Well, I *am*, of course! ... But once my meeting's out of the way, we could stay on and enjoy Manhattan together. Can you face the idea?'

'I could, dear Andrew, but not right now,' she said hoarsely. 'I'm sickening for something – either the cold to end all colds, or a dose of flu. You'll have a much better time without me, and the truth is that I couldn't manage a transatlantic flight at the moment.'

'You even *sound* wretched, my poor love,' he had to agree. 'What a pity; it seemed such a lovely plan. I'll come straight back instead, and take care of you.'

'No...' She had to stop herself from shouting, '...promise me you'll stay and sample all the hospitality that's sure to be showered on you. I'm going to get myself down to Nether Hamdon tomorrow and enjoy some pampering there.' She wished him bon voyage and rang off quickly after that, abandoned all thought of supper and crawled into bed instead. With a clearer head, she thought she might have tried to decide whether life was working out some master plan all on its own or simply being awkwardly, bloodily perverse as usual. A New York tryst with Andrew would surely have settled their future once and for all; but now she was only conscious of the relief of not having to make up her mind quite yet – she could be ill first in peace.

The familiar drive to Somerset the following morning was a strain, despite the thinness of the Sunday traffic. It seemed a long time before Stonehenge rose into view on her right, and longer still before she could turn off the A303 and thread the lanes that led to her parents' village. With the car safely turned into their drive, she ducked her head against the steering wheel, suddenly weak with relief at no longer having to concentrate. But inside the house she managed a smile at her mother's concerned face.

'I nearly gave up half an hour ago – thought I'd turn into a lay-by and die peacefully there! But a dose of flu didn't seem quite enough to die for.'

'It's those trips to Russia,' Monica Kirkby complained. 'Why can't that wretched firm send you somewhere else? Still, tell me later, love; you must go straight to bed. I'll come up when I've got your things from the car. Your bed isn't the least bit damp, of course, but there's a hottie in it just to make sure. What a good thing I came straight home from church – your father's still there doing his churchwarden's bit.'

The gentle monologue, so typical of her mother, followed Kate reassuringly up the stairs ... She was home; she could lower Kate Kirkby's bright smiling guard at last.

The bout of influenza proved severe, and it was four days later before she felt strong enough to exchange her bed for an armchair by the sitting-room fire. The calendar said April already, but the English spring was as reluctant to appear as usual, and she could see her mother working in the garden still muffled up in old tweed trousers and an anorak.

The old house felt peaceful and friendly, as it always did, but she wasn't sorry when her father came into the room to share the firelit afternoon with her.

'Lovely to see you downstairs again, sweetheart. It seems an age since you were here.'

'But you and Mummy are both all right?'

The sudden anxious question made him smile at her. 'We're more all right than you are, she thinks! *Is* anything wrong, Katey?' It was his childhood name for her, used whenever comfort had seemed to be needed.

'Post-influenza depression,' she suggested wryly, 'with added complications! Do I ask not to be sent back to Russia because my Intourist colleague is in rather a state about me? Do I leave the firm and marry Andrew Carmichael before he gets tired of asking me to? Or do I pretend that the last trip *wasn't* specially significant and carry on regardless? I'll be as right as rain when I've worked out some answers!'

He would have liked to ask what had been significant about the trip, but decided that she would tell him if she wanted to. 'Any help needed?' he simply asked.

It was her turn to repeat a childhood saying. 'Let me manage on my own, please!'

Her father nodded but thought he could safely say one thing. 'I liked Andrew when you brought him down. I know he mystified your mother, but they'd make friends in time.'

Kate's grin reappeared, acknowledging that Andrew and Monica Kirkby had indeed mystified each other. One of them couldn't tell a camellia from a cotoneaster, and the other didn't understand that to live west of Hammersmith Broadway put her unbearably far from the centre of things.

'He *is* likeable,' she agreed, and then ended the conversation by talking of some village matter.

The following morning she accepted breakfast in bed, but came downstairs afterwards in time to see her mother ushering someone into the hall – Linette Faringdon, with her arms full of spring flowers.

'I forgot that people who live in the country are likely to grow their own,' she said, smiling ruefully. 'Silly of me – I had to beat a path through the daffodils outside!'

'You weren't to know that my darling mother is the village champion. Mummy, meet Linette Faringdon, one of the group I took to Russia recently and successfully brought back alive!'

'Miraculous,' Monica told Linette with a smile. 'She was half-dead herself with influenza when she arrived here; she's getting better now, though. If you can stay to lunch, talk to Kate while I go and see about it.'

'Oh, how nice this is,' exclaimed Linette, looking round the room she was led into. 'We have a ghastly drawing room "designed" by one of my mother's friends!'

'It's what comes of living in Eaton Square,' Kate pointed out with a smile. 'Now tell me how you knew how to find me.'

'I kept trying your flat number – thought you must have left again on another trip. Then my father spoke to Andrew Carmichael about some business thing. He was just back from New York and said you'd been too unwell to go with him. He thought you might still not want visitors, but I decided to risk it.'

'I'm very glad you did; it's lovely to see you,' Kate said warmly. She saw Linette hesitate and wondered what was coming next.

161

'Andrew was kind enough to take me out to dinner last night. We both enjoyed it very much – me letting my hair down about Ranald McEwan, and him talking about you!'

'An entertaining evening, to be sure. Where ... where is our Caledonian giant, by the way – already striding across India?'

'No, he's chained to a desk in London, like a bear with a sore head! Some little frontier dispute with Pakistan is taking precedence over what he considers more important matters, and visiting experts would get in the way.'

'If you've seen him since he returned from Scotland, did he mention visiting Jenny Kemanskaya's parents?'

'Said he'd been to Edinburgh, that's all. Perhaps that's why he wasn't his usual self: I seemed to be boring him rigid, which isn't how he usually behaves – we click very well.'

She smiled as she said it, but it was a sad smile, and Kate felt a stab of anger against McEwan. It would be kinder to leave Linette alone than to blow hot and cold with her. He was too experienced not to recognize that he mattered to a girl who badly needed an anchor to a rootless life. She'd thought better of him – had thought of him altogether too much, she realized sharply. Let the damned man go to India soon and stay there, for all their sakes.

'What other news?' she made herself ask. 'I've been out of touch down here.'

'I expect the Grants tried to get hold of *you* as well – a golden-wedding party. I refused – said I was coming to see you; so it left my father free to drive down to Sussex and take Lucy. Rather clever of me, I thought!'

Kate looked at her doubtfully for a moment. 'Perhaps, but I'm not sure that you should meddle, Linette.'

'Because Lucy's not one of the sophisticated, hard-as nails women my father's used to? I know that, and so does he; it's what he loves about her.'

'Then meddle on, little one,' said Kate, as her father came in to meet their guest.

Eleven

Easter arrived in wind and driving rain. Monica Kirkby prophesied in a voice of doom that there wouldn't be a spring flower left standing in the garden to decorate the church with; but the parish ladies worked their usual miracle and it looked beautiful. Then, on Easter morning, the wind veered, and suddenly the sun shone from a sapphire sky.

The old hamstone church was crowded and even Job himself, Kate reckoned, would have been hard put to it not to rejoice at the familiar triumphant shout: 'Christ is risen, He is risen indeed.'

She found herself with more people to pray for than usual; the Kemanska family now came after her own, but she also asked for happiness for gentle Lucy, and for Linette not to be driven back to her Parisian life by sadness over McEwan. It even seemed a pity not to hope that Phyllis Newcombe *would* be invited by the Women's Institute to show them all her Russian photographs!

Then, after another peaceful day or two at home, it was time to return to London. Not all the questions in her mind were answered, but she was certain about one thing when she reported back for duty to her boss. His contemplative stare wasn't encouraging.

'You look more pale than interesting; I thought you were supposed to be fit for work again.'

'I am, but I'm hoping that I could be useful somewhere other than in Russia. My dear mother reckons I've seen too much of the frozen north.' It wasn't much of an argument to use, but she was anxious not to drag Sergei's name into it.

The man in front of her didn't smile, but then he very rarely did. 'Would I earn Brownie points with "dear mother" if I gave you the Sicily trips to look after this summer?'

'I rather think you would,' Kate agreed cheerfully. 'The only snag is that my Italian is minimal.'

'You learned Latin at school – I checked on your CV.'

'Ten years ago,' she protested, 'and I doubt if they quote Cicero much to each other in today's Syracuse.'

'Don't make difficulties,' said the man who'd never sullied his mind by learning a word of anyone else's tongue. 'You can have a fortnight in the language laboratory; I'm *told* you're a quick learner.'

He was careful to sound unconvinced in case she guessed how much he valued her. The company had been his brainchild from the beginning, but he knew that its great success rested largely on the shoulders of people like Kate.

'It will be interesting,' she commented, 'exchanging one Mafia-run society for another.'

'Maybe, but watch the Italians, Kate; they've been at it longer.'

She grinned as she went away, and an hour later found herself back in school. Over dinner with Andrew that night she described the first day's work, but waited rather anxiously for the question she thought he was certain to ask.

'It means that you're going to carry on travelling, I suppose. Is that true, Kate?'

She nodded, thinking that she should have begun with what she must say now. 'Just this one last summer; then I shall be ready to hang up my courier's cap. But there was time while I was unwell to realize what a selfish cow I've been! Don't laugh, please, or pretend it isn't true. I *hope* you'll still be waiting for me at the end of the summer, because settling down together is what we've been going towards, but you're free as air, Andrew. If I can slay you with a cliché I never thought to use, I hope we always stay best friends, whatever happens; but some sharp-eyed woman may pinch you before I'm through and, if so, it will only be what I deserve.'

A rueful smile touched his mouth. 'I run a risk as well: another sharp-eyed male might pinch *you*.'

'No,' she said decidedly, 'there's no chance of that.'

'Then we've got nothing to worry about,' he said, and leaned across the table to kiss her mouth.

The following evening she heard from Linette Faringdon. 'Kate, you *can't* not be in London on Saturday. You have to come to an engagement party.'

'For Lucy and your father, by any wonderful chance?'

'The very same, and without any help from me! My clever parent could see that Lucy oughtn't to be left unguarded; someone else might have snapped her up. It's sweet to watch them together: *he* smiles all the time, and *she* gets prettier and prettier.'

'It's lovely news – perhaps something for Three Cs to put in their brochures from now on: "A tour with us and lifelong happiness guaranteed"!'

'Not in every case,' was Linette's wistful

167

qualification. Then she suddenly became brisk again. 'The party starts early, Kate – sevenish – because Andrew has to rush off to some dreary City dinner he can't get out of. Now, must go; I've still got to track down Ellie and Dirk.'

McEwan hadn't been mentioned, Kate realized as she put down the telephone. The likelihood was that his Indian trip was on again, and Linette had momentarily sounded forlorn because of it.

On Saturday evening, however, when she arrived with Andrew – he resplendent in City dinner rig of white tie and tails – McEwan *was* there, filling the room all by himself, as usual. A neat dark suit and college tie made him look more or less reduced to conventional mode, but he still put her in mind of a mountain eagle tethered among a flock of singing birds. He was a hard man to ignore, but it was what she intended to do – a resolution that turned out to be unnecessary because, as the party got under way, he took no notice of her at all.

Lucy moved among her guests – mostly old army friends of Nigel Faringdon's – with the gentle grace that was her hallmark; but her face shone with happiness. She'd come into her kingdom at last, and Kate told her so when they got a few quiet moments together.

'I owe it all to you,' Lucy said tremulously. 'I'd have turned tail at Gatwick but for you, and never met Nigel at all.'

'My only contribution was to talk you into getting on the plane!' Kate pointed out with a smile. 'What happens now – will you live here when you're married?'

'We shall keep this flat, because Nigel often needs to be in London, and it's home to Linette; but we'll sell my cottage and find something else in the country.' Lucy's happiness was dimmed for a moment. 'Kate, my only worry is that I might be a disappointment to them – I do so want *them* to be happy. I'm sure I can make them comfortable, but happiness is more difficult.'

'My advice, for what it's worth, is to keep them busy making *you* happy,' Kate suggested. 'It will go against the grain, I know, but just *try* to be difficult occasionally!'

Smiling again, Lucy was whisked away by Nigel, and Kate blinked at the sight of Ellie surging towards her, a large and joyous vision tonight in pink satin.

'You're going back to Amsterdam, Linette says,' she complained reproachfully. 'London won't seem the same without you and Dirk.'

'Often you must come on visits, Kate ... and little Linette, too.' She looked across the room at Nigel's daughter, apparently glued to McEwan. 'She's happy tonight, not so? Well, for three pins I should be lovink our large friend myself.'

'Two pins, Ellie dear,' Kate corrected her, seeing that Dirk wasn't nearby to do it; but the Dutch lady was right otherwise: in her beaded dress, reminiscent of a 1920s flapper, Linette looked beautiful, but there was more to notice than that. Clinging to McEwan's arm, the girl radiated happiness. Had he put away the memory of Jenny Maitland – decided that he was a marrying man after all? Kate couldn't persuade herself to believe it. He was simply bored in London, and letting Linette keep him flattered and amused. It was inexcusably selfish behaviour, but, unable to say so, she said goodnight to her hosts instead. She was at the door when the man she'd been berating in her mind sauntered up to her. 'Your young man's gone, I see; perhaps I'd better take you home.'

'No need, thanks,' Kate said, smiling sweetly. 'We aren't in Moscow now; I can find a cab outside the door.'

'Perhaps true, but we could even exchange a few words on the way; you haven't spoken to me since you arrived.'

It was rich, she thought, coming from a man who hadn't even noticed she was there. On the doorstep, ignoring what he'd said, she lifted a hand to flag down a passing taxi, but McEwan caught hold of it and towed her to a car parked by the kerb. She had no option but to give in to force majeure, but got into the car with the evening's anger finally brimming over.

'It's what I particularly like about Highland gentlemen: our slightest wish is their command.'

He turned to look at her, with a hint of hurt surprise. 'You're cross, shepherdess; I wonder why. For the moment, though, just tell me where to go.'

'I live at the unfashionable end of Chelsea Bridge. Andrew's just across the river, in the more expensive bit.'

'Of course – where else?' McEwan agreed so pleasantly that she couldn't decide whether the remark was snide or not. 'He cut a dash tonight, I have to admit. I don't think that even you should keep a catch like that hanging about.'

It was one thing to think so herself, quite another to have the man beside her point it out as well. She didn't answer him except to tell him tersely where to turn, but a sidelong glance at him confirmed what she suspected: he was merely amused.

Outside the house that she indicated he broke the silence himself, managing to sound wistful. 'Would a cup of coffee be forthcoming, I wonder, in return for the lift home?'

She was minded to say a blunt no, but a different thought suddenly occurred to her. Ranald McEwan was feeling bored again; Kate Kirkby, though not the delightfully young, impressionable creature that Linette was, would nevertheless be better than no one at all. Her turn had clearly come to keep him entertained.

'A *quick* cup of coffee,' she agreed briefly. 'That's the extent of the offer.'

'Terms accepted,' he said with a faint smile. 'Lead on, shepherdess.'

Her sitting room was very pleasant, but it was undeniably small. As a setting for Ranald McEwan it now looked absurd. 'Perhaps you'd better sit down before you knock yourself senseless on the ceiling,' she suggested. 'Coffee will be along in a minute.'

When she came back with it, he was sprawled in an armchair, frowning over one of her volumes of poetry.

'I can never get the hang of Browning, can you?'

'I like to think so; perhaps *you*'d do better to stick to Robbie Burns instead.' She was pleased to have got the better of him for once, but had a question of her own to ask. 'Did you see Jenny's parents in Scotland?'

'Of course – that's why I went. They were ... demolished, I'm afraid, is the word, by the knowledge that she's now there for good. There was only one grain of comfort for them: they *could* remember Nikolai Kemanska, and be persuaded that he will most certainly take care of her.'

Kate nodded, and sat thinking about the little household in Kalynka Prospekt, unaware that she was being studied by her guest. He found her beautiful in her simple black dress, and he liked the way her hair was drawn back severely by a velvet ribbon. The style suited her, but it revealed the thinness of her face.

'Linette said you'd been unwell,' he commented suddenly. 'Why was that?'

'Only a sharp dose of flu, but it gave me an excuse to go home to Somerset and be spoiled for a bit.'

'Nice parents?' he enquired. 'I expect they are.'

'*Very* nice. My father's an expert on longcase clocks; he repairs and restores them so lovingly that you might think they were living things. My mother's genius is for creating a garden. What was once a field now stops people in their tracks with wonder.'

'Brothers and sisters?' McEwan's questionnaire continued.

Kate shook her head. 'Twin boys who died almost as soon as they were born; that's why my mother took up gardening. It was her way of coping with the pain of losing them.'

It seemed to end his search for information and, since his coffee was almost drunk, she hoped he would soon go home. He'd accepted her terms, and there wasn't the least need to feel nervous; but in the quietness of the room she couldn't fail to be aware of him. He was altogether too large and powerful and uncontrollable, like some unpredictable force of nature. To restore some feeling of being still in charge, she asked a hurried question herself.

'Is the Indian trip postponed for long? If so, you probably hate being desk-bound in London.'

'I do, but it's not for much longer, thank God. I'm being shipped off to Ethiopia instead next week. I haven't been there and I'm rather looking forward to it.'

Kate was startled into speaking without thought. 'Linette didn't mention that this evening.'

'She didn't know; it was only fixed up yesterday.'

Winded for a moment by sheer rage, Kate sat trying to translate it into words. Words wouldn't be enough, of course; she wanted to pummel him with her fists, to cause hurt that would make him admit his own callousness.

'You *will* think to mention that you're going away?' she asked in a voice that barely trembled. 'Or is it your plan to just disappear from London?'

He smiled, with what she thought was barefaced smugness. 'Of course I shall mention it when I telephone; I was always taught to say thank you for a party – weren't you?'

It was the moment she'd been waiting for. 'But you *weren't* taught not to hurt people in other ways. It's perfectly all right to monopolize a girl who's had the misfortune to fall in love with you, to let her flatter and amuse you while you're at a loose end, and then just to clear off...'

It was as far as she got before he roared, 'Stop shouting at me, woman. We'll talk about this quietly...' He heard the volume of his own voice and tried again, more pianissimo: 'We'll discuss this quietly or not at all. Being one of the Highland gentlemen you despise so much, I'll let you begin.'

'Linette is deeply in love with you,' Kate said, more or less quietly. 'When she's with you, it's so obvious to the rest of us that I can't believe you aren't aware of it yourself. But having warned her that you're a roving man, your conscience is clear; you think you

175

can make use of her for as long as it suits you.'

'I *did* give the warning,' he commented.

'And how do you suppose that struck her, if not as an irresistible challenge? Linette's young enough to nurse the strange idea that men can be persuaded to change! I got treated to a show of righteous indignation when I reminded you once before how vulnerable she still is, but you just don't care. There – have I said my piece quietly enough?'

He nodded. 'It was quiet enough, just all wrong! Linette is in love, certainly, but not with me. Her heart is set on Andrew Carmichael.'

A profound silence filled the room while Kate grappled with what he'd said. 'You're mad,' she finally managed to insist. 'She scarcely knows him, for one thing; for another, she doesn't even see anyone else when you're around.'

'It's true that she keeps the fiction up very well; but the fact of the matter is, she's using me. I'm the trophy everyone is supposed to think she wants, because they know that Carmichael already belongs to you. Far from being the mixed-up adolescent you seem to think she is, I'd say she's handling the situation rather well!'

'I don't believe you,' Kate muttered over

the dryness in her throat. 'It's no surprise if she likes Andrew: most people do; but she isn't acting when she smiles at *you*.'

McEwan looked genuinely puzzled for a moment. 'I thought women were supposed to be able to understand each other, even if they remained a mystery to us mere men. But you haven't fathomed her at all. She's just like her father. Nigel Faringdon had appropriated Lucy by the time we left St Petersburg. Linette fell for Carmichael just as quickly, but she needed for pride's sake to be sure that *he* at least wouldn't know, even if you guessed the truth.'

'So, motivated by simple kindness, you joined in the charade, and she won't mind a bit when you go traipsing off to Africa! Forgive me if I don't believe your story. You'll tell me next that you've had a miserable time being nice to a stunningly attractive girl.'

'No, I enjoyed her company; men, being selfish creatures, are never helpful for nothing.'

'Andrew is,' she said swiftly. 'I judge men by him.'

'Of course – young Lochinvar himself! He's damned hard to live up to. You'd be doing the rest of us a kindness if you'd take him off the market.'

Kate walked to the door and held it open.

'Thank you for the lift; now please go.'

McEwan sauntered to the door, then halted there, apparently reflecting. 'I feel sure there's something else I ought to do – stand in for your missing paragon perhaps?'

She heard the words but didn't understand his meaning. The next moment it was too late; she was caught in his arms as easily as he might have trapped a bird. His mouth found hers in a kiss that hurt, then overwhelmed her. Released at last, white-faced and trembling, she made one final effort against him.

'Highland gentleman to the end, with generations of marauding renegades and thieves behind you, I expect.'

'Something like that, beloved,' he agreed not quite evenly. 'Forgive me if my performance didn't match Lochinvar's!' Then, with a little farewell nod, he walked out of the house.

She stumbled to the nearest chair and collapsed into it. A hand dragged across her own mouth did nothing to wipe away the memory of his, and beyond that there seemed to be no effort she could make. The tremors that racked her body would cease soon; then she'd be calm, sensible Kate Kirkby again, well known for remaining cool and collected under all the trials and tribulations of a courier's life. By the time

McEwan was back from Ethiopia – he was *sure* to come back, of course – she'd be safely in Syracuse or Palermo. She would disregard a kiss that had been simply intended to teach her a lesson for condemning him. She knew she wasn't wrong about Linette, nor need she feel anxious about herself. At the end of the summer there'd be nothing to stop her leaving Three Cs to settle down happily with Andrew near the golf course of his choice. Little as she wanted to meet McEwan again, she hoped he would be around to see it happen.

Twelve

Her boss had been right, Kate discovered after a fortnight's intensive but enjoyable work in the language laboratory. Helped by wisps of Latin left from schooldays, Italian wasn't hard to grapple with. It also rolled very pleasantly off the tongue, and was obligingly understood by the waiters at the trattoria Linette took her to one evening.

'I'm glad you agreed to come,' Linette said when their orders had been taken. 'You've been hiding from us since the party.' She examined her companion's usually vivid face, thinking that it looked thin and strained. 'You make one of the idle and fairly rich like me feel guilty – you work too hard. Why not give up Three Cs, Kate? Andrew's dying to keep you in luxury.'

'Worn out and ancient as I am, it's very tempting,' Kate agreed wryly. 'But the truth is that idleness wouldn't suit me; I'm not used to being "kept", and I do want to see Sicily – Mafia stronghold, or the legendary Garden of Persephone? Andrew knows that

I plan to retire at the end of the summer, and I don't think he minds waiting a bit longer.' Then she risked a question of her own. 'What about you – do you miss Paris? It's a sinfully seductive city.'

'It is,' Linette admitted slowly, 'but I shan't go back to *la vie bohêmienne*, if that's what you're bothered about.'

'Your mother's still there,' Kate reminded her.

'I know, and I shan't lose touch with her, because I have the feeling she might need me one day; but I don't want the messy life her friends lead – not now.' She was silent for a moment, then began again. 'The trip to Russia was an eye-opener in all sorts of ways. I rediscovered my father, of course; but everyone else helped, too – you and Lucy, and the nice Grants ... people who are real and good, unlike the strange creatures I'd been hanging out with.'

'What about McEwan, whom, I notice, you don't mention! Doesn't he count?'

Linette answered the teasing question seriously. 'Oh, he counts all right. He *matters*, Kate. I shan't forget a morning in St Petersburg when I made some silly remark about the old peasant women kissing the ikons in the church we'd just left. Ranald shrivelled me – hoped I'd wait until I found some better rules to live by than Jesus

Christ's before I sneered at other people's beliefs. He was quite right, but then he always is.'

'Not always,' Kate couldn't resist saying. 'He's human, like the rest of us.' But she couldn't allow herself to say that he'd been wrong most of all about Linette herself.

'The two of you didn't take to each other – I wonder why not?' her companion said next.

'Wrong chemistry, let's say, but more probably a clash of temperaments. Bossiness is an occupational hazard for couriers, and McEwan is also much given to telling other people what to do. I bet it's exactly what he's up to now, striding across Africa!' Kate managed to smile at the thought, then decided it was time to change the topic of conversation. 'What have you all been doing since the party?'

'House-hunting in Sussex. Well, garden-hunting's nearer the truth. We saw three that faced the wrong way, according to Lucy, one so neglected that even *her* heart failed at the thought of it, and one so perfect that there'd have been nothing for her to change!'

'My mother would understand completely,' said Kate. 'So you're still looking.'

'No, we found one in the end that was "just right", like the little bear's porridge!

Fortunately the house that goes with it is rather nice, too; so it's all going through.' Linette's attractive grin appeared. 'My father dimly suspects, and I'm quite sure, that our lives are about to be made over in the gentlest, quietest way imaginable; but the truth is that we're looking forward to it. The wedding is in mid-May, by the way, and you *must* be here for it.'

'It should be all right; by then I shall just have survived my first trip to Sicily. I'm going next week to be shown the ropes and discover how much I still have to learn about the island.'

Their waiter reappeared to put coffee on the table, but when he'd gone, Linette switched topics again.

'I'd like to go back to Russia when I've got somewhere with its strange language. I want to call on the Kemanskas again, but it seems unfair to talk in English when it means that poor Ludmilla gets left out.'

'You were managing rather well with her at Jenny's wedding party,' Kate remembered with a smile. 'We could go back together and be more adventurous next time – take the long train-ride down to Bokhara and Samarkand, even visit the blue mosques of Isfahan, which is a line of poetry in itself. It's something I've wanted to do since I first read about them.'

Linette, she realized, was looking at her curiously again. 'You're forgetting Andrew. He won't expect you to go off roaming with me.'

It was true, of course; she knew that she *did* tend to forget Andrew when he wasn't there. 'He has to be away a lot himself; he's in Brussels at the moment,' she could at least point out. 'But first of all I promised the Engelsmans that we'd pay *them* a visit in Amsterdam. We could go straight after the wedding; you'll be feeling a bit flat then after all the excitement.'

'Lovely, Kate; let's do it,' Linette agreed cheerfully. But she wasn't as carefree as she wanted to seem. Hard as she tried to conceal it, some sadness shadowed her eyes, and Kate thought the reason wasn't hard to fathom. Here was a girl who'd have gone gladly to the world's end if McEwan asked her to go with him; but perhaps in her heart of hearts she knew the truth. He travelled best who travelled alone, and his choice would be always to remain solitary. The damnable part of it was that he couldn't easily be forgotten even when he wasn't there – the memory of him hovered now in both their minds; she could sense Linette's ache of longing.

'I'll fix things with Ellie and let you know,' she said firmly. 'But now I must say *buona notte*. I've still some homework to do before I go to bed; Sicily's had rather too long a history!'

She left London two days later, while Andrew was still away, and spent the next fortnight in the explosion of warmth and colour that was the Sicilian spring. Palermo, the island's capital, was an unsettling mixture of grandeur and decay, but she was enchanted by the ghost-haunted sites of classical Magna Graecia – Syracuse, Selinunte, and Segesta – and the magical landscape itself overshadowed by its sleeping volcano. These were images worthy of being kept and set beside her memories of Russia.

Lucy's marriage to Nigel Faringdon took place a day or two after she got back to London. She drove down to Sussex with Andrew on a May morning lovely enough to compare with anything a Mediterranean island had to offer. An English spring hadn't the same exuberance, she explained to the driver, but ...

'Or the same vulgar excess, to put it another way,' Andrew interrupted, but she shook her head.

'Unfair, because it *was* stunningly beautiful, but then so is this. I know all *isn't* right with the world, but I can't help feeling that God must be in His heaven on a day like this.' She smiled at the idea, then fell silent, because the man who claimed he couldn't understand Robert Browning had just been allowed to elbow his way into her mind again.

It was a charming wedding, the bride as pretty as a picture in cream silk and wide-brimmed hat selected for her, Kate suspected, by her future stepdaughter. Linette herself wore blue, the same colour as her eyes, and Andrew agreed quietly, when asked, that she was also worth looking at. After the reception, held in the garden of a nearby hotel, Nigel and Lucy set off for a honeymoon in Florence. Linette drove back to London with Kate and Andrew, and it was he who suddenly began to talk of their forthcoming visit to Amsterdam.

'I'm not sure you should go by yourselves. I can't land myself on the Engelsmans, but why don't I escort you to their door and then find myself a room somewhere?' No immediate answer came from the back of the car, and at the next stop for traffic lights he turned round to look at his passengers. 'No chorus of delight, apparently. Don't spare my feelings – if you'd rather go without me, just say so.'

Aware that the silence had become awkward, Kate was still thinking what to say when Linette finally answered for both of them.

'Of course, come. An escort was all the weekend needed, wasn't it, Kate?'

She was bound to agree and promised to let Ellie know about the change of plan, even though three – five with the Engelsmans – seemed to her a less than ideal number.

They took the Friday evening flight, and found Dirk waiting at Schiphol airport, beaming with the pleasure of their visit. His welcome, and Ellie's refusal to hear of Andrew staying anywhere else, seemed to put the weekend on the right, happy footing. The Engelsmans' home was a pleasure in itself – a tall, steeply gabled house overlooking a tree-lined canal. Radiating kind hospitality, Ellie's only regret was that they hadn't brought Ranald McEwan as well.

'We miss that large man,' she said wistfully over their late supper. 'Be sure he comes next time, dear Linette.'

The girl agreed to do her best but quickly changed the subject by admiring a collection of Delft pottery on the beautiful old dresser in the dining room. She was her bright, vivacious self, but it seemed to Kate that a determined effort was having to be made; Linette was obviously missing the 'large man' too. Her philosophy might once

187

have been: 'Who cares about tomorrow if today be sweet?', but she wasn't the same girl now, and the present moment wasn't quite enough for happiness.

The following morning they split up, Kate opting for a visit to the Rijksmuseum with Dirk, while Andrew escorted Ellie and Linette on a shopping expedition. In the museum Kate made a beeline for the Vermeer paintings, stood looking at them for a long time, and asked to go back again before they left.

'They mean something special to you,' Dirk murmured beside her. 'May I ask what?'

'I'd have a roomful, if I were stupendously rich,' Kate said longingly. 'They're full of light, of course, and just beautiful in themselves; but they're the serenest paintings I know. I can't argue with Lucy Faringdon for wanting to see the Botticellis in Florence, but I love these quiet Dutch ladies best.'

'I also,' Dirk agreed, happy with a view that matched his own. He smiled at his guest, but noticed something that must be discussed with Ellie when the visit was over. Kate Kirkby had seemed to him not unlike the women in Vermeer's paintings – luminous and tranquil of heart. She wasn't tranquil now, and he regretted that he had no right to ask her why not.

They rejoined the others for lunch, and inspected the purchases that had been made. Andrew owned up to buying some beautiful Dutch pewter, and Linette had been entranced enough by the silver filigree work on offer to blow serious money on a necklace of turquoises beautifully set in silver.

'I wavered ... didn't I, Ellie?' she asked, to excuse the extravagance. 'It was Andrew's fault really: he said it was perfect for someone with my colouring.'

'He's right,' Kate agreed cheerfully, 'and you may rely on him in such matters. Our Mr Carmichael's judgement is never at fault!'

'You're a golden girl, Kate, according to him, and I'm silver; I hope he's talking about colour, not worth!' But she smiled as she said it, as if his verdict had pleased her.

It was Ellie who spoke of McEwan again, asking the others where he was.

'Tramping across Ethiopia,' Kate answered, 'no doubt bullying any unfortunate native who comes his way.' But the remark sounded so unfairly snide that she tried to soften it. 'That's the English way of saying that he's probably working himself to the bone, trying to stop those poor people messing up their environment.'

Ellie looked so moved by this more heroic

image that Dirk gave her hand a little pat. 'My wife knows that I love her more than life itself, but she hankers a *little* after this man who makes her, she says, feel small and fragile.'

Kate was careful not to catch Linette's eye, but even so it wasn't possible to suppress a rising bubble of mirth, and her grin grew helplessly into a chuckle. An elephant, pink and perhaps on the small side, as elephants went, had as much chance as Ellie of seeming fragile. She could hide her mouth behind a napkin, but her laughing eyes met Ellie's across the table and they both exploded into laughter, setting the others off as well.

At last, with order restored, Kate got up and walked round to her hostess's side of the table to drop a kiss on her hair.

'Perhaps *not* as delicate as a fairy, but we wouldn't have you any other way. Stay as you are, please, Ellie.'

Dirk nodded approvingly. 'What a lovely, subtle language English is.' Then, as if reminded of Russia by the talk of McEwan, he went on to speak of the Kemanskas, deploring the waste of clever men like Anatoly and his son.

'They're not quite the outcasts they were, I think,' Andrew pointed out. 'The system *has* been liberalized, and Russians no longer get banished to Siberian labour camps for stepping out of line.'

'They are still victimized nevertheless,' Dirk insisted. 'Both the men we met are highly trained physicists, but Anatoly can't get a job at all, and Nikolai teaches in a low-grade school. What kind of liberalization is that?'

'I think the problems now are economic, rather than political,' Kate suggested quietly. 'The *result* isn't any better, because the research institute the Kemanskas worked at closed down for lack of funds; but at least they don't live in an atmosphere of fear and suspicion, as they did before.'

Dirk didn't argue the point, because Kate's face was now shadowed by the memory of Kalynka Prospekt, and Ellie did her best to wipe the sadness away.

'It was a fine wedding party, not so? When they are forgetting their worries, the Russians wonderful hosts make.'

With lunch over, there was a boat-ride round the canals, and in the evening they dined out, recommended by their hosts to sample the delicious rice dishes brought back by the colonialists of the old Dutch East Indies. There was music as well, of course, because – like many large people – Ellie moved lightly and loved to dance. She'd been thoughtful enough to even up their numbers by inviting a colleague of Dirk's, a shy, bearded man who steered Kate round the floor as if holding a piece of delicate china. He found himself completely at ease with this lovely, russet-haired English girl who smiled at him so charmingly. Her heart was kinder than her younger companion's, whom he suspected of finding him too Dutch and boring.

Henrik wasn't Fred Astaire, Kate admitted to herself, but she enjoyed talking to him. It was a happy evening altogether and she said as much when Ellie and Dirk left the floor and came back to their table. She looked idly across the room as she spoke, to where the others were dancing, and it was in that precise moment that the pleasant evening was suddenly transformed. Linette, in the beautiful aquamarine dress that so perfectly matched her new necklace, was absorbed in some enchanted world of her own; held in Andrew's arms, she was oblivious of anyone else on the floor or of anyone else in the room.

Unaware that she hadn't even finished what she was saying, but certain that she was watching something she wasn't meant to see, Kate dragged her glance away from the couple on the floor. She met Ellie's eyes instead and the dismayed puzzlement in the Dutchwoman's face confirmed that she hadn't been mistaken. Linette *had* given herself away, betrayed by the music, the strain of pretending, and the sheer joy of being in Andrew's arms. The music stopped and Kate had to watch again because it seemed necessary to know what would happen next. Andrew stood holding Linette for a moment, said something to her that made her open her eyes and faintly smile at him; then she released herself and they came back to the table.

The brief episode was over and so, almost, was the evening. No one felt like dancing again and, after the long, full day, they agreed that it was time to go home to bed. Linette was quiet on the journey back to the house, but she thanked Dirk and Ellie sweetly for a wonderful day and then said goodnight. Kate forced herself to share the nightcap Dirk suggested, in order to prove to Ellie that nothing was wrong, but climbed the stairs to her own attic bedroom at last, leaving Andrew still with their unflagging hosts. She closed the door thankfully behind her, then opened the casement window and sat staring out; but instead of the starlit night she saw Linette's face, entranced and beautiful.

She felt proud of Andrew, she told herself. He was too perceptive not to have understood, but with his usual kindness and perfect manners he'd handled a situation that would have embarrassed most men to death. For Linette she felt the utmost sadness – a hopeless infatuation did no girl any good, but she *was* especially vulnerable, whatever McEwan said.

McEwan! The thought of *him* was what she'd carefully been avoiding. How loudly, confidently, she'd insisted that he was wrong about Linette; how blindly she'd maintained that his 'story' was a convenient fiction she refused to believe. If he ever returned from darkest Africa and she had the misfortune to meet him again, she would have to apologize. It wasn't a prospect to look forward to, because he'd be like one of those people who rubbed a puppy's nose in the puddle it had just made, explaining that it was for the poor creature's own good to be humiliated.

She went to bed at last with the conviction that she must leave Linette to Andrew. While she herself spent the next few months travelling back and forth to Sicily, he could safely be left to handle a lovesick girl gently. He'd know exactly how to deal with someone so much younger than himself. It was a comforting thought with which to turn out the light and end the day.

They flew back to London the following afternoon and it was only when Linette smiled at Andrew as he fixed her seat belt that Kate was suddenly struck by a different thought that wasn't comforting at all, but extraordinarily unsettling. She'd assured her dear Lochinvar – the man she'd so stupidly undervalued all along – that while she came and went she must risk having him snapped up by someone else. It wasn't very likely to happen, of course, but how richly, damnably, hoist with her own petard she would be if the girl who did the snapping turned out to be Linette Faringdon.

Thirteen

While the summer's new routine established itself for Kate – a fortnight's visit to Sicily followed by a rest week in London – the Faringdons moved into their Sussex home. The 'just right' garden went with a pleasant, half-tiled house in a village not far from Petworth.

It was familiar territory to Lucy but something else again, in Lisette's vernacular, for a man whose hunting grounds had been exclusively in Knightsbridge, Mayfair and St James's. Nigel Faringdon was heard to say occasionally that, as soon as the leaves began to fall, they'd retreat back to Eaton Square, but his daughter doubted it. His visits to London now were as brief as he could make them. He was becoming a country gentleman, and she suspected him of wishing in his heart of hearts for a winter that would find them snowed in at Badger's Mount.

Lucy was equally content. Her great fear had been that a spinster lady of fifty-two would seem a very inadequate wife; but under Nigel's gentle guidance she'd found only joy in embarking on married life; it had all seemed so natural and delightful.

With her cup of happiness overflowing, she even took in her stride one morning the discovery that she shared a shopping centre in Petworth with Phyllis Newcombe, not seen since they'd parted company at Gatwick on the way home from Russia. When they accidentally bumped into one another, Lucy admitted with a blush of pleasure that she and her husband – the word still filled her with incredulous happiness – were now living nearby.

'I saw the wedding announcement,' Mrs Newcombe commented, '...quite a surprise at your age, I thought.'

'It was,' Lucy was ready to agree, 'but dear Kate did warn us that Russia had strange effects on people's lives!'

Phyllis, whose life had remained obstinately the same, allowed herself a pitying smile. 'She was trying to make the best of it, poor girl. How sick she must be of borsch soup, not to mention Lenin and statistics about the production of gas turbines!'

It was Lucy's turn to smile. 'Don't feel sorry for her; Lenin's a thing of the past. At this very moment she's probably standing on a sunlit Sicilian headland, showing her lucky group the remains of some marvellous Greek temple.'

Irritated by the correction, Phyllis offered a tit-bit of her own. 'It's strange that I should run into you just now: only a week ago I happened to see Linette as well.'

'She comes down most weekends,' Lucy agreed happily.

'We were both at Covent Garden,' Mrs Newcombe pointed out, '...for a wonderful gala performance. They didn't see me, but your stepdaughter was there with the very good-looking man who turned up on our last night in Moscow.' She gave another acid smile. 'One gets so confused – I thought *he* belonged to Kate Kirkby, while Linette was much taken with that large Scot who was pretending to be interested in Russian ikons!'

Flustered into nearly blurting out something about the wedding and remembering just in time that Phyllis hadn't attended, Lucy did her best. 'All four of them are good friends, but Ranald has been away in Africa. The others spent a lovely weekend in Amsterdam recently with the Engelsmans. You must remember them!'

'How could one forget?' Phyllis agreed with a hint of malice that even Lucy couldn't miss.

'Such *nice* people,' Lucy insisted with

unaccustomed firmness, and then launched into the first lie she could remember telling. It had been an unexpected pleasure meeting Phyllis again like this, but now she simply had to hurry away.

She hurried as far as her car, drove out of town, and then pulled into a quiet lane to do some necessary thinking. Linette had been down the previous weekend. It was strange that she hadn't mentioned the visit to Covent Garden; a gala performance was usually worth talking about, and she would have known that they'd be interested in news of Andrew Carmichael. He *was* a handsome man, and Kate was often away ... Here, Lucy took herself in hand. Phyllis Newcombe's innuendo must be ignored. She was a lonely widow, poor thing, entitled to be a little spiteful now and then.

On firmer ground now, Lucy decided that it was good for Linette and Andrew to be the friends she'd claimed they were; there was no harm in that. A man who flew to Moscow just to spend an evening with Kate was clearly devoted to her, and only a blind woman could miss Ranald's attraction for Linette. It was just a pity that he had to be away so much. Calm again, Lucy put the car in gear; she could now finish the drive home thinking only how unkind it was to hope she needn't make a habit of bumping into

Phyllis Newcombe.

She told Nigel of the meeting, but excluded any mention of the gala performance; it was for Linette to tell them about it if she wanted to.

'I'm afraid to guess that you invited Phyllis to tea,' Nigel said, smiling at his wife. 'Your kind heart insisted that she's probably lonely!'

'My heart wasn't quite kind enough,' Lucy admitted with a twinge of shame. 'The truth is that I don't like her very much.'

'Then leave her alone, my love; you're not absolutely obliged to like everyone you meet. It even seems that Linette doesn't like Ranald McEwan very much at the moment. She rang while you were out. He's back in London, but when I suggested that she bring him down she was very sniffy – said that she preferred to come alone!'

'I wish I was more experienced in these matters,' Lucy regretted. 'Dare we ask her what's wrong?'

'Knowing my darling daughter, we shall be told,' Nigel said, and was soon proved right when Linette arrived the following evening.

She made an amusing story of it, but only, Lucy thought, because the alternative was to burst into tears.

'I knew it was Ranald's birthday – I'd

spotted the date in his passport when we were coming back from Russia. A celebration seemed called for, and I invited him to dinner. I knew Kate was due back, so that I could ask her and Andrew Carmichael as well. *He* agreed to come, but she turned it down; she made some excuse, but I think she didn't want to see Ranald again. It left me having to find another girl to take her place.'

'Not too difficult, surely?' her father suggested. 'You know heaps of girls.'

'Well, the one I chose didn't work and it was a perfectly disastrous evening. Angela Browning, whom I hope never to have to see again, is prettier than most, but she isn't very bright. I hadn't really noticed it before, but the more she talked, the sillier *she* got and the more deadly, politely, bored Ranald became. Even she was defeated in the end, and I almost wept with relief when dear, kind Andrew offered to drive her home. I had a short, sharp row with Ranald, and that was the end of a far from happy evening!'

She managed a smile but even the recollection had hurt, Lucy thought, and she cast around for something else to talk about. It seemed permissible to speak of her own meeting with Phyllis Newcombe, whom Linette had occasionally enjoyed crossing

201

swords with in Russia.

'She was full of a gala evening she'd attended at Covent Garden,' Lucy said, almost unthinkingly, and then wondered what subconscious worry had prompted the remark. There was a moment of silence, as if Linette waited for her to say something more; but Lucy merely busied herself with pouring their after-dinner coffee, and her stepdaughter launched instead into a recital of life in London that couldn't, apparently, have been more hectic or happy. What with lectures at the V & A on Russian art, and German classes at the West London Poly, to be fitted into a busy social round, there was scarcely a moment to spare.

Throughout the weekend she talked as persistently as her friend Angela had done. She wasn't silly in what she said, but even so Nigel smiled wryly at his wife when she'd said goodbye and driven back to London.

'It's suddenly gone blessedly quiet! She isn't usually such a chatterbox – she was rather strung up, I thought. I hope the falling-out with Ranald isn't serious; he's such a good man for her to have picked.'

'If Kate's in London at the moment, we could ask her down,' Lucy suggested. 'She's very good for Linette.'

'Then you must ask Carmichael too: the poor man scarcely sees her at all.' Nigel smiled at his next idea. 'Why not the birthday party that didn't happen? It would persuade Linette to patch up her quarrel with Ranald, and we'd have a nice weekend house party.' Lucy's expression made him go on. 'Something wrong with that plan? You're looking thoughtful.'

Unable to explain her faint fear of what might be wrong with her husband's suggestions, she took refuge in a small evasion. 'Only because Linette seems to think that Kate and Ranald don't get on. It mightn't be a very peaceful weekend.'

'You'll smooth them down, my love,' he said with great affection. 'It's known as "the Lucy treatment"!'

She accepted the tribute with a blush of pleasure and objected no more, but when Kate and Andrew accepted her invitation, she was careful to warn Linette that they were coming to be introduced to Badger's Mount. She half-hoped that her stepdaughter would think of something else she'd rather do; but such faint-heartedness got its just reward. Ranald drove Linette along the drive in time for Saturday lunch, ten minutes before Kate and Andrew arrived.

The day was fine, but it had been a persistently rainy month of June; the result was that the old red-brick-and-tiled house seemed to be bowered in greenness. A rampant 'Madame Alfred Carrière' swarmed almost up to roof level, scattering its perfume on the air, and the borders that Lucy had left undisturbed for the time being were crammed with cottage flowers, campanulas and sweet williams and pinks making their own tapestry of colour.

While the flurry of greetings was in progress, Kate watched Linette – not too carefully, she hoped – as the girl kissed Andrew's cheek. She *would* do that, of course – it was what fellow-guests did; but Kate couldn't help wishing that the quiet weekend Lucy had invited them for hadn't got changed somewhere along the line. It was hard for Linette to have to watch her and Andrew together. She turned away and now found herself standing beside Ranald McEwan. He was looking round with a faint air of wonderment that she thought she could understand.

'Does it seem almost indecently lush and green after Ethiopia?' she asked quietly.

The question made him stare at her instead. 'Something like that – shades of Norman Douglas back from Calabria, as it then was, imagining he was a caterpillar crawling through a never-ending bed of lettuces!' McEwan's grey glance wandered over Kate's tanned face and sun-gilded hair. 'You're very bronzed and glossy; Sicily obviously suits you.'

He was darkly burned by the African sun himself, but she couldn't return the compliment: he looked tired and thin, and the bright light revealed more silver than she remembered in his dark hair. 'I'm enjoying the summer,' she said after a moment.

'No undercurrent of violence to disturb your customers?'

Kate frowned over what to say that would be fair. 'It's there, of course, but I doubt if visitors are aware of it. The island certainly doesn't have Russia's blood-soaked history, and there's a lovely anarchic gaiety about Sicilians, even if they still happen to be poor.'

He nodded, accepting that what she said was true, then unexpectedly returned to where the conversation had begun. 'I wasn't sneering at this breathtaking greenness, by the way.'

'Nor was I,' said Kate. 'And perhaps we can also agree that it's lovely to see Lucy and Nigel so obviously happy.'

The smile that she'd been offered so rarely changed his face. 'It must be a record, shepherdess; we've never lasted this long without falling out!'

She would have smiled back, acknowledging some kind of truce that had been struck, but Lucy was waiting to show her guests indoors. McEwan watched them walk towards the house, the small figure of their hostess flanked by Andrew Carmichael, elegant still in country clothes, and a slender girl in a cream-linen dress that beautifully set off her bare, brown arms and legs.

Lucy's fears proved needless; the weekend was a success. In apparent harmony with each other again, Linette and Ranald stayed together during an afternoon of rambling round Petworth House. Nigel led Kate round the picture collection, about which he was very knowledgeable, and Lucy introduced Andrew to the gardens.

During supper they reminisced about Russia, laughing over Ellie's misdemeanours, and remembering the wedding party at Kalynka Prospekt. It was impossible to know from looking at McEwan, Kate thought, whether it still hurt to be reminded of Jenny, when it was he who recalled Lucy's success with Anatoly, and Linette's heroic exchange of toasts with Ludmilla.

The following morning Kate went with Nigel and Lucy to the communion service, and they returned to find the other three locked in a cut-throat game of croquet on the lawn. The two women settled down in deckchairs to watch, while Nigel went to produce the cooling drinks that would obviously soon be needed.

'Linette seems to be happy again,' Lucy remarked to Kate. 'She said your visit to Amsterdam was a great success, but she's been on edge since then – bright one minute, cast-down the next. Nigel says it's because she misses Ranald very much when he's not here. I'm not an expert in these matters, but I only see them as dear friends.'

Fearing that she was becoming desperately artful, Lucy wondered what the quiet girl beside her would say. It took Kate a long time to say anything at all.

'I suppose, like the rest of us, she needs the assurance of coming first with someone else; without that the world seems rather a lonely place.'

'*You* must certainly feel sure of it,' said Lucy, smiling at her. 'What a gesture it was of Andrew's – that surprise visit to Moscow!'

Kate absently agreed, her mind not on what her hostess had said, but fixed instead on the tableau in front of them. McEwan was deliberating over his next stroke, the mallet looking like a toy as he waved it about. But at this critical moment, instead of watching the game, the other two were staring at each other, unable, Kate realized, at that moment to do anything else. Even the sternest self-control sometimes faltered;

it had now for both of them, and they were lost. Then, when McEwan called out, reminding one of them to play, Andrew struck wildly in the wrong direction and had to apologize for not concentrating enough.

Kate turned away from the trio on the lawn and stared down at her brown hands instead; they weren't trembling, she noticed. It was even possible to manage a little smile when she saw that Lucy was looking at her anxiously.

'Are you going to settle down with Andrew when the summer is over, dear Kate? You can see how happily I'm married – anxious to recommend matrimony to everyone else!'

'It was roughly the plan,' Kate agreed, marvelling that she could still say it calmly when the plan had just disintegrated in front of her. 'I've seen so little of Andrew recently that perhaps it's not safe to assume he still wants to marry me!'

In spite of telling herself that she wouldn't watch the croquet players again – Linette laughing at something Andrew had just said – she was doing it. The compulsion was painful but necessary, like needing to touch an aching tooth. Then Lucy's quiet voice spoke again beside her.

'I'm very fond of Linette – of course I am: she's Nigel's daughter. But I'm aware that she's a taker where people are concerned.'

Lucy's smile apologized for what she was going to say next. 'When she falls in love, she wants a man's whole attention; but she chose the wrong man, because Ranald McEwan can't be possessed that way. I think she realizes that now and, to make herself feel better tries to ... to *borrow* what belongs to someone else. You mustn't let her borrow from you, Kate – that would be unfair.'

There was so long a silence that she spoke again herself, rather ruefully. 'Perhaps you think I have no right to imagine I understand her; I never fell in love at all when I was young.'

Kate could smile at her now, loving the honesty that had prompted the remark. 'What I think is that for someone who's come to the aches and pains of love rather later in life than usual, you understand them very well!'

But Lucy's sensible advice had come too late. Linette wasn't in the business now – if she ever had been – of 'borrowing' Andrew while she sorted out her life with someone else. She wanted him for himself, for good, for now and always.

It would have been a relief to say, as Lucy had, that Linette was being greedy and unfair in trying to grab the man Kate herself had learned to value at his proper worth and anticipated spending the rest of her life

with; but the *truth* would have been to tell
Lucy that it wasn't unfair. She'd blithely
insisted to Andrew that he was a free man,
entitled to love whom he pleased while she
worked out what her own heart wanted.
Kate Kirkby had been too confident by half,
and McEwan for one would have said that
she deserved the empty future she was
suddenly staring at.

She couldn't have explained it to Lucy, in
any case, but there was no need; the croquet
game had ended, and Nigel was bringing
out a tray of pre-lunch drinks. The sun
wasn't less warm than it had been a few
minutes ago, and Lucy's garden was no less
beautiful. Kate got up and wandered away
to inspect the water lilies that were opening
in the ornamental pond. She was watching
the tiny pulsing throat of a frog sitting on a
broad lily leaf when McEwan sauntered
across the lawn towards her.

'You were being very idle with Lucy – why
not have joined in the game?' Deep-set eyes
in a bony, sunburnt face examined her too
intently, and she had the unnerving feeling
that she was being accused of not joining in
something more important than a game of
croquet. 'Perhaps you lack the competitive,
killer streak?'

'That's probably it,' she agreed with an
effort to sound casual. 'Who needs it any-

way? That little frog looks happy enough; I doubt if he knows he ought to be up and doing.' She smiled as she said it – an inconsequential end to a brief exchange that hadn't really been important – and then strolled back to the others grouped round the terrace table.

Late in the afternoon she left with Andrew to drive back to London. He was untalkative, but it was understandable: the returning traffic was heavy enough to need a driver's full concentration. When he stopped the car outside her door, she didn't ask him in and he didn't invite himself.

'Another early start tomorrow?' he asked instead.

She nodded. 'Almost the last one, though; the season is nearly over. It's been a fascinating summer, but I shan't be sorry when it's done. I've been foot-loose long enough.'

Andrew's taut expression didn't change, but his voice was gentle. 'Settling-down time at last, Kate? We've waited for it long enough.'

She only answered by kissing his cheek, then let herself out of the car. He drove away with his usual little farewell toot on the horn, and as usual she waited until he'd turned the corner before she went inside the house.

She felt immeasurably tired, but there

were clothes to be packed ready for departure in the morning, and a note to Lucy and Nigel to be written. It brought McEwan to mind – the man who'd been taught always to thank his hosts for a party. She felt strangely certain that their conversation by the lily pond *had* been intentional. He knew the truth now – not only about Linette but about Andrew as well. Perhaps he was even feeling rather sad on his own account; after all, he'd admitted to enjoying Linette's company.

Kate put the thought aside and forced herself to concentrate on the one final thing she must do before she could end a painful day. Her third attempt at a letter to Andrew was suitably brief, friendly, and firm: he was to forgive her, please, for so much indecision, but she now knew that even deep affection wasn't quite enough to marry on. She wanted him to find someone else to be happy with, and hoped that he very soon would.

She posted the letter at Gatwick the following morning, and then went to meet the people clustered round the Three Cs desk. It was another day and another tour; for as long as it lasted, mercifully, she didn't have to think about anything else at all.

Fourteen

A fortnight later, at the end of another tour, Kate drove down to Somerset instead of going back to London. She said, when she got to Nether Hamdon, that it was time she checked up on dear but elderly parents.

'Elderly but not yet infirm,' Monica Kirkby insisted, hugging her daughter. 'It's a very becoming tan you've got, but you're getting too thin; have the customers been more awkward than usual?'

'The customers have been much the same, but Sicily's had its hottest summer in years; that makes the work a bit more tiring.' Kate smiled at her mother. 'Tell me *your* news. No parish battle-lines drawn over hymns ancient as opposed to modern, no sneaky developer trying to pinch green fields for a new housing estate?'

'Battle-lines are *always* being drawn,' Monica pointed out. 'They're a necessary part of village life, to stop us vegetating completely. Even your father, the most peaceable man I know, enjoys an occasional

213

tussle with the Deanery office!'

Then she smiled as he came into the room, to kiss his daughter and to pour the pre-dinner sherry. 'I'll take mine to the kitchen – supper's nearly ready. Come when I call, because the soufflés won't wait while you talk!'

Left with Kate, Henry Kirkby examined her carefully; it was his habit, honed by years of looking at delicate mechanisms. He thought he saw signs of strain beneath the surface appearance of sun-tanned well-being, but he approached the subject of his daughter's life with caution. She wouldn't snub him, but she might smile and evade an issue she preferred to leave alone.

'The season's changing, Katey; we had the first touch of frost last night. Didn't I hear a rumour back along that Andrew Carmichael was persuading you to give up travelling at the end of the summer?'

'Rumour was mistaken as usual,' she said calmly. 'Well, perhaps it wasn't at the time, but I changed my mind – about Andrew, I mean. I'll stay with the firm until the end of the year; then I'll have to have a think about what to do next.'

He wondered about her change of mind, but smiled at the phrase she'd used. It was left over from childhood and the small girl who'd often needed to 'have a think' about

214

some problem she was determined to solve on her own.

'Come down for Christmas,' he suggested, '...settle the future after that.'

She agreed that she would, then Monica called from the kitchen. The soufflés were ready; it was time to move into the dining room.

The next morning dawned fine, a golden late-September day that demanded to be spent out of doors, and they set off to visit some of the lovely gardens in the vicinity of the village: Barrington, Tintinhull and Forde Abbey. Over dinner that evening Kate promised to take her mother to meet Lucy Faringdon one day; the two women would need no company but each other, she explained to Henry.

'I've told you how she and Nigel Faringdon met on our last Russian trip. They're very happily married now, and fortunately Nigel's daughter, whom you met at Easter-time, gets on brilliantly with her new step-mother. I think they're both an education for each other in different ways!'

'What with your Dutch friends as well, that trip wasn't like all the others, was it?' Monica commented. 'The people you met then haven't since disappeared; they seem to have been worth remembering.'

Kate agreed slowly that it was true, and

215

then found herself embarking on the story of Jenny Maitland, now Kemanskaya.

'What about the "Caledonian giant"?' her father asked. 'He doesn't sound an easy man to lose sight of either.'

'I met him again at the Faringdons' new home,' Kate said briefly. 'He roams about the world a lot ... likes to tell other people what to do.'

'*Not* your cup of tea, by the sound of it!'

Kate's expression was suddenly rueful. 'We fell over each other quite literally the first time we met at Gatwick. *Our* relationship never really recovered from that, but I think his friends probably value him very highly.'

It was all she intended to say about Ranald McEwan and she firmly changed the topic of conversation back to village affairs. She was on the point of leaving the following day when Andrew Carmichael's name cropped up again.

'You know me – the fool who rushes in where angels wouldn't,' Monica said apologetically. 'Am I allowed to ask whether we're going to see Andrew here again?'

'Perhaps as a friend, but not as a son-in-law,' Kate answered after a moment's hesitation. 'Six months ago I could have married him but didn't very much want to; by the time I made up my mind, it was too late: I think that he will marry Linette Faringdon!' She smiled at her mother's anxious face. 'Don't agonize about me – I'm sad, but not going into a terminal decline. Perhaps next time I'll find someone who knows a thing or two about gardening, just for your benefit!'

'Let him know a thing or two about you; I'm not sure that Andrew did,' her mother said unexpectedly.

On the drive back to London she couldn't help wondering what Andrew's response to her letter would have been – hurt, regret, ill-concealed relief? A few months ago she could have made a guess and expected to be right. Perhaps what her mother had said was true; perhaps it was still more true that they hadn't really known each other. It was a lesson she needed to remember in future.

Her letter box yielded an assortment of mail when she got home, but there was nothing at all from Andrew. From so courteous and kind a man the omission was hurtful, brutally underlining the fact that she must get used to life without him. His solicitous telephone calls had been a source of irritation in the past; now, she'd have been grateful just to hear his voice enquiring how she was.

Later that evening there was a ring at the door bell instead, and for a moment she felt sure that he'd come in person to say a tender goodbye; but it was a girl who waited there, looking far from sure that she'd be welcome. Kate found it hard to smile, or infuse the slightest warmth into her voice.

'Linette ... this is a surprise! I'm only just back from Sicily ... well, there and then a weekend in Somerset. Are you on the way to somewhere else, or will you come in?'

'I'd like to come in, but I'm not sure you want me. If that *is* the case, I'll go away again.' She tried to smile but her face looked strained and pale, and suddenly Kate felt ashamed of her own cool welcome.

'Stay and share my frugal supper,' she suggested more naturally, '...unless you've already eaten.'

Linette shook her head. 'I'll share anything you like – bread and cheese will do.'

'I've come back with both,' Kate said cheerfully. 'My mother's good home-made bread, and some of the delicious Brie that's made in Somerset instead of France; there's even wine from a neighbour's vineyard. What more do we need?'

She thought she was chattering too much, but Linette was beginning to look more at ease. Then, sitting at the kitchen table, with the wine poured, her guest started in on what she'd come to say.

'I've brought a message from Andrew first of all. He was suddenly needed at a financial wizards' coven in the Hague; otherwise he'd be here himself. His own idea was to leave you a note, but I asked him to let me come instead.' Her huge eyes were fixed on Kate's face. 'We gave ourselves away, didn't we? – that's why you wrote.'

It was bravely direct, Kate thought, and deserved an honest reply. '*You* gave yourself away in Amsterdam; at that point I had no idea how Andrew felt. Then, down at Badger's Mount, it was suddenly crystal clear: the two of you scarcely knew the rest of us were there, although you tried very hard to remember us now and then!'

'Don't joke about it,' Linette said gravely. 'When you do that I know it still matters, because it's how you deal with serious things.'

She was Nigel Faringdon's daughter – clever and perceptive, Kate remembered from the past. Whilst she debated how to reply, Linette went on herself.

'Your letter said you'd changed your mind about settling down. Is that *true*, Kate ... do you really not want to marry Andrew?'

Her voice combined disbelief and hope in a mixture that made Kate finally smile. 'Marrying each other was an idea we ... rather got used to,' she tried to explain. 'It might even have happened one day, and we'd have jogged along together contentedly enough. But what you and he share has nothing to do with jogging along: you'll make each other profoundly miserable or ecstatically happy!'

'Happy, I think,' Linette insisted, with the perfect confidence of youth. 'We can't *not* be happy together.'

'Then that's the future settled, and we'll drink to it in good Somerset wine. My letter need never be referred to again.'

Linette's mouth smiled, but her eyes still looked troubled. 'We need to refer to *you*, though; what will you do?'

Kate made a heroic effort to sound cheerful. 'For the moment what I said I *wouldn't* do. But the firm is very short of Russian-speakers, so I've agreed to cover the northern tours until Christmas. After that I'll insist on a reward – some cruising up or down the Nile, perhaps – I can never remember which it is.'

'I know; we'll all come too – me and Andrew, Daddy and Lucy, and Dirk and Ellie as well. Perhaps *not* dear Phyllis, though!' Lucy's face was sparkling now, sadness and doubt about Kate wiped away by the beauty of this new idea.

'You don't mention the great McEwan, not that I can imagine him cooped up on a small boat,' Kate pointed out. 'Where *is* he, by the way?'

'Just back in London; he and Jenny's brother share a flat in Dolphin Square. He's been visiting his Highland hideout. Have you heard him talk about it? His voice changes when he does; he can even make a kind of poetry out of describing it!'

Yes, he could, easily enough, Kate knew. He'd described it once to her, and ever since she'd been able to see, in her mind's eye, a lonely white house tucked into a stretch of windswept turf that ran down to the grey-blue waters of the Sound of Sleat. It would be peaceful and solitary enough even for a man who needed other people as little as McEwan did.

'He's off again tomorrow,' Linette said as she got up to leave. 'The Indian trip is on again, and he's flying out early in the morning to Madras.' Then she wrapped her arms round Kate in a warm hug. 'I needed to see you,' she explained unsteadily. 'It didn't seem fair to be happy unless we could be certain *you*'re all right. You're sure you are, Katey?'

'Thank you for asking, but I'm fine,' she answered solemnly. 'And if you don't leave it too long, I'll still be spry enough to dance at your wedding!'

'It *won't* be long,' Miss Faringdon said firmly. 'I shall see to that.'

She kissed Kate, promised faithfully to

keep in touch, and floated away on a cloud of happiness, now certain that Ranald had been wrong for once when they'd quarrelled after his ill-fated birthday dinner party. As usual he hadn't minced his words, and the accusation that he'd flung at her had hurt. Andrew belonged to Kate, he'd said, and it was a treacherous friend who showed a man so clearly that *she* was available instead. They'd patched the quarrel up, but she wondered what his reaction would be to her actually marrying Andrew. If he stayed too long in India, it would be a fait accompli by the time he got back.

Kate closed the door after her departing guest, then stood still for a moment, knowing that what she was about to do next was not the act of a normally rational woman. It wasn't born of thought at all, only of instinct operating at some subconscious level. She'd been aware long since that an apology was due to McEwan; Linette's visit, and the certainty of her marriage to Andrew, had merely driven the message home. She should have apologized when they were at Badger's Mount together, and might have done, if only Linette had been involved; but he'd guessed about Andrew, too, and her mean little soul had shied at admitting that she'd kept him waiting too long.

She picked up the telephone directory,

cursing herself for not having asked Linette for the number; but agitation was stilled by the discovery that he *was* listed: R. A. McEwan, Rodney House, Dolphin Square. The clock chimed eleven – late to ring anyone, of course; but she'd gone beyond caring. Her apology had to be made, and the longer she put it off, the worse her discomfort would become. She absolutely refused to be left with it unsaid while he ambled around India. Even if she had to wake him up, he must listen to what she had to say.

He wasn't there to waken, however; she could hear the hollow sound that a telephone always seemed to make when it was ringing in an empty room.

She dragged out the directory again and rang Heathrow. British Airways had no morning flight to Madras. Air India did, and by dint of shamelessly using her Three Cs credentials she got the reservations clerk to admit that they were holding a seat for R. A. McEwan on the flight taking off at 8 a.m. Passengers had been advised, she added helpfully, to stay in one of the airport hotels overnight.

Kate abandoned the search – the damned man could be sleeping anywhere in West London. She set her alarm clock for four-thirty and went to bed.

★ ★ ★

The pre-dawn traffic was heavy, but she was making good time. If the gods were kind she'd be able to spot McEwan's unmistakable figure as he went to check in. The words she'd say were ready in her mind: he *hadn't* used Linette selfishly; the girl *was* deeply in love with Andrew; and Kate Kirkby regretted that she'd doubted these things and perhaps shouted at him like a fishwife. Then, with her apology made, she could wish him a successful trip and return home feeling at peace with the world; her sin of omission, as the Bible neatly put it, would have been rectified.

The gods were not minded to be kind. Half an hour later she was sitting in a traffic jam on the M4, and the impatience inside her was growing into a fever. The traffic crawled to another stop and she looked at the dashboard clock yet again, aware that she was running out of time; but she was stuck in the queue, unable to go any faster and just as incapable of turning round. She changed gear, inched forward again, agonized a lot, and even found herself weeping a little; it *mattered* – mattered more than anything else she could now think of that McEwan shouldn't set off without her seeing him this one more time. She finally crept off the motorway on to the slip road leading to the airport. There was little hope of finding the car park; the car must take its chance while she fled into Terminal 4.

'Eight o'clock flight to Madras?' she asked desperately.

'Called through long ago – you're terribly late,' said the Air India girl behind the desk.

'Not travelling,' Kate gasped. 'I wanted to see a passenger.'

'Hopeless, I think ... well, how important is it?' Bloody silly question, the ground stewardess said to herself; the face of the girl in front of her was stained with tears. 'We'll see if there's anything we can do.'

She took Kate's hand and raced her through the crowd, waved cheerfully to the man behind the passport desk as they hurtled past, and almost fell down several flights of stairs. The board for AI 459 to Madras was already down, and the departure lounge was empty. Still reluctant to give in, the stewardess charged the length of the hall with Kate at her heels.

'Madras?' she shouted to a colleague the other side of the gate.

'Flight's boarded ... already taxiing, I think. You're much too late.'

Much too late. The words penetrated Kate's haze of distress like some dreadful knell, sounding the death of hope. She'd had that small last chance, and lost it.

'You all right?' the stewardess asked

quickly. 'I'm sorry we didn't manage it.'

'I'm grateful to you for trying ... pity I got held up on the motorway.' A pity! Dirk Engelsman was right: the English language was a strange and wonderful thing. She gave the girl a faint smile, and climbed the stairs. The car hadn't been towed away, and all she had to do was drive herself back to London – not quite all, she silently amended. She might also have to work out why that mad airport dash had seemed so vitally important. It was tucked away in the corner of her mind where matters were lodged that couldn't be faced immediately.

But it made itself felt that night. She woke sweating and nearly distraught from a nightmare in which some disaster hovered, not identified, not quite arrived; but waiting to descend. She *could* identify the place her dreadful dream was set in; these brown-faced people that she could see were accustomed to the disasters that seemed to happen all too frequently in India.

She got out of bed and went downstairs, made tea that she didn't want, for something to do, and then sat at the kitchen table thinking of McEwan landing among the people she'd been dreaming about. She knew now why it had seemed to matter so much to reach him before he left. Her affection for Andrew had been real enough;

but it had nothing at all to do with the onslaught of emotion that she now struggled with. Trust McEwan, she thought, always larger than life himself, to involve her in *this* kind of turmoil.

Fifteen

Night-time terrors were like the moon, fading in the light of day. Kate watched the eastern sky slowly brighten and could tell herself that she was calm again. Nothing would be quite the same from now on, but she could face the future, as other women had done who couldn't have what they wanted.

There'd been a lot to discover during the long, sleepless night – her own fallibility, for one thing; and since she'd been so terribly wrong about herself, God alone knew how often she'd managed to misguide other people as well. The ache of loneliness she'd grown familiar with in recent weeks had nothing to do with missing Andrew. She'd given her heart away instead to a self-sufficient, solitary man who might once have wanted Jenny Maitland but didn't want anyone else. Through all the years to come she must visualize him only in her mind's eye, content with his own company when he wasn't busy trying to save the world. He

wouldn't need what lesser mortals craved –
the touch of someone else's hand, shared
warmth, shared laughter.

She couldn't imagine learning not to
measure everyone she met from now on
against him. If the ache of loneliness grew
too intense, she might have to try; but for
the moment she would make do with her
memories of Ranald McEwan. They'd been
so carefully hoarded, she now realized, that
her subconscious must have known that this
moment of discovery had been waiting for
her all along.

A little late for work that morning, she
reported in and found herself unexpectedly
summoned to face the boss.

'Sorry to be late – rather a bad night,' she
apologized briefly.

His inspection of her pale face didn't last
long. 'I can see it was,' he agreed and abandoned the subject. He wasn't an inhumane
man, only one who believed that people
who weren't his customers could and
should be responsible for themselves, by
and large. It was a view Kate shared and she
would have been taken aback if he'd enquired tenderly about the reason for her late
arrival.

'Not Russia next week, Kate,' he told her.
'I want you to stay here for a fortnight,
knocking some new recruits into shape.

You're our most experienced courier now; it's time you began to take an interest in how we run this place – maybe the training programme needs an overhaul. Does it appeal?'

'Not indefinitely,' Kate answered after a moment's thought. 'I've enjoyed working with the customers – by and large!' Straight-faced, she borrowed the phrase he was so apt to use himself and got a reproving stare.

'Cheeky, but *good* with the customers,' he commented as if to himself, and then very faintly smiled. 'Clear off now and get to work on the hopefuls. I don't care if they can read *War and Peace* in the original: they've got to learn how to handle people.'

Against expectation the next fortnight flew past and she even found herself enjoying the role of guide, counsellor and friend to half a dozen nervous would-be couriers, some of them too nervous, and some too confident.

It was only when the two weeks were up and she was getting ready to leave for her own next tour of duty that there was a ring at her door bell one evening. Andrew Carmichael stood there, as he had so often in the past, with a bottle of wine in an elegant small carrier.

'No flowers this evening, Kate; Linette said you were about to go away.'

'Tomorrow, in fact. It's lovely to see you ... Come in.'

She poured the whisky that she knew he preferred as an after-dinner drink, and then sat down opposite him. 'You look frazzled – too much work?'

'Too much of everything in Brussels – meetings followed by interminable dinners, followed by late-night lobbying and fixing! It's how the EU is run, God help us.' Then his long thin hand waved the bureaucrats aside. 'Dear Kate, I've been away for weeks, and all the time I wanted to be here instead – to thank you for your letter, and to ... say goodbye, I suppose.'

He took a sip from his glass, then put it down again and it seemed to Kate that it was her turn to say something.

'You know that Linette came round, sweetly anxious to make sure that I wasn't being too noble about managing without you in future. Reassured on that point, she could allow herself to be happy – she *is* happy, wonderfully so, and you must be, too.'

Andrew examined her face across the small width of the hearth. Not seen for some time, it had surely become more beautiful – thinned down, because he could now see the shadow beneath her cheekbones – and more disciplined. Her smile came less readily, and there was a new air of self-containment about her; it was harder to know what this Kate was thinking.

'I expect it seems mad,' he began diffidently. 'I often had the feeling that I was too dull a stick-in-the-mud for *you*, and here I am now proposing to marry a girl only a little more than half my age, who is accustomed to being spoiled, and scarcely understands that most of us have to toil quite hard for a living! Put like that, our marriage sounds little short of lunacy, I'm afraid.'

'But I can put it differently,' Kate suggested, smiling at him. 'Linette is like her father – that was once pointed out to me, and it's true. She has all Nigel's sharpness of mind, so she'll learn very quickly to cope with your sort of life, but she also has his warmth of heart. All *you* have to do is to love her in return and take care of her – both of which you can easily do. I don't see any lunacy in that.'

Andrew's face relaxed into its charming smile, but he grew serious again. 'Kate, we shall stay friends, because I can't imagine losing touch with you; but what I want to say now can't ever be said again. The dearest hope of my heart was that you'd learn to love me as much as I loved you. It was a stupid hope, of course, because love doesn't come with careful learning; it's the *coup de foudre* or it's nothing at all, and the lightning didn't strike for you. I shan't stop loving you, but it won't hurt Linette; in fact, in a funny sort of way it makes it easier to love her more. Does that sound like nonsense, or a downright lie?'

If anything, it sounded too wistful, she thought – Andrew still looking back over his shoulder. 'No, because I agree,' she answered. 'I might not have done a few years ago, but at the ripe old age of twenty-five I *am* learning a thing or two. We don't have to parcel love out – a bit more here or there meaning a bit less left for somewhere else; that's not how it works at all. Unlike money, it multiplies with spending, and if that doesn't gladden an actuary's heart, what will, I wonder?'

It was a cheerful note to end the conversation on, she hoped. 'Where are you going to live?' she asked next. 'In Eaton Square?'

'No, in my flat, at least to begin with. Linette likes it, and she knows that the view of the river means a lot to me. Nigel will sell his; he and Lucy can stay with us if they need to be in London.' Andrew set down his glass and stood up. 'A Christmas wedding, my young woman says; will you be here, Kate?'

'Can be, I'm sure, though I've promised to

233

be at home for the festival itself. I like Christmas in the country – still can't help feeling that the cattle in the fields *are* kneeling down when the bells ring out "on the midnight clear".'

'Soppy date!' said Andrew, smiling at her with the affection that he hoped *was* still permitted. 'Now I must go, my dear. Let us know when you get back.'

She promised that she would, kissed him goodnight as any friend might, and let him out into the street; but she didn't immediately return to the packing he'd interrupted. He wasn't entirely right about the flash of lightning that ignited love; it didn't always happen like that – hadn't happened when she'd cannoned into McEwan at Gatwick one morning. She couldn't have doubted even then his strength and vigour, and the sheer presence of the man; but how slow she'd been to learn about his lurking humour and honesty and insidious charm.

It was a temptation that often had to be resisted; thinking about him was a self-indulgence she couldn't afford. Better to concentrate her mind on Andrew and Linette instead. Their marriage would work, she felt sure; but it would work more easily if they were left alone to settle down into being man and wife. She'd sensed in him a faint echo of regret that life hadn't provided the prize he'd yearned for most; but she refused to feel anxious about them. He would learn to count himself lucky with Linette; it was only a matter of time before she blotted out for him the memory of any other woman.

The pattern of departure morning at Gatwick was much the same as Kate remembered it from nine months ago: a group of pleasant-looking people, overdressed for a warm lounge in cold-climate clothes, sat around her, waiting for the flight to be called. Her mind kept wandering back to an earlier departure, and had to be ruthlessly called back to order. The job was the thing – get on with it, cheerfully, she insisted to herself.

When they arrived in St Petersburg, the city was freshly covered with its first fall of snow of the winter. The night felt much colder than in England and, although the Neva wasn't yet frozen over, everyone had already settled into the usual winter wardrobe of heavy coats, boots, and fur hats. The hats always appeared so simultaneously that Kate imagined there must be an insistent memory of some old Party diktat which said that fur hats would be worn from such and such a day. The fur ran up the scale, from rabbit at the bottom to mink or sable at the top, and neatly indicated the standing of its owner. She'd tried to tease Sergei once on the subject of hats in a society he claimed was classless, but he'd refused to discuss the matter on the grounds that the question was frivolous. She felt sad about him, torn between thinking that he loved her a little and knowing that he ought to disapprove of her a lot.

However, he wasn't at the airport to meet them and, feeling sad and relieved at the same time, Kate found another Intourist representative waiting, a blonde girl called Nadia, who had occasionally helped out when Sergei needed an assistant.

'If this means you've been promoted, congratulations!' Kate said with a smile.

'I am your guide now, yes.' Nadia did not smile – hadn't done so in the whole of Kate's acquaintance with her, but perhaps things would improve.

A week in her company was enough to confirm that Nadia was many things, but *not* a girl who smiled. She was efficient, informative, and determined. No statistic was left unstated, not one statue of Lenin overlooked, and her future with Intourist was obviously assured. But an enquiry about Sergei was turned aside, and when Kate persisted and said it would be nice to meet him and say hello, Nadia said stiffly that it

would not be possible. He was now con-
ducting the tour that took visitors across the
continent on the Trans-Siberian railway.
Her indifferent voice said that she had no
interest in what had become of Sergei
Ivanov, and anger suddenly made Kate
blunter than usual.

'Fewer Westerners to be contaminated by
in Siberia – is that the reason?'

Anger or irony – it didn't matter which;
Nadia was impervious to both. 'It is a
chance for him to see more of our great
Motherland. Sergei is lucky.'

Kate reminded herself that she was lucky
too, to the extent that under Nadia's cold
blue gaze no arrangement would have dared
to go awry. Even their journey to Moscow
went without the slightest hitch; there was
no Ellie Engelsman always getting lost, no
unhappy girl provoking drunken soldiers.
There was no large infuriating man to
rescue them and destroy her own peace
of mind at the same time. She managed very
well not to keep looking for him, but he
was now the constant companion of her
thoughts whenever she could allow her
mind to wander from the job in hand. On
the long train journey she stared at the
snow-covered landscape outside the window and saw instead the burning plains of
India: McEwan was in the picture, towering

over a crowd of bird-like Indians. The fierce summer sun was on his face as he taught them, with passion as well as expertise, how to feed themselves.

'Kate ... I've brought you a glass of tea...' A voice at her elbow dragged her thoughts away from India and she smiled her thanks at a fatherly member of the group who thought she looked tired.

There *was* a setback when they arrived in Moscow, which Kate accepted the more cheerfully because it seemed to irritate Nadia so much. Their reservations at the Intourist Hotel overlooking Red Square had been cancelled at a moment's notice because more rooms were needed for the visiting delegations to some international conference. The sudden change of plan wasn't unusual in Russia, where Kate often suspected officialdom of playing havoc with people's lives whenever it felt bored with other things. She would have put the point of view to Sergei, but not to Nadia, who was now explaining to her bus-load of weary passengers that they would be *more* comfortable at the Hotel Kosmos than at the Intourist.

'But we *shan't* be overlooking Red Square,' a voice called defiantly from the back of the bus – this season's Phyllis Newcombe, who had been studying her map of the city and was determined not to be cowed by Authority.

'Not as near the centre of Moscow,' Nadia had to agree with reluctance.

Kate had different reasons for regretting the change. The Kosmos held too many memories, and when she went into the restaurant for breakfast the next morning, she was assailed by a terrible longing to weep because McEwan wasn't there to help himself to her bread and butter.

The tour followed the programme usually mapped out and Kate had to possess her soul in patience until the free afternoon arrived. Then, with all her flock happy, she took herself in a taxi to Kalynka Prospekt, praying that the Kemanska family would still be there.

It was Ludmilla Kemanskaya who opened the door. Her mournful Russian face, not forgotten once seen, looked suspicious of the unexpected visitor; then, slowly, recognition dawned. She didn't smile, but her expression changed.

'Jenny's English friend,' she murmured. 'You've come to see *her*, but she's not here. She and Nikolai have a place of their own now. It's almost nothing – just one room but...' The sentence faded away and her shrug indicated that they'd all learned to make do with almost nothing.

'I also came to see you and Anatoly,' Kate insisted gently. 'May I come in?'

The door was held open, and she walked into the sitting room; it was as bleak as she remembered it – no, worse: Jenny's canary was missing now.

'You and Anatoly are well, I hope,' Kate began formally.

'Well enough. We shall be grandparents soon; it's something to look forward to.'

Try as she might, Kate could detect no warmth in the woman in front of her for a daughter-in-law who'd undertaken to share her son's harsh life. As a result, it was hard to feel any warmth for *her*, but she soldiered on.

'I brought some small things for you from England,' she said diffidently. 'Accept them, please.' Out of her satchel she took tobacco for Anatoly, because she remembered seeing a rack of pipes, and for Ludmilla a parcel containing a thick, soft cardigan in a beautiful hyacinth blue. It was unwrapped and stared at for so long that Kate feared she'd made a terrible mistake – injured pride in some way that couldn't be forgiven; but when Ludmilla looked at her at last, her eyes were full of tears.

'Lovely, Katerina,' she murmured, stroking the softness of the wool.

'I hope it fits,' Kate said, trying not to

weep herself. 'I had to guess the size.'

Ludmilla put it on, and then went to stare at herself in the small mirror hanging on the wall. Smiling now, she turned to face Kate. 'Anatoly will be back soon. Will you stay and take a glass of tea? I can give you Jenny's address, but she won't be there now. She teaches, like Nikolai.'

'I'll try to call one evening, then,' Kate said, 'but it depends on the group I'm looking after. May I leave their presents with you just in case I don't get to see them? Give them my love, please.'

Ludmilla brought the tea and, with the small hospitable gesture, she became – as she had at Jenny's wedding party – the woman she'd once been.

'You must look after these people all by yourself, Katerina? That seems wrong to me – too much for a young girl.'

'Not all that young,' Kate pointed out with a smile. 'In any case, I have a Russian colleague as well, but she isn't very popular with the group. We've yet to see her smile, and she clearly despises us for being decadent Westerners. I thought *that* attitude had died long since, but my theory is that Nadia was brought up by a grandmother who forgot to mention that my country did take a share in fighting the Nazis.'

Ludmilla shook her head. 'Attitudes *don't*

die here; they get buried for a while, then reappear again. I expect you think that communism is dead also; not so, Katerina. The Party is important still.'

Kate thought it was all too probably true, and held out little hope for families like the one Jenny had married into; but all she could do was promise to call whenever she came to Moscow in future.

'But not to bring presents,' Ludmilla said firmly, '...just for friendship, Katerina.'

Kate agreed that it would certainly be for friendship, kissed her hostess goodbye and, unable to wait for Anatoly any longer, went away. She didn't succeed in seeing Jenny either. The next morning a mishap occurred that was always liable to disrupt the best-run tour. An elderly lady slipped on some ice beneath the snow, fell and broke her hip. Going with her to the hospital, arranging a special journey home, and keeping the rest of the tour on the rails took all a harassed courier's time and energy.

She thankfully parted company with Nadia at the airport three days later. The other girl still didn't smile, but she *was* moved to say that the injured lady had behaved well – quite like a Russian, in fact – and the others had given no trouble. It wasn't effusive praise, Kate thought, but at least this stern upholder of the Motherland

242

no longer openly despised them; chinks were beginning to appear in Nadia's armour. She might even be surprised into smiling next time.

Sixteen

Three weeks later, though, it wasn't Nadia waiting for their arrival from St Petersburg, but Sergei Ivanov. At first glance he looked unchanged, still wearing his old blue quilted jacket, still thin and wary; but his face lit up as soon as Kate walked towards him, nothing else remembered for the moment except that she was there, smiling as only she could smile.

'Sergei ... it's lovely to see you,' she said and meant it. 'Are *you* looking after us? I was expecting an awe-inspiring girl called Nadia.'

'Tonight only,' he confessed. 'I offered to come instead. She has a birthday ... something to celebrate with her fiancé. We have not told the Agency, of course.'

'I shall look at her differently tomorrow; the girl's human after all,' Kate said cheerfully. 'Now, let's get my people to the hotel and talk afterwards. They're tired and hungry.'

When her flock had been fed and safely

disposed in their rooms, Sergei agreed to something he'd never accepted before: a drink in one of the hotel's cafés.

With glasses of the inevitable tea set in front of them, Kate spoke first. 'Nadia told me that you'd been transferred to the Trans-Siberian railway tour. At least no one can get lost – the courier's everlasting dread! But it's a tiring job, I imagine.'

'Tiring and rather terrible,' Sergei agreed unexpectedly. 'Always as a boy I wanted to cross Siberia; it represents something very special for the Russian people. The railway itself was one of our great achievements.'

'So it still is,' Kate insisted gently when he went on looking agonized.

'Yes, but we know the truth now. After all the lies we're *learning* the truth. The railway was built by thousands – no, millions – of slaves. Criminals or innocent men and women, it made no difference: most of them died. Most of what we were taught was a lie. Do you have to say that about your own country?'

His voice shook as he asked the question, and his tormented expression reminded her of what Ludmilla had said. Things *didn't* change in Russia, and Sergei could have stepped out of any one of Dostoevsky's novels. An almost mystical devotion to Mother Russia couldn't quite withstand the knowledge, once forbidden, of the horrors that had been inflicted on her people.

'You can't compare your country and mine,' Kate answered at last, 'and you can't compare our very different people. We've done great things and some bad things in a long history, but it hasn't been soaked in blood and sacrifice in the way that yours has.' She reached out across the table to clasp Sergei's hand in her warm one.

'Nothing can minimize the horrors, but nothing can diminish the achievements either. The Russian people defeated Hitler – that has *never* been a lie.'

Sergei lifted her hand to his mouth and kissed it. 'It's time I went,' he said unsteadily, '...you are tired of today's travelling. I probably shan't ever see you again, but I shall love you always in my heart.' Then he stood up, made a little, formal bow and walked out of the café. It was a theatrical departure – Sergei wasn't a Slav for nothing, she remembered – but that didn't mean it was insincere. She knew that his grief was very real and that she, to some extent at least, was its cause. It was a thought to take sadly to bed; but, as always, she ended the long day by praying for someone else. India, she couldn't help but fear, was a dangerous place. She needed a whole flock of angels to keep watch over McEwan there.

The following morning Nadia was waiting for the bus as usual, but looking less than usually intimidating.

'Nice birthday party last night?' Kate ventured with a friendly smile.

It didn't have the effect she intended. The Russian girl's face, never very expressive, went completely blank. 'I suppose you're going to report it to the Agency,' she suggested, sounding angry and hopeless at the same time.

'Then you suppose wrong,' Kate said very decidedly in a tone of voice Nadia hadn't heard her use before. 'Now, *smile* at these nice people, and let's get on our way.'

It took a moment or two for the command to register, but at last Nadia's set expression wavered into something that could be called the beginnings of a smile. She watched the people waiting to board the bus, the queue orderly, the voices good-natured and the faces gentle. 'Yes ... nice,' she finally agreed, with a faint sense of wonderment.

That evening it was Nadia's turn to shepherd them to the Bolshoi. Kate saw them off, then flagged down a taxi and asked to be taken to the address Ludmilla had given her – Ulitsa Nezhdanovoi, a lane leading off the busy Tverskaya Street. It was a good deal more attractive than Kalynka Prospekt and her heart rose a little at the sight of it;

247

but Ludmilla was right: the apartment Jenny led her into a little while later certainly wasn't 'very much' – a bed-sitting room, and a kitchen and bathroom shared with another couple.

'Dear Kate, it's wonderful to see you,' Jenny said, after wrapping her in a hug. 'We'd almost given up hope when Ludmilla told us about your visit. The presents were wonderful too. Nikolai's books were the best thing you could have brought him, and I'm wearing my new sweater, as you see!'

'I didn't come sooner because I spent the summer going backwards and forwards to Sicily,' Kate explained. 'Then, just when I was hoping to come here one evening after seeing Ludmilla, I spent it in a hospital instead with a lady who'd fallen and broken her hip. Still, forewarned by your mother-in-law, I've brought some really useful things this time: baby clothes! Congratulations, Jenny dear.' She looked round the room and asked a tentative question: 'Will you be able to manage here with a baby?'

'Not for long, but the couple we share with are getting an apartment of their own; with their room as well, we can manage beautifully.' Jenny's pale, thin face flushed with pride. 'Nikolai's clever – he makes everything we need. You can see how well organized we are!'

It was true, Kate agreed; the room wasn't large or lavishly furnished, but it was spick and span and welcoming, and space had even been found for the canary in its cage.

'Tell me what happened to the nice people who came to our wedding,' Jenny said while she made tea. 'There was the pretty girl who seemed permanently attached to Ranald; Ludmilla was very impressed by the way she could drink vodka, I remember.'

'Linette is about to get married, but *not* to McEwan; and her father has already married the shy lady who made such a hit with Anatoly. The Engelsmans – whom you can't have forgotten – are back in Amsterdam, but they're still our good friends.' Kate hesitated a moment, and then went on: 'I expect you have news of McEwan – know that he went off on a long trip to India.'

She wasn't aware that her voice had changed when she spoke his name, or that Jenny looked curiously at her; but she found herself wanting to confess to that futile, agonized journey to Heathrow that had failed so entirely in its object. Jenny, she thought, would have understood, because Jenny knew what loving meant; but the confession would have been even more absurd than the journey itself had been. Instead, she mentioned what came to mind whenever she thought of McEwan.

'He spoke once of his home – not where your parents live in Edinburgh, but the private place that seems to mean so much to him.'

'Oh, Achnavour,' Jenny said immediately. 'Well, it *is* very beautiful – just a small hamlet that runs alongside a sea-loch. Ranald's land is at the seaward end, facing the Sound. A factor looks after it for him, but it's where he'll finish up when his travelling days are over. He quotes a line from a Yeats poem about it, a place where "peace comes dropping slow"! It's a pity he's such a loner; most people who *are* seem not to be very good with other people, but I don't know anyone who doesn't fall for him.'

Yes, it was a pity, Kate thought with a stab of pain, and it was also unfortunately true that falling for him seemed so unavoidable. 'I envy him – the peace,' she managed to say. 'It's what we're all looking for.'

Then she was silent for a moment and, looking at her more closely, Jenny was aware of the change in a girl she'd remembered very vividly. Something had left an imprint on Kate, but, whatever it was, she didn't intend it to be touched on. Happiness she'd have spoken about herself, so it was a grief of some kind that she kept hidden away. Aware of the silence in the room, Kate roused herself to break it and unearthed a scrap of paper from her bag.

'My address in London; I insist on knowing when your baby is born. Time things right and I'll be in Moscow to attend the christening – at least, I assume there are such sacraments here?'

'There will be for our child,' Jenny said firmly. 'As it happens, the church at the end of this street has never ceased to function; it's a rare achievement in post-revolutionary Russia.'

Kate was reminded of another question, but this one was more difficult to ask. 'Speaking of achievements, how are you getting on with Ludmilla nowadays? When I called on *her* it took a little while to break the door down, but I had the feeling that we finished up friends.'

'You did well then,' Jenny said seriously. 'To begin with she saw me as another misfortune in her life. We've made a little progress since then, but she won't be able to resist a grandchild – no Russian can.'

'And are *you* all right ... happy?' Kate risked asking.

'I have Nikolai,' Jenny answered.

Kate smiled at her, and reluctantly stood up. 'I'd love to wait and see him, but my flock will soon be back from the ballet, all bursting to tell me how marvellous it was. Are there any messages I can take home for you?'

'Thanks, Kate, but we're in touch; I telephone every fortnight or so. Just call in when you can; it's lovely to have a natter in English.'

Kate promised that she would, kissed Jenny goodbye and let herself out into the street. It was still only November but already very cold, and the long months of winter stretched ahead. She shivered at the thought of Jenny carrying her unborn child through the worst weather of the year, then remembered the quiet certainty of the answer she'd been given. Jenny had Nikolai; she needed nothing else for happiness.

Back in London the following week, there were urgent messages waiting for her from both Linette and Lucy Faringdon. The Christmas wedding Andrew had spoken of was being hurried through at the beginning of December. He was being transferred to New York for a three-month visit. Linette refused to be left behind and insisted on going as his wife. The wedding, having to be arranged so quickly, would be very simple, but neither of them minded that. Kate was required to be present, though, because she was the one guest they couldn't do without.

There was no reply from the London flat when she telephoned, but a call to Badger's

Mount found Lucy at home. She sounded bemused but not unhappy, and laughed when Kate said she sympathized with anyone forced at the moment to live with Linette.

'It's really not as bad as that,' Lucy felt able to insist. 'She's excited, of course, but if she shows signs of being unreasonable, dear Andrew steps in; he seems to know just how to handle her, which Nigel says is more than *he* ever did!'

'A successful marriage is clearly in store!'

There was a moment's silence at the other end before Lucy spoke again. 'Are *you* all right, Kate dear? You sound a little tired, I think.'

More probably she'd sounded snide, she thought, and any woman less kind-hearted than Lucy would have said so. 'I'm fine,' she answered hurriedly, 'and you've been clever enough to fix a wedding day I can manage.'

'Then nothing will go wrong, if our shepherdess is here – do you remember, Kate, how Ranald always used to call you that? Such a dear man – it's a great pity he won't be here.'

Kate ended the conversation as best she could, and put down the telephone wondering who else would suggest that something was a pity about McEwan. The only real and terrible pity, perhaps, was that she'd ever met him at all. No, that wasn't – couldn't – be true. She walked across the room and stared at herself in the mirror above the fireplace. No sign yet that she could see of embittered spinsterhood, but if the Prayer Book's 'envy, hatred, malice and all uncharitableness' were not to lie in wait, she *must* learn to share other people's happiness, not feel jealous of it, as she had done a moment ago.

It was finally arranged that on the day of the wedding she would drive down to Sussex with Dirk and Ellie, who'd flown over to London the night before. Ellie, never one to languish unseen, had chosen as her wedding outfit a cape of Prussian-blue velour and a white fur hat. The English weather for once sportingly agreed to co-operate and provided a December morning of brilliant, frosty sunlight that, as Dirk said, matched his darling perfectly.

He had a charming compliment for Kate as well – in hunter-green coat of superbly military cut and matching velvet beret – and in this happy mood the three of them set off for Sussex.

It was a beautiful wedding in the parish church at the end of the lane, and from there the guests walked back to the house for the sumptuous buffet lunch that Lucy had provided. Linette, in white silk with a toque made of what seemed to be swan's feathers on her dark hair, looked like a princess in a Russian fairy tale. She was beautiful enough to blind a husband to any other woman, and Kate thought she need worry about Andrew no longer. If he still had any dreamy memory of hankering after someone else, it would soon be lost in the real and wonderful need to love his wife.

A brief honeymoon in Vermont before going to New York meant an early-afternoon departure for the bride and bridegroom. When they'd been waved away, Kate walked back into the house with Nigel Faringdon, and heard him give a heartfelt sigh of relief.

'Wedding stress as bad as that?' she asked with a smile.

'Stress, certainly,' he agreed, more seriously than she'd expected. 'I hid the morning papers, but I was on tenterhooks in case someone mentioned the disaster in India – it was on the morning's news.'

'What ... what sort of disaster?' Kate heard a voice ask that she didn't recognize as her own.

'A train-crash of some kind. India's a huge country, and no doubt a thousand trains run up and down it every day; but I knew that just the thought of Ranald being there would spoil Linette's happiness.'

Kate didn't answer – couldn't for the moment find anything to say at all. Her mind clung instead to what Nigel had just claimed, and kept repeating it like a saving mantra: India *was* huge, huge, huge; but the whiteness of her face startled him into speaking again himself.

'I shouldn't have mentioned it, Kate; I've upset *you*, quite needlessly, I'm sure.'

'Quite needlessly, quite needlessly' ... Now these words rang in her brain like the echo of a hollow laugh that wouldn't go away. She pulled herself together with a tremendous effort and spoke almost normally. 'All the same, I'm glad Linette didn't know. Now I must go in search of Ellie; Dirk said they needed to be back in London by five.'

It was a quieter trio who made the return journey, with Ellie nodding off in the back of the car while Kate forced herself to concentrate on navigating Dirk back to London. She loved them both, but she was thankful when they said goodbye outside her house. She watched them drive away and then walked to the nearest shop to buy a selection of the day's papers. Back indoors, with them spread on the kitchen table, she read the reports of a terrible accident in which a crowded train on its way from New Delhi to Kashmir had been derailed and had caught fire.

McEwan had gone to Madras in the *south*, she told herself. He'd gone to visit India; there'd been not the slightest mention of Kashmir. By the time she went to bed she was almost convinced that her dread was due to the lingering memory of a nightmare weeks ago. She managed to believe it for the next two days, until she read an eyewitness account of the disaster, which included a paragraph she nearly overlooked. Most of the passengers had been Indians, but among those who hadn't survived was a visiting delegation of Americans and Britons – agronomists and other such specialists – who had been making an extensive tour of India. Their names were being withheld while relatives were traced. Dry-eyed – no tears could help her now – she read the paragraph again, then folded it up very carefully and put it away in a drawer.

Seventeen

She had to set off again for Russia. It was her job, and in any case she desperately needed to be busy. The manner of McEwan's death was something her mind refused to contemplate; it took refuge in anger instead. Disasters were occurring all the time – natural or man-made, they regularly defeated the power of prayer. But *this* insane waste of human life and goodness couldn't be accepted; it was too wickedly wrong to be forgiven.

A note to Lucy and Nigel before she left London was more bearable than a conversation, and in Moscow a week later she cravenly stayed away from Jenny Kemanskaya. The Maitlands were not McEwan's blood relatives; perhaps they hadn't been informed. She couldn't talk about him, not even to Jenny. There were so few memories to cling to, they had to be hoarded like miser's gold.

The tour covered its familiar ground, the group was no more troublesome than usual, and Nadia was no more affable. The only remarkable thing about it was its ordinariness when she had expected a world with McEwan no longer in it to look entirely different.

It was almost Christmas when she got back to London, just in time to set off again for Somerset. There was something to be said for perpetual motion, but she knew it for what it was: an excuse not to stop and think about the emptiness of her life. The excuse couldn't be relied on at Nether Hamdon, where the days went in a more gentle rhythm.

Her mother's greeting when she arrived warned her of the different effort that would have to be made. 'Darling, you look so tired. You must do nothing while you're here … except help us with the high bits in the carols; our sopranos do their best, but they're dangerously weak.'

Kate agreed to manage the descants, but insisted on helping with the decoration of the church as usual. She chose to do the font and, as she garlanded it with holly and ivy, thought of Jenny's baby, due to be born in the early spring. It seemed to her that she managed very well; she smiled and talked just as usual, she thought. But Monica Kirkby explained to Henry in the privacy of their bedroom that night that Kate was missing Andrew Carmichael.

'She was *very* fond of him, and I'd swear he was deeply in love with *her*; so can you explain to me why our daughter is clearly grieving and he is now married to another girl?'

Henry, who couldn't explain it at all, pointed out something else instead. 'It was a different world when we were young, my love. The competition is fiercer now, the rewards much higher, and the penalties for failing more severe.' He smiled at his wife as she sat frowning at herself in the dressing-table mirror. 'Agonizing about Kate won't do a particle of good. She's here with us and it's Christmas – that's *some* comfort for whatever ails her.'

Kate would have agreed with what he said. The unfolding of the Nativity story, known but never wearied of, brought its unfailing peace. The beauty of the starlit night as they walked home after Midnight Mass reminded her of what she'd been in danger of forgetting: joy and laughter weren't gone from the world because Ranald McEwan was dead. She'd find them again some time – could even hear what *he* would have said: 'You can't give up on life, shepherdess.'

At least an immediate problem had, she discovered, solved itself. At some level where instinct operated instead of conscious thought, a decision had been taken: she knew what she had to do next. She explained to her parents that she had a visit to make before returning to London.

'It's on your way back?' Monica asked tentatively.

'Well, not quite,' Kate admitted with a faint smile. 'I've a slight detour to make to the Western Highlands – a small place called Achnavour! Rather to my surprise, I've found it on the map.' She appreciated her mother's heroic effort to pretend that a detour of several hundred miles was a perfectly normal way to behave, but knew the time had come to mention McEwan.

'I'm haunted by a place I've never seen,' she confessed slowly. 'It meant a great deal to someone I met months ago on a trip to Russia.'

'But he's no longer there?' Monica suggested.

'He died in a recent rail disaster in India.' Kate shook her head at the horrified expression on her mother's face. 'You weren't to know, and it's time to talk about him. I'm no worse off than I was before, because even if he needed a woman in his life, he wouldn't have needed *me*: we did nothing but quarrel! But he told me once about Achnavour, and I just need to see it for myself.'

She set off the next day, broke the journey

for a night at Callander and, early the following morning, headed north-west for Fort William and the road to Kyle of Lochalsh. The day was overcast and drizzly but not at all bad for almost the last day of December. She made good time and felt pleased with herself for not getting lost and for finding the turn-off at Shiel Bridge. It was still only early afternoon when she passed through Glenelg, followed the road round the coast and saw Achnavour below her, a huddle of buildings alongside a sea-loch opening on to the Sound of Sleat. The memory of what Jenny had said guided her through the little community and it wasn't hard to spot McEwan's house tucked into a fold of the surrounding hills, half-turned away from the road, towards the sea.

She parked the car some distance beyond it, on the springy turf beside the single track that the road had now become. Then she stared at what had been his view: the silver waters of the Sound, Eigg and Rhum shadowy on the horizon, and the southern tip of Skye nearer at hand. The drizzle was becoming heavier, but even that seemed right, too; this must be how McEwan had often seen it, veiled in a silver-grey curtain of rain. Imagination could paint it in the colours of sunlight easily enough, and how beautiful it would then be.

At last she turned back towards the house, protected from the north wind by its encircling hills. It wasn't quite the small croft she'd visualized so often, but a simple whitewashed house, nevertheless, that properly belonged to the landscape around it – cool in the high days of summer that the West Highlands must sometimes have, warm and secure in winter storms.

She was jolted by the unexpected sight of a car parked near the house, then remembered what Jenny Kemanskaya had said. It must be the factor who was there, still looking after the affairs of his dead master. She was tempted for a moment to knock and explain that she had known Ranald McEwan. Then, even as she thought about it, the porch door opened and a schoolboy came out with luggage to put into the car. Kate heard him call to someone still in the house, and waited to see the factor emerge; but it was a woman who walked out first, then waited for someone else to join her.

Kate felt sharply disappointed by her mistake: it was the wrong house after all, even though it seemed so much as if it should have been the right one. She was about to turn away when the man the woman waited for came out and stood beside her. And it wasn't the wrong house, and McEwan wasn't dead, because it was he who now put his arms round the woman and kissed her. Then he installed her in the car, waved goodbye to the boy, and stood watching as they drove on to the track, fifty yards away from where Kate now crouched behind a drystone wall.

It was the coldness of the rain trickling down her face that finally made her move. Her heart was behaving erratically and her legs seemed stuffed with cotton wool, but she made it back to the car and collapsed into the driving seat with her head against the steering wheel.

For the moment only one thought clamoured in her brain: McEwan wasn't dead. He couldn't be; she'd just seen him. She wasn't light-headed from fatigue, wasn't hallucinating even; because ghosts didn't embrace real people. He was alive, and it should have been all the joy she needed, but she felt sick with anger instead. The Maitlands seemed to matter to him, and so did the woman and child who'd just left; but the rest of them could go on mourning a death that hadn't taken place because he couldn't be bothered to tell them he was still alive.

She lost count of how long she sat there, shivering and inclined to spurts of half-hysterical laughter. How wrong she'd been yet again, imagining McEwan solitary and self-sufficient in his Highland retreat; but at last the discomfort of her wet clothes and the rivulets of water that still trickled down her face from her soaked hair couldn't be ignored any longer. It was time to get herself on the road to London.

She put the car in gear and tried to reverse back on to the track, but the wheels spun uselessly on the sodden turf. She tried again, forwards this time, and, sobbing with relief, felt the tyres grip and move the car. Fifty yards further on there was even a turning place; she was back on the road and facing in the right direction.

But the road was no longer empty: McEwan now stood there, waiting for her, calling out her name. She could stop, run him down, or trust herself to the treacherous grass verge. With a sharp swerve she was past; then she hauled the car back on to the road again and slammed her foot on the accelerator pedal. He was still standing there, bare-headed in the rain: she could see him in the driving mirror.

It was a nightmare journey in the dying afternoon light, up and down the snaking, rain-drenched curves of the Mam Ratagan. Safely back at Fort William, she knew she was no longer safe to be on the road. She *must* stop and sleep. The lights of a hotel beckoned; she drank the soup a waiter put in front of her and then, slain by exhaustion, abandoned the rest of the meal and fell into bed. It was the last night of the year, and the revelry downstairs had continued into the small hours, a tired-looking waitress told her in the morning. She'd slept through it, and now could resume her journey while most people were still sleeping off the effects of their parties. Hurrah for sobriety and virtue, she suggested to the waitress, and doubtfully the girl agreed.

Back in London by the evening, she managed to park for once outside her own front door. She was lifting her large holdall out of the boot when it was suddenly taken out of her hands by the man who'd come to stand beside her. The street light fell on his dark head this time, not the Highland rain.

'I wish you wouldn't keep appearing, like the Demon King,' she muttered crossly, and then ducked her head because her voice was coming from a long way away, and there was only blackness in front of her. It lasted only a moment, and before he could pick her up she lifted her head and managed to scowl at him.

'I don't know what *you*'re doing here; it's been a long day and I'm not entertaining this evening.'

'I've brought food – enough for both of us,' he said as if she hadn't spoken. 'I expect you'll not have bothered to eat all day; hunger's making you tetchy!'

She couldn't decide whether to laugh or weep at a word that didn't quite cover her turmoil of emotions; but he saw her mouth quiver, and spoke in a different tone of voice.

'Kate, I want to talk to you, but perhaps you're too tired tonight. If so, I'll just feed you and then go away; but I shan't go until I'm sure you're all right.'

She saw no point in arguing, even though tiredness seemed the least of her problems. If she went inside without him, he would doubtless hammer on the door, and although Londoners weren't renowned for taking an interest in their neighbours' lives, McEwan wasn't a man to pass unnoticed. She unlocked the door, scooped mail off the floor, and led him into the kitchen. It seemed a long time ago that she'd been there, believing that she'd seen him for the last time. The memory of it was enough to revive her anger, even though she could now see that his face looked shockingly thin and drawn.

'We thought you were dead,' she heard herself say, although she meant to be quietly dignified and calm so that he would go away. 'You didn't think to let us know that you got off that doomed train?' Her voice shook, despite the effort she made to keep it steady, and she collapsed into a chair at the table because her legs would support her no longer.

He saw the extreme whiteness of her face, and delved into the bag he'd brought in. She pointed mutely and he unearthed a corkscrew and glasses; then, with restoring wine poured, he sat down himself. How many months since he'd seen her? It seemed a lifetime ago. He wanted not to talk at all, just to pick her up and hold her against his heart; but that wouldn't do, of course. She was barricaded in behind a wall of anger and hurt that he might never be able to dismantle.

'After you left yesterday I rang Lucy Faringdon,' he said quietly. 'She told me about the newspaper report; until then I didn't know that any of you would imagine I'd been anywhere near that train. I *wasn't* on it; at the very last minute I decided to fly up to Kashmir. After the accident I rang my boss in Geneva, then went to find out what had happened to my colleagues. It was indescribably terrible and chaotic, and I spent days searching through the survivors scattered among the surrounding hospitals; but the truth was that all my friends had died. Since then I've been visiting their families.'

There was a long silence in the room before Kate spoke again. 'I had a nightmare that something terrible was going to happen,' she murmured. 'I'm so very sorry about your friends.' The other things they might have said didn't seem important now, and his haunted face required them to return from horror to simple normality.

'You brought food, you said,' she reminded him quietly. 'It doesn't matter if you don't feel like eating it.'

'Of course it matters; you're as thin as a lathe, and my only excuse for being here is to look after you.'

While she laid the kitchen table he unpacked his carrier bag: what he called *real* Scottish smoked salmon, a brown loaf, lemons, and cheese – a simple meal, he said, with a return to the old McEwan, but better a dinner of herbs, etc., etc. ... and she hastily agreed.

'How did you get here?' she asked, when the salmon had been eaten and they were nibbling cheese.

'I drove down overnight,' he answered. 'Now it's my turn to ask a question: what were *you* doing in Achnavour?'

She thought wildly of saying that she'd been passing by and decided to drop in; but it seemed not only implausible, just downright absurd. At last she offered as much of the truth as she could. 'You spoke of it one day and, when I went to see Jenny Kemanskaya in Moscow, she said how beautiful it was. I wanted to see it for myself, that's all.'

He nodded, and she thought the difficult ground had been skirted very easily, because he began to talk of something else.

'Lucy told me about the wedding. She seemed to think you hadn't minded Carmichael marrying Linette. Was that true?'

'Yes; I think they'll be happy together. For the next month or two they're living in New York.' At last the apology that had weighed on her could finally be made. 'I wanted to admit before you went to India that you were right about her loving Andrew, but I was too late: you'd already gone.' Intent on what she was going to say next, she didn't see him smile. 'I called on Ludmilla the next time I was in Moscow; Jenny and Nikolai had got a flat of their own by then, and eventually I got to see her, too. The flat is tiny, inadequate by our standards, but she's serenely content about the child she's expecting.'

'And what about you – are *you* content?' McEwan asked suddenly. 'Is Russia still fascinating?'

'I went back because we're short of Russian-speakers, but the truth is that I find it too saddening now to be fascinating. There's been too much suffering inflicted on those people, by megalomaniac tsars or the monsters who came after them.' Her eyes were full of remembered grief, now, as she stared at McEwan. 'I saw Sergei again briefly. He's harrowed to his Russian soul by what he's now learning about the past.'

'Poor wee sod,' McEwan said gently, as he had once before. He refilled their glasses and then stared at the golden wine he was about to sip. 'Having got to Achnavour, why did you take off as though the hounds of hell were after you?'

It had to be a lie now, and she must pray that it would be forgiven. 'I thought that going there wouldn't be an intrusion – we believed you were dead. But there you were, standing in the road, and I'm afraid I lost my head.' Her glance skimmed his haggard face and looked away again. 'Now I've reminded you of India again – I'm sorry. There seems to be more sorrow in the world sometimes than we can rightly bear. Don't *you* think that?'

'I think it, but I know it isn't true,' he commented slowly. 'The fact is that we can bear whatever we have to.' He put down his glass and stood up. 'You look transparent with weariness and it's time I went away, but will you have dinner with me tomorrow night at Rodney House in Dolphin Square?

Robin Maitland and his wife are in London, and I'd like you to meet them – also, she's a much better cook than I am!'

Kate agreed and asked what time she should be there.

'I'll collect you at seven,' McEwan said, and smiled when she insisted that she didn't need fetching. 'I know, but fetched is what you're going to be.' His hand touched her cheek in a fleeting caress. 'Now go to bed; you look done in.'

He was gone before she could recover from the unexpected gesture and thank him for the supper he'd brought; but lying in bed later on, she was still wide-awake, still watching the road unwind itself behind her car, and still remembering the woman and the boy at Achnavour that McEwan hadn't mentioned.

Eighteen

The following evening, dressed with more care than usual, she was ready when his car drew up at the door.

'Punctuality,' he observed as she got in, '– not quite as important as obedience, but nevertheless an "excellent thing in a woman"!'

She was reminded of their earliest encounters and warned of his change of mood. Whatever effort it cost, sadness was going to be set aside for this evening. In this frame of mind he'd be difficult to deal with, and she had secrets to keep from his amused, considering glance.

'Robin Maitland is Jenny's half-brother, and a scientist of some kind,' she remarked calmly. 'What else should I know about him?'

'Only that he's a very nice man – someone to ride the water with, as we say in Scotland. Janet is his childhood sweetheart. We grew up together, with Jenny as the fourth member of the quartet.'

He said it calmly enough, but she was missing now, and Kate remembered the anguish in his face when they'd walked out of the Kemanskas' flat, leaving her behind. It must have seemed desperately wrong that the foursome shouldn't stay intact for ever and ever, as the Lord's Prayer always ended up. Kate asked no more questions about the Maitlands, and McEwan seemed content to concentrate on the evening traffic.

The apartment she was shown into was pleasant but impersonal, one of the many in the huge blocks that made up Dolphin Square. It had the air of a place that its owners stayed in but didn't count as their home. She was warmly welcomed, though, by a man who immediately reminded her of Jenny: same slight build, same directness of manner. Janet Maitland was different, a pretty, fair-headed woman who smiled easily. One of the four had needed to be a less complicated human being, Kate reckoned, and it was obviously she.

Almost as they arrived the telephone rang and McEwan went to answer it, leaving Kate barely introduced to her hosts; but Janet wasn't at a loss.

'You're Ranald's shepherdess! Did you know he called you that?'

'Yes, when he wanted to suggest that bossiness was an occupational hazard for

274

couriers. We can't help it; we're meant to tell the poor, driven customers what to do!'

'It sounds an awe-inspiring job to me,' Janet said frankly. 'But you don't look in the least fearsome – does she, Robin?'

Her husband inspected Kate, then shook his head. 'Not fearsome; charming, I'd say. But we were expecting that. Jenny insists that Nikolai and Anatoly both fell in love with Kate Kirkby!'

She smiled at the compliment, but grew serious again. 'Even though you're both in touch with her, you must wonder what her life is really like. It's harsh, compared with the comfort and security we have here; but her happiness is bound up in Nikolai and the child she's expecting, and she has a kind and gentle father-in-law. Ludmilla Kemanskaya is a harder nut to crack, but your sister will manage it in the end, and then Ludmilla will lay down her life for Jenny if need be. That's the sort of woman she is.'

'I'll tell my father and stepmother that,' Robin said quietly. 'They're planning a surprise visit to Moscow when the baby's born.'

Janet left them to attend to matters in the kitchen, and McEwan came hurrying back into the room; but he found the usually shy Robin Maitland talking to Kate with the ease of an old friend. Her sophisticated glamour – very apparent tonight – should have been enough to reduce Robin to almost total silence, but it wouldn't have mattered, McEwan thought morosely, if he hadn't come back into the room at all.

Janet's dinner restored him – the succulent venison casserole she had cooked to perfection, and a tarte au citron to which he was also very partial. The easy conversation around the dinner table was enjoyable as well until Janet asked where Kate's next assignment would take her.

'It seems I'm to stay in London for a while, training new staff. As couriers go, I'm considered ancient and experienced now.' A rueful twinkle lit her eyes for a moment. 'But I also suspect my boss's intentions!'

'You mean he fancies you?' Janet suggested. 'Poor Kate; how embarrassing for you, unless you don't mind being fancied.'

'I rather do mind,' she confessed, 'but I should hate to hurt George's feelings. He's not quite the proverbial rough diamond with a heart of gold; he *is* a self-made man, tough and successful, but he isn't cocksure. I shall have to invent some admirers who absorb all my spare time. I respect him and enjoy working for Three Cs, but I've no ambition to become Mrs George!'

'Then I'd better call one day and make a lot of fuss about taking you to lunch,' said

McEwan, frowning at her. 'Better a large admirer in the hand than two in the bush.'

Kate agreed that he would certainly be hard to miss, and then the conversation moved on. But after dinner, invited to re-powder her nose, Kate found the subject returned to by her hostess.

'Ranald doesn't like the sound of your boss, I'm afraid.'

'He doesn't like not to interfere,' Kate suggested instead. 'McEwan can't bear to see the rest of us floundering about in the muddles we keep making.'

Janet Maitland considered her guest in silence for a moment, wondering why the comment had been so tart. 'We know him as Ranald,' she pointed out. 'Why do you always call him McEwan?'

'I suppose because he told me to.' Kate's entrancing smile appeared as a memory came back to her. 'I once made the mistake of saying *Mr* McEwan; he almost choked on the morsel of black bread – mine as it happened – that he was eating at the time!'

'I can imagine.' But Janet's amusement quickly faded. 'He looks haunted, poor, dear man. The men who died on the train were his friends and colleagues – especially his chief assistant, Peter Mackay. He's too sensible to blame himself for being alive when they are not, but he won't ever quite get over their loss. He made himself go and visit their families when he got back. Peter's son, Alexander, is his godchild. The boy and his mother, Morag, spent Christmas at Achnavour. Ranald couldn't bear them to spend it grieving alone.'

Kate thought of the woman she'd watched saying goodbye to McEwan, and remembered her own jab of jealousy; it seemed unbearably shameful now – something never to be admitted to.

'Jenny said that he'd finish up at Achnavour when he grew tired of roaming the world,' she commented instead. 'Do you think that's true?'

'I'm sure of it – that's where his heart is. It was his father's and his grandfather's house – lonely, rather, in my own view, but not in his.'

Kate knew that it was true. The house wasn't entirely isolated – Achnavour had other settlements as well – but he wouldn't have minded if it were. She'd known that about him all along; there was no reason now to feel that she wanted to creep away and weep her heart out in some dark seclusion of her own.

'It's time I went home,' she suggested with heroic casualness. 'You said you'd got an early start to make for Edinburgh tomorrow. Is there the slightest use in telling

McEwan that I can take a taxi?'

'Save your breath to cool your porridge – I should,' Janet recommended. 'He'll have made his mind up to see you to your door. Come and visit us, Kate; we'd like you to, and it would give my parents-in-law pleasure to have you talk about Jenny.'

She agreed that she would, and a little while later found herself, as predicted, back in McEwan's car.

'This is silly,' she said crossly. 'A double journey that is quite unnecessary.'

'Why so peevish, shepherdess?'

Why indeed? There was no true answer to that, but while she cast about for a reasonable fib the lights in front of them changed and he could then turn and smile at her.

'Shouldn't you be thinking how to thank the kind gentleman who's taking you home – a nightcap, perhaps, or a little snack of some kind?'

'You can't be hungry – not after the dinner I saw you consume.'

'All right, no snack,' he agreed regretfully. 'It was a very pleasant evening, but we haven't had our talk yet, and that's something I *do* need, Kate.'

She was silenced by the change of tone, and he said nothing more himself for the rest of the short journey.

'Coffee or whisky?' she asked when they

were back in her small sitting room.

'A dram, please, I think.'

She lit the fire, and a lamp or two, and put the decanter and a glass beside him. 'Help yourself; none for me, though.' From an armchair across the width of the hearth she watched him pour out a small measure of whisky. The lamplight fell on his dark hair, frosted with silver, and tired, fine-drawn face. She had no idea how old he was, she realized, but probably less old than he now looked. His life was always arduous, but recent events had left their mark; he looked bone-weary and sad, and suddenly she wanted to tell him the truth.

'Janet mentioned your godson this evening. I saw him with his mother at Achnavour – they were just leaving when I arrived.'

McEwan stared at her, but didn't comment again on the way she'd ignored him, standing there in the road. 'Morag is a widow at thirty-three, and Alexander has no father,' he said instead. 'If Peter Mackay hadn't been working for me, he wouldn't have been anywhere near that damned train.'

'But you will take care of Alexander and Morag,' Kate pointed out gently, 'just as James Maitland took care of you.' She saw the despairing sadness in his face and realized that there was a limit even to McEwan's strength. 'Your friends could equally have been killed in some way that had *nothing* to do with you,' she insisted. 'What you said last night is true: the world's sorrows have to be borne, because that's all we can do.'

There was a little silence before he spoke again. 'What are your sorrows, Kate? You have them, I know, because your face is sad when you forget to smile. Does Sergei's unhappiness matter to you that much, or did you relinquish Andrew Carmichael just because you thought Linette needed him?'

She shook her head, wondering how much more of this conversation she could stand without blurting out the truth. 'Sergei *will* survive, because somehow the Russians do, and I didn't relinquish Andrew: I lost him, and deserved to. He asked me to marry him often enough.'

The large man opposite her took another sip of whisky and then deliberately put down his glass. 'You won't get a lot of offers from *me;* it's only the one chance you'll have to turn me down.'

It was McEwan doing what he enjoyed most, she tried to tell herself: joking with a perfectly straight face. Just for a split second she'd almost fallen into his trap, all but given herself away. It was a cruel game to play, but he wasn't to know that, of course.

'It's not a laughing matter,' she said

hoarsely. 'Suppose I'd called your bluff – where would you be – "Benedick, the married man"?'

A little smile touched his mouth, but she couldn't read what it meant. 'A laughing matter it's not, I agree, when a confirmed bachelor of thirty-eight gets seduced into throwing his hat into the matrimonial ring! It *was* a serious offer, shepherdess; I can't have you marrying George.'

She stared at him with huge, imploring eyes. 'I gave myself away by going to Achnavour, but there is *nothing* you need do about it, even though you have this strange compulsion to save the entire world. You would have shared your life with Jenny, I think; but without her you're content to walk alone. That's what you must go on doing.'

'All wrong, Kate,' he answered gently. 'Jenny is the sister I didn't have – greatly loved because who could fail to love her? But she isn't the girl I want to be the companion of all my days. That, alas for me, is a termagant with russet hair and lovely honest eyes who knocked me off my feet the very first time we met! Don't you remember, my dearest love?'

'Yes ... I do remember,' she said unsteadily. She was very inclined to weep, but tried to smile instead. 'I remember something else as well: a woman's place is in the home, you said, staying obediently put, and bringing up the children!'

'We can take them with us,' he said generously, '– well, some of them at least!' Then his face changed. 'Kate, *are* you saying yes?'

'I must,' she agreed with a catch in her voice. 'You said it was the only chance I'd get.'

She could see the sudden blaze of joy as he looked at her, but there was laughter as well. 'This is an unbearably decorous conversation we're having. Perhaps I should do something about it.'

He got up and lifted her bodily into his arms and then settled back with her in his own chair.

'This is roughly how we first met,' she said reminiscently, 'but you weren't so co-operative then. You couldn't wait to get me off your lap, as I recall.'

'I hope to get much more co-operative yet.' His arms tightened their hold, and his mouth found her smiling lips. Breathless and bemused, he finally lifted his head. 'I don't suppose you have the slightest conception of how much I love you, but there'll be time enough to prove it to you; there isn't a great deal to do in the evenings in Nigeria.'

'Nigeria?'

'My next port of call. Shall you mind it

283

very much? – you're looking rather doubt-ful.'

'I shan't mind it wherever it is. I was just thinking of Jenny and Nikolai – wishing *their* lives could be easier.'

McEwan was now looking alarmed. 'We don't often, if ever, get sent to luxurious watering places, sweetheart. You aren't exactly in line for a life of luxury yourself.'

She smiled with great contentment. 'If you're trying to back out, it's too late. You made me an offer!'

'So I did. But, Kate, there *is* something serious to say. When it's time to stop travelling, I want to go on with my work at Achnavour. A lot of our country is unworkable – that's why Scotland's so wildly beautiful; but there's land that should be used, and I'm going to find out how it should be done. You've seen Achnavour; is it too much to ask that you should be happy in so isolated and lonely a place?'

'I dreamed of living there even before I saw it,' she confessed. 'And one of these days we'll bring Jenny's children over to enjoy it with ours. We'll bring Anatoly and Ludmilla too, and teach *her* to smile and be happy.'

'But a wedding first, don't you think?' McEwan suggested.

'And, even before that, a visit to Somerset

to meet my parents. Then we'll reconvene some of Tour 245: Lucy and Nigel, Linette – plus Andrew, of course – and certainly dear Ellie and Dirk.'

'Reconvene as many as you like, my dearest,' McEwan said largely. 'But I shan't mind if you forget to invite Mrs Newcombe.'